autoLISP

IN PLAIN ENGLISH

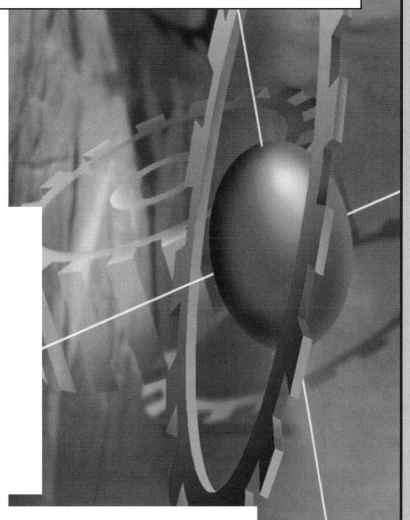

autoLISP

IN PLAIN ENGLISH

A PRACTICAL

GUIDE

FOR NON-

PROGRAMMERS

Fifth Edition

George O. Head

VENTANA
PRESS

AutoCAD Reference Library™

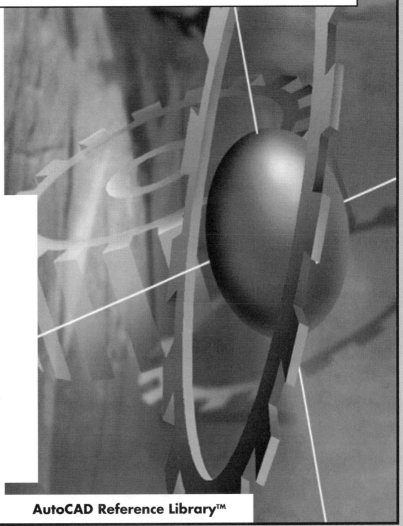

AutoLISP in Plain English: A Practical Guide for Non-Programmers, Fifth Edition

Library of Congress Cataloging-in-Publication Data

Head, George O., 1945-
      AutoLisp in plain English : a practical guide for non-programmers / George O. Head. -- 5th ed.
          p.   cm.
      Includes Index.
      ISBN 1-56604-140-6
      1. AutoLISP (Computer program language) 2. AutoCAD (Computer file) I. Title.
      QA76.73.A84H42 1994
      620'.0042'02855369--dc20   94-41201
                                                  CIP

Book design: Karen Wysocki
Cover and icon design: Tom Draper Design
Index service: Mark Kmetzko
Technical editor: Brian Matthews, Architectural Technology Dept. Head, Wake Technical Community
    College
Editorial staff: Angela Anderson, Walter R. Bruce, III, Tracye Giles, Marion Laird, Pam Richardson,
    Jessica Ryan
Production staff: Cheri Collins, John Cotterman, Bill Hartman, Dan Koeller, Dawne Sherman, Marcia Webb
Proofreader: Valeria Nasir

Fifth Edition 9 8 7 6 5 4 3 2 1
Printed in the United States of America

For information about our audioproducts, write us at Newbridge Book Club, 3000 Cindel Drive, Delran, NJ 08375

Ventana Press, Inc.
P.O. Box 2468
Chapel Hill, NC 27515
919/942-0220
FAX 919/942-1140

Limits of Liability and Disclaimer of Warranty

Trademarks

Trademarked names appear throughout this book. Rather than list the names and entities that own the trademarks or insert a trademark symbol with each mention of the trademarked name, the publisher states that it is using the names only for editorial purposes and to the benefit of the trademark owner with no intention of infringing upon that trademark.

About the Author

George O. Head is president of Associated Market Research, a business and management consulting firm for architects and engineers, based in Rhode Island. He is a co-developer of A/E Solutions, a project management and financial accounting software package for architects and engineers and a developer of Auto Mechanical, a comprehensive mechanical AutoLISP program for mechanical draftsmen and engineers. He is the author of *The AutoCAD 3D Companion* and co-author of *1000 AutoCAD Tips & Tricks* and *The AutoCAD Productivity Book* (all published by Ventana Press), and author of *Managing, Marketing and Budgeting for the A/E Office* (published by Van Nostrand Reinhold).

About the Technical Editor

Brian Matthews, department head of Architectural Technology at Wake Technical Community College, Raleigh, NC, and director of its AutoCAD Training Center, has been responsible for organizing and creating courses in several areas of AutoCAD and AutoLISP application for the past nine years. His courses are taught as part of a two-year degree for engineering technology curriculum students. He has also been coordinator and instructor for several AutoCAD—Industrial Extension Service programs at North Carolina State University. He was technical editor for the seven books in the Ventana Press *AutoCAD Reference Library*. Readers with technical inquiries can reach him at 919-662-3476, via fax 919-669-3369 or via Internet at bmatt@wtcc-gw.wake.tec.nc.us.

CONTENTS

CHAPTER 12 Advanced Entity Manipulation 157

CHAPTER 13 Working With Strings 169

CHAPTER 14 Extended Entity Data 179

Why Learn AutoLISP?

AutoLISP helps you modify AutoCAD, save time and boost productivity. It lets you and third-party developers write customized programs to control every aspect of the drawing, the database and third-party applications. More important, it lets you solve your particular problem and do it exactly the way you want. This can save you hours and weeks of time—which is the reason you purchased AutoCAD.

If you're like most AutoCAD users, you'd like to use AutoLISP to solve everyday drawing problems—without spending your entire career becoming an AutoLISP expert! You'll be glad to know that creating AutoLISP programs doesn't have to be a difficult, confusing endeavor. AutoLISP can be taught in plain English and anyone can understand it.

What's Inside

AutoLISP in Plain English will help you create simple, useful programs that make you more productive in your daily work. You may want to create customized text entry programs, make global changes in your drawing or simply write programs that eliminate excessive steps in a particular drawing situation. After reading this book, you should be able to construct such programs in a short time.

This book assumes you know little or nothing about AutoLISP or programming, and dozens of well-documented examples accompany the tutorial chapters. At the end of each chapter is a working (and useful!) AutoLISP program illustrating each point covered in that chapter. Each line of the sample program is then taken apart and discussed in detail so that you're never lost.

Six new chapters have been added for the Fifth Edition. This new section contains advanced AutoLISP, intended for AutoLISP users who want more instruction. If you have worked in AutoLISP and have written your own programs, this section is for you. It provides you the information you need to work with files, tables and advanced list construction.

The advanced section shows you how to error-check your programs and effectively work with strings and advanced entity manipulations. The chapter on Extended Entity Data is the easiest to understand of any instruction materials in publication. Throughout the Advanced AutoLISP Section, you will find valuable AutoLISP utilities to help you get your job done.

Basic AutoLISP

Chapter 1, "Getting Started," shows you how to enter and run a simple AutoLISP program, using the most basic commands.

Chapter 2, "Managing Lists," explains how to take a list apart and create new lists.

Chapter 3, "Controlling the Program," introduces many basic statements that let you select or enter data from your keyboard, mouse or digitizer.

Chapter 4, "Angles & Distances," covers angles—the heart of programs that deal with parallel lines, coordinate geometry, mechanical and civil engineering, computer-aided manufacturing and more.

Chapter 5, "System Variables," explains the manipulation of AutoCAD's most useful system variables.

Chapter 6, "Programming Techniques," outlines the thought processes involved in creating a program from scratch. You dissect a useful program and learn, step by step, a typical process for program development, testing and debugging.

Chapter 7, "Managing Entities," introduces you to the most useful aspect of AutoLISP—entity selection and change. You actually alter AutoCAD's database and begin to use AutoLISP in high gear!

Advanced AutoLISP

Chapter 8, "Advanced AutoLISP," teaches you file management with AutoLISP, the essence of communicating with the outside world.

Chapter 9, "Accessing Tables," provides you with the insight you need to go right to the heart of the AutoCAD database. The AutoCAD tables provide a storehouse of information about the drawing that you can tap into.

Chapter 10, "Error-Checking," gives your programs the professional touch. No longer will the user of your programs be wondering what happened to the program. This chapter will make you a much better programmer.

Chapter 11, "Advanced List Concepts," expands on how large amounts of data can be manipulated with AutoLISP. After all, LISP stands for List Processing, and you must know how to effectively use lists. You learn not only how to store data in lists and take the data apart, but also how to change information in the lists and get to any part of a list whenever you need to.

Chapter 12, "Advanced Entity Manipulation," picks up where Chapter 7 left off. You learn new ways to work with entities and selection sets, including complex entities of Polylines and Blocks.

Chapter 13, "Working With Strings," gives you the tools you need to work with text data. You learn how to put text together, take it apart, substitute one for another and handle multiple conversion functions.

Chapter 14, "Extended Entity Data," is the easiest-to-understand explanation available in print. This powerful feature of AutoCAD and AutoLISP gives you the ability to attach up to 16k of information to any entity in your drawing. Once you learn how to work with Extended Entity Data, attributes will look like a thing of the past.

Chapter 15, "Tips & Tricks," presents special tips and tricks for programming, testing and debugging as well as shortcuts that can save you hours.

Chapter 16, "Miscellaneous Commands," wraps up those AutoLISP commands that don't fit nicely in a tutorial but are still important.

Chapter 17, "Fifteen Programming Examples," is designed to help you learn by example. Fifteen ready-to-run programs show you AutoLISP in action and enhance your AutoLISP library.

Three appendices cover how to use EDLIN, how to modify AutoCAD's ACAD.PGP file and how to set up your prototype drawing file.

About Release 13: As AutoCAD becomes more complex with additional platforms being introduced, books that help AutoCAD users must address the new as well as the older releases. Those who have used AutoCAD over the last several years and are comfortable with previous releases need to be aware of the productivity enhancement features of Release 13.

This new edition of *AutoLISP in Plain English* may be used effectively with all releases from 10 through 13. AutoCAD users, therefore, can benefit from this book regardless of the release used.

Whatever version you're using, *AutoLISP in Plain English* is the book you need for learning AutoLISP. And it increases in value as you move up to Release 13.

How Well Do You Need To Know AutoCAD?

A basic knowledge of AutoCAD is assumed throughout the book. However, you needn't be a CAD expert. If you can load AutoCAD, produce some lines, circles and arcs and save the drawing, you have the prerequisites to begin learning AutoLISP!

This book will give you a much better understanding of the *AutoLISP Programmer's Reference Manual*. In addition to writing programs that will make using AutoCAD easier, you'll advance along the AutoCAD learning curve, further increasing your speed and output.

Software & Hardware Requirements

Software: *AutoLISP in Plain English* can be used with Versions 2.18 through Release 13. Versions 2.17 and lower don't have the AutoLISP interpreter and therefore won't work.

Each new version of AutoCAD adds new features to AutoLISP not found in previous versions. Beside each command, the book indicates the version in which the command originated. No indication means it was available beginning with Version 2.18.

Throughout the book, EDIT (a text editor available free with Versions 5.0 & 6.0 DOS) is used to create AutoLISP programs. If you're experienced with another text editor (WordStar, WordPerfect, etc.) you may use it when creating AutoLISP files. If you have a DOS version prior to DOS 5.0, you can also use EDLIN.

For more information on how to use EDLIN, refer to Appendix A or your DOS manual.

Beginning with DOS 5.0, EDIT becomes a strongly recommended alternative to EDLIN. The obvious advantage of EDIT over EDLIN is that EDIT is a full-screen editor with search and replace capabilities. Although EDIT looks and feels like a real word processor, it produces ordinary text files as AutoLISP requires. If EDIT is available to you, use it.

Hardware: If your equipment runs AutoCAD, it can run AutoLISP. It doesn't matter which platform you're using—DOS, Windows, SUN, etc. AutoLISP works with all of them.

How To Use This Book

AutoLISP in Plain English is a learning book, not a reference guide—so use it in front of your computer! The chapters show you step by step how to write useful programs and illustrate by example how each command works.

As you're programming, you'll want to refer to the examples in this book, but they don't cover all AutoLISP commands and functions. For a complete listing of AutoLISP commands and nomenclature, refer to the *AutoLISP Programmer's Reference Manual* and the *AutoCAD Reference Manual*.

You'll get the most from this book when you use it in the following way:

1. Read the explanation about each command.

2. Type in the example(s) that accompany each command and compare what happens on your computer with the books explanation.

3. Read the line-by-line explanation of the sample program at the end of the chapter until you understand what each line does.

4. Type (or load from the *AutoLISP in Plain English Companion Disk*) the sample program at the end of each chapter. Run the program in AutoCAD to see how it works.

5. Modify the program as suggested in each chapter to see how the changes affect the program's operation.

6. When you've learned a concept, think how you could use it to write a small program.

7. Reread the AutoLISP Programmer's *Reference Manual*. To your amazement, you'll now understand it!

8. Check out other programs you find in magazines, on third-party software or from user groups. You can learn a great deal through others' creative solutions. And you may well find an easier way to create your own specialized program.

Rules of the Road

As stated previously, this book gives you a working knowledge of Auto-LISP and shows you how to write simple AutoLISP programs. You'll find the book sometimes takes liberties with the technical jargon of the programming language. For example, an AutoLISP command is technically called a **function**. But for this book's purposes, it's better to communicate in a language everyone understands, rather than get bogged down in technical accuracies.

As you advance, you'll want to consult the many good technical references available on LISP and AutoLISP.

So that everyone is speaking the same language, the conventions and notations used throughout this book are listed below:

- <RETURN> means to press RETURN or ENTER on your keyboard. Don't type these statements with the code.

- At the beginning of each chapter you should be in AutoCAD's drawing editor at the Command line.

- You may type commands and programs using uppercase or lowercase letters in DOS, Windows or NT environments. AutoLISP in a UNIX environment is case-sensitive. LISP programmers generally use lowercase, so that's what this book uses.

- **Type:** means you're to enter line(s) from the keyboard at AutoCAD's Command line.

A Note About LISP & AutoLISP

LISP was one of the first high-level programming languages invented, which means the programmer is able to develop the program using English-like expressions. When first learning LISP, you may sometimes doubt just how English-like those expressions really are! But AutoLISP is not LISP.

The version of LISP AutoCAD uses is called a **"subset"** of the language. Autodesk developers chose commands that were appropriate, left some behind—and even changed some of them. If LISP didn't have an appropriate command, Autodesk made one up! Therefore, AutoLISP is truly a unique language specifically designed for AutoCAD.

If you read a book that doesn't explicitly refer to AutoLISP, you'll be learning a language that won't work with AutoCAD. You may wonder why Autodesk didn't choose BASIC or some other familiar language as its internal programming tool. As you read this book, you'll see that Auto-LISP's unique ability to assign a list of values (such as X, Y and Z coordinates) to a single variable makes LISP an excellent choice.

You're on Your Way...

...to dramatically increasing your AutoCAD productivity using AutoLISP. You'll write your first AutoLISP routine in the next few pages. With some work and diligence, AutoLISP's power will become apparent to you, and you'll soon be creating simple programs that can make you the master of your own application. Let's get started.

CHAPTER 1

Getting Started

Preliminaries

Welcome to *AutoLISP in Plain English*. You'll find this book a valuable learning tool for AutoLISP, the programming language of AutoCAD. This Fifth Edition, entirely rewritten and updated for Release 13, lets you learn AutoLISP at your own pace.

But for those of you who are already *self-taught* in AutoLISP and have previous versions of this text, there's a bonus. An extra section of six new chapters have been added.

This new section is called "Advanced AutoLISP." It's intended for those who have learned AutoLISP and are ready for more. If you have worked in AutoLISP and have written your own programs, this section is for you. It provides information you need to work with files, tables and advanced list construction. It shows you how to check your programs for errors and work with strings and advanced entity manipulations. It also includes an easy-to-understand explanation on working with Extended Entity Data.

This new edition ends with a "Tips & Tricks" chapter and a "Miscellaneous Commands" chapter. Whether you're a basic or an advanced AutoLISP user, you'll find valuable AutoLISP utilities to help you get your jobs done.

1.1 Basic Settings, Units & Limits

Unlike past releases of AutoCAD, Release 13 doesn't require DOS environment settings before you begin running AutoLISP programs. The AutoCAD Release 10/386 to the Release 13 versions have automated memory management for both AutoCAD and AutoLISP. This feature permits your AutoLISP programs to share the memory pool with any other aspect of AutoCAD so you can run virtually any size AutoLISP program.

For your sample programs throughout this book, you'll want to set up a 24" x 36" prototype drawing. Use the MVSETUP.LSP bonus file supplied with AutoCAD. Or after you've completed this chapter and for the sample programs in this book, refer to Appendix C and create a prototype drawing and set the **UNITS** and **LIMITS** as suggested.

1

GETTING
STARTED

For your convenience, the companion disk contains three prototype drawing files, which are already set up.

1.2 Creating an AutoLISP Program

AutoLISP programs are created as simple text files, which means they're written using a text editor. A text editor is a program that lets you enter text and write out to a file without the special control codes used by many word processors. To avoid WordStar's control codes, for example, use its "nondocument" mode. In WordPerfect, use the (Ctrl-F5) DOS text file in/out mode. The DOS EDIT text editor will let you save your program in the correct format, without having to worry about control codes.

Throughout this book, DOS EDIT is used to write AutoLISP programs. One of the advantages of using DOS EDIT, in addition to its being free, is that it's easy to call up from inside AutoCAD. And after you've saved your AutoLISP program, EDIT returns you to your drawing in the drawing editor. (Appendix D contains a short lesson on EDIT basics and also gives you some tips on using EDIT in Windows and NT while working on your AutoLISP programs.)

However, through a file called **ACAD.PGP** (explained in Appendix B), you can set up any text editor to do the same thing. Or, if you have a favorite word processor, you may want to use it instead of the DOS EDIT function. If you have not yet changed the ACAD.PGP file, now is a good time to do so, before we start.

It's important to remember that you must use either EDIT or a text editor in the DOS Text mode to create AutoLISP programs. Now, let's create a simple AutoLISP program. Enter AutoCAD's drawing editor and, from the AutoCAD **Command:** prompt line,

Type: `SHELL <RETURN> <RETURN>`

You are placed into a DOS screen. Remember, to get back to AutoCAD, type EXIT.

Type: `EDIT TEST1.LSP`

If EDIT.EXE is in your DOS path, then you're now ready to type your program.

```
Type:    (defun myprog1 ( ) <RETURN>
         (prompt "My program") <RETURN>
         ) <RETURN>
         Press the Alt-F X <RETURN>
```

The above sequence saves the program file and exits EDIT. You may also use the DOS 6.0 pull-down menu. Pick EXIT, located under the FILE pull-down menu, and answer YES to save your file and exit. This sequence saves **TEST1.LSP** from the DOS EDIT and returns you to the DOS prompt.

To return to AutoCAD's Command line, type **EXIT** at the DOS prompt. Now let's run the program you just created.

```
Type:    (load "test1") <RETURN>
```

```
Response:  myprog1
         AutoLISP is confirming that it loaded your program called myprog1.
```

```
Type:    (myprog1) <RETURN>
```

```
Response:  "My program"
```

Congratulations, you've just written your first AutoLISP routine! Now a few words of explanation.

All AutoLISP programs must contain the suffix **.LSP**. Otherwise, AutoCAD won't access them when loading. For example, in AutoLISP Program Lesson 1 at the end of this chapter, the example program is called **LES1.LSP**.

1.3 Tracking Your Work With the Semicolon

When you begin a line with a semicolon, nothing you write on that line is loaded into the program. It's used only for documentation and explanation of your program, in much the same way the **REM** statement is used in BASIC. When the program is loaded, remarks after the semicolon are ignored and not loaded. However, you can access and read those comments through your normal text editor.

You should get into the habit of thoroughly documenting your programs. Write notes about what you're doing, what the variables are, or how you might revise your program in the future. Those notes will be most helpful when you want to debug or revise the program. Remarks don't take valuable memory in AutoCAD, so feel free to write as much as you want!

A semicolon doesn't have to come at the beginning of the line. For example,

```
(prompt "This will print"); This is a comment.
```

From where the semicolon begins, the rest of the line is a comment statement. The comment statement ends where you place your next carriage return. Therefore, if you want the next line also to be a comment line, start it with another semicolon.

1.4 Parentheses ( )

Parentheses are vital to writing AutoLISP programs. All commands are surrounded by parentheses. AutoLISP uses parentheses to **nest**, allowing you to write a command that acts on (evaluates) another command. In turn, that command can act on another command. As you add parentheses, you're nesting commands deeper and deeper.

Remember to leave the nest with an equal number of parentheses. The easiest way to do that is to simply count them and add left parentheses (and subtract right parentheses). For example,

```
(xxx (xxx (xxx )  (xxx )  )  )
1    2    3      2 3     2 1 0
```

At the first (, count **1**, then (count **2**, then (count **3**, then) count down to **2**, then (count up to **3**, then) count down to **2**, then) count down **1**, then) count down **0**.

By counting up with left (open) parentheses and down with right (closed) parentheses, you should end up at zero, which means you've correctly closed all your parentheses. That method doesn't guarantee the commands or programs are correct, but if the parentheses aren't closed correctly, your programs are guaranteed not to work!

Finally, all parentheses needn't be on the same line. For example,

```
(xxx (xxx)
(xxx (xxx) (xxx))
)
```

The pattern above is as correct as the previous example. As you begin to work with AutoLISP, you'll find indentation more readable, allowing you to understand and track your work more easily.

If you haven't closed your parentheses properly, AutoCAD gives you the following message at your Command line: **1>**

To correct that, simply enter another) parenthesis to close the LISP argument. AutoLISP responds by executing the command. Let's try it:

Type: `(load "test1" <RETURN>`

Response: `1>`

See what happened? Let's correct it.

Type: `) <RETURN>`

Response: `myprog1`

Note that after you entered the missing parenthesis, the AutoLISP file loaded properly.

Three types of errors can cause the **1>**: a missing right parenthesis, a missing quotation mark or a missing apostrophe. The missing parenthesis is the most common. If including the extra right parenthesis doesn't work, try the quotation mark or the apostrophe.

A **2>** error means you are missing *two* parentheses. The number before > increases according to the number of missing parentheses that AutoLISP needs to finish the statement.

NOTE: After you've corrected the problem, your program still may not run in a normal fashion. But at least you'll get back to AutoCAD's Command line!

When you get one of these errors, it's easier to exit with **CTRL-C** and begin typing again.

1.5 How to Load Your Programs

The file containing your AutoLISP program must be loaded into AutoCAD before the program can run. Here's the way to load your program from the Command line:

`(load "file name") <RETURN>`

Note the importance of enclosing the load command in parentheses. If you don't, AutoCAD will try to load a shape or text file (because **load** without the parentheses is a valid AutoCAD command).

Remember that nearly all AutoLISP commands can be entered directly at the Command line if they're enclosed in parentheses. Also, remember to enclose the name of the AutoLISP file in quotes.

Although the file itself must have the required **.LSP** extension, you *do not* add **.LSP** to the file name when loading the program—that's understood with the **(load...)** command.

Once loaded, the program prints the name of the last function in the file on the screen.

1.6 (defun   Define Function

In AutoLISP, a *function* is simply the program. Unlike other languages, the file name is *not* the program. In fact, one AutoLISP file may have several programs inside. When the files are loaded, the programs (functions) are available at any time. The words *program* and *function* are used interchangeably throughout this book.

The name of the program or function must be defined in the first statement, which is done by using the command **(defun**.

(defun is the first actual command in the program. The name of the program isn't closed off with parentheses immediately. In fact, the last parenthesis in the program is the one that closes **(defun**.

(defun is followed by the name of the function (or program):

```
(defun drawline
```

drawline is the name of the function. After you've named your function, you have three choices. First, you may do nothing, by simply using **( )**. For example,

```
(defun drawline ( )
```

You're saying that all variables you plan to use in the program are *global*. A global variable is one that doesn't lose its value after the program ends. For example, if **R** were defined as **17.52** in one program, it would still be **17.52** when the next program started. Thus, we say it's global.

Second, you may wish all your variables to be local. For example, if **R** were defined as **17.52** in one program, it would have value only for that program; i.e., it's local to that program. If you want a variable to be local, list it after the name of the program and precede it with a **/**. For example,

```
(defun drawline (/ pnt1 pnt2)
```

Remember, **drawline** is the name of the function. In the above example, it's followed by variables that are used in the function as local variables. A local variable is one that has value only for that program while that program is running. A function that contains variables not stated and listed must be followed by **( )**.

Also remember that the closing parenthesis is at the *end* of the function. Since more than one function may be included in one file, each function begins in this manner and ends with a closing parenthesis.

Your third option is to list a variable without the */*. That means a variable is set up to receive a value passed to it from outside the program. For example,

```
(defun dtr (a)
```

That function might be one that converts degrees to radians. To use the function, the program must know the number of degrees. Here, you start the function by typing *(dtr 32.234)* at AutoCAD's **Command** line, which converts **32.234** degrees to radians. The **32.234** would be immediately assigned to the first variable mentioned after the *(defun dtr*, which was *not* preceded by a */*. That's known as *passing an argument to a program.*

Finally, you can combine all three options. For example,

```
(defun drawline (a / b r d)
```

drawline is the name of the function. Variable **a** receives the first value passed to it from outside the program. Variables **b**, **r** and **d** are all local variables. All other variables not mentioned are considered global variables.

Another option can be used with **(defun**. If **C:** precedes the name of the function, you don't have to use parentheses when the function is called. That's important because AutoCAD now thinks of that function as an AutoCAD command that can be used in the (Command...) statement. In fact, when the function is preceded by **C:**, it can be used like any other AutoCAD command such as **LINE**, **ARC**, **CIRCLE**, etc.

At first, you might think of the **C:** as your **C:** drive, but it has nothing to do with the **C:** drive. When using AutoLISP, **C:** is simply a designation that AutoCAD should treat that function as any other AutoCAD command. For example,

```
(defun C:drawline ( )
```

define **fun**ction with the name **drawline**. The C: before **drawline** says to treat the function as an ordinary AutoCAD command. The ( ) following drawline says there are no local variables and all variables used in the program should be global.

1.7 Using Variables

Variables are like **X** and **Y** in algebra—they represent other values, making it a simple matter of storing data that can be manipulated later.

In AutoLISP, variables may be any collection of letters or numbers, as long as they begin with letters. Generally, the rules for variables in Auto-LISP are the same as those for most languages (such as BASIC). Use only letters A–Z and numbers 0–9.

Examples of legal variables:

    a
    arc1
    point1
    pnt1
    d3

Examples of illegal variables:

37	Must begin with a letter.
1point	Must begin with a letter.
pnt*3	May contain only letters A–Z. * is not a legal character.
a$	A valid variable in BASIC, not AutoLISP.

One major difference between an AutoLISP variable and a variable in another language is that the former may contain more than one value in a single variable. A value can be anything, such as

Real Number	Decimal number such as 134.2039
String	John Jay Jones
Integer	Counting number 3 or 9 or -5
Pickset	A special type of data explained later in this book

Therefore, a variable can store just about anything. In AutoLISP, those variables are called *symbols*. For your purposes, variables and symbols are synonymous; throughout this book they're referred to as variables.

Local variables are used just for that function. In other words, if you define variables in the (defun command using the /, those variables maintain values only within that function. If you use the same variable name in other functions, the variable will have *only* its *own value* for *that one function* and won't conflict with other functions with the same variable names.

There are two situations in which you may want global variables instead of local variables. First, you may want other functions to use the values created by a function. Second, and most important, when debugging, you'll often want to ask about the value in the variables when a program crashes.

If local variables have been created, their values will be nil (meaning no value) when the program crashes. However, if they were established as global variables, they retain their values until replaced by values in another program. Therefore, variables should not be declared until the program has been thoroughly debugged. More on this in later chapters.

Unlike a local variable, an argument is a variable that is given a value before the program begins. For example,

```
(defun drawline (d1 / pnt1 pnt2)
```

d1 may be a beginning distance when the program is called (meaning when it begins). In

```
(drawline 3)
```

d1 begins with the value of **3**. **pnt1** and **pnt2** are local variables. All local variables begin with /.

If there are no arguments to pass and you don't want to declare local variables, then in

```
(defun drawline ( )
```

( ) tells the program that no local variables have been created and no arguments have been passed at the beginning of the program.

1.8 Lists

A list can be assigned to a variable containing multiple values. Each value is called an element. The ability to manipulate lists of data gives AutoLISP its power in AutoCAD.

For example, a 2D point in your drawing is described by the value of the **X** coordinate and the value of the **Y** coordinate. In AutoLISP, that point can be described by a single variable: a list of two elements, the first being the **X** value and the second the **Y** value.

A list in AutoLISP is set off with parentheses and might look like this:

```
(7 9)
(3 5 9 7 2)
(3.2039 6.9029 8.2039)
```

If the value of a variable is a single value not set off in parentheses, such as **6**, it's not a list. Let's take a single 3D line entity as a complicated example of a list.

The line contains information on the beginning **X, Y, Z** coordinates, the ending **X, Y, Z** coordinates, the layer, the line type, the line scale, and the fact that it's a **LINE** (type of entity) as opposed to a **CIRCLE** or an **ARC**.

Everything used to describe the single entity can be expressed by a single variable. That variable is a list that contains all those elements. Such a list might look like this:

```
((- 1 . <<Entity name: 60000014>>) (0 . "LINE") (8 . "LAYER1")
(10  563.0 484.0 0.0) (11  1162.0 745.0 0.0) (210 0.0 0.0 1.0))
```

The above is actually how a simple line is stored in the AutoCAD database (a very simple entity list!), as discussed in more detail in Chapter 7, "Managing Entities." For now, it suffices to note that AutoLISP is an ideal language because it lets you store the entire definition of an entity in a single variable.

1.9 Starting Your Programs

After you've written your program and loaded the file that contains it, the rest is easy:

```
(drawline)
```

Now you enter the name of the function, surrounded by parentheses, at AutoCAD's Command line. If the function requires up-front data, then enter

```
(drawline 3)
```

The program may be entered either from the AutoCAD Command: prompt line or added to your menu or Toolbar. Remember that the file must be loaded first and the program name must be surrounded by parentheses unless the function name is preceded by C:.

Let's take a look at the commands used in AutoLISP Program Lesson 1.

1.10 (graphscr) Graphics Screen

The above command is used to shift the screen back to the graphics screen (if it's in the text screen) on a single-screen system. Nothing will happen if you're already in the graphics screen. You should put this command at the beginning of the program to be sure you start on the graphics screen when the program begins.

If you have a single-screen system, depending on your version or platform, pressing **F1** returns you to the DOS text screen. Or **F2** returns you to the Windows text screen.

Be sure you're in the text screen and at AutoCAD's Command line:

Type: `(graphscr) <RETURN>`

See how you went to the graphics screen? Try it again, but this time start from the graphics screen. What happened? If the answer is nothing, it worked!

1.11 (prompt) General Print Statement

This command is used simply to print text on the Command line. A line feed isn't included, so two consecutive prompt commands will print the text on the same line. Any printing after the prompt must either have the **(terpri)** command or **\n** within the quotation marks to guarantee that the next prompt will be on the next line. At AutoCAD's Command line,

Type: `(prompt "Hello how are you ") <RETURN>`

The message in quotes is printed at the Command line.

1.12 (terpri) Terminate Print and \n

This command is a line feed that causes the next printed text to appear on the next line. It generally follows the **prompt** command.

Type: `(prompt "Hello how are you ") (terpri)`

AutoLISP has other ways to terminate lines, such as \n before the next printed statement.

Sometimes you'll want the next prompt to appear on the same line, similar to the way it's done in AutoCAD. At other times you'll want the next prompt to begin on the next line.

Type: `(prompt "Pick a point: ")(prompt "Pick 2nd point: ")<RETURN>`

Note how the two commands appear on the same line.

Type: `(prompt "Pick a point: ")(terpri)(prompt "Pick 2nd point: ") <RETURN>`

The two statements now appear on different lines.
The other way to issue the line feed looks like this:

Type: `(prompt "Pick a point: \n") (prompt "Pick second point: ")`

The most common procedure is to place the **\n** before the string.

`(prompt "\nPick a point: ")(prompt "\nPick second point: ")`

This guarantees that every line begins on a new line, regardless of what came before it.

Remember that the **\n** must be enclosed within the quotation marks and must be a lowercase letter.

`(prompt "\n")` actually has the same effect as `(terpri)`.

One of your goals in writing AutoLISP programs is to emulate the look and feel of AutoCAD commands as naturally as possible. Those commands let you put continuing commands on the same line or separate them as needed.

1.13 (setq) Set Quote or Set Equal

(setq) takes any AutoLISP object and any designated symbol, and makes the object "equal to" the value of the symbol. The above is an *assignment* command; i.e., it assigns the value of one variable or constant to another variable. **(setq)** is the same as **LET** in very old versions of BASIC.

`If A=5 and B=6 then LET A=B`

In BASIC, the above example would change **A** to **6**, the value of **B**.

IMPORTANT NOTE: **(setq)** is the primary assignment command in AutoLISP. In AutoLISP, the = isn't used as an assignment. = doesn't exist except in **(if...)** and other nonassignment statements. It cannot make one variable equal to another. Only **(setq)** can do that. The order of the **(setq)** statement may seem a little strange at first.

`(setq a b)`

That statement assigns the value **b** to the variable **a**. The first variable after **(setq)** is the one that receives the value. That which follows is the value assigned to the first. Note how similar it is to BASIC's **LET** statement:

```
Let A = B (let A be assigned the value of B)
(setq A B) (set A to the value of B)
```

You needn't assign only values to variables. You also may use constants, numbers or strings such as:

```
(setq a "Hello how are you")
```

Now if you print **a**, you'll get **Hello how are you**.

```
(setq a 7)
```

Now **a** has the value **7**. Let's try a few. At AutoCAD's Command line,

Type: `(setq a 7) <RETURN>`

Type: `!a <RETURN>`

A 7 should appear on your screen. Notice how the **!** is used to print the value of variables. Any time you want to know the value of a variable, simply enter the **!** followed by the variable, and the value will print.

Type: `(setq b "John") <RETURN>`

Type: `!b <RETURN>`

The word **John** should appear on your screen. Finally,

Type: `(setq a b) <RETURN>`

Type: `!a`

The word **John** should now appear on your screen. In this example, you've assigned the value of one variable to another variable. Both **a** and **b** now contain the same value.

1.14 (getpoint)   Pick a Point

The above is an input request to pick a point. Nothing further will happen until you pick a point on the screen. If you use **(setq)** with the **(getpoint)** command, then the **X, Y** and **Z** coordinates of the point picked are assigned to the variable named by **(setq)**.

You also may include a message following **(getpoint)** so the user will know what you want done.

Type: `(getpoint) <RETURN>`

What happened? The answer obviously should be nothing. But that's not quite true. Your computer is simply waiting for you to pick a point.

Now pick a point on the screen. The coordinates will appear at the Command line, between parentheses.

Type: `(setq a (getpoint "Pick first point: ")) <RETURN>`

(setq...) assigns to the variable **a** the **X, Y** and **Z** coordinates of the point picked through the **(getpoint...)** command. Note the message in quotes following **(getpoint...)**. That message will appear on the Command line. A **(terpri)** is necessary if you want the next message to be on the next line.

NOTE: A better way to write it would be

`(setq a (getpoint "\nPick first point: ")) <RETURN>`

Notice also that **(getpoint...)** is nested with its own parentheses. All commands must begin with a parenthesis even if they follow another command. Remember to count parentheses to make sure they're all closed.

Type: `!a`

The resulting value of **a** is now a list of three values—the real number of the **X** coordinate, the real number of the **Y** coordinate, and the real number of the **Z** coordinate.

This is a good time to point out a unique feature of AutoLISP. Other AutoLISP manuals use the term "returns" such as **(getpoint...)** returns a list of three reals. In plain English, that means when you issue commands in AutoLISP, you generally produce a value that is available for you to use. If you don't use it, you lose it!

Therefore, the way to use a value that's been produced (returned) is to **(setq...)** the value to a variable (save it to a variable). So when a book says **(getpoint...)** returns a list of three reals, it's really saying that when you issue the command **(getpoint...)**, it will produce—in the form of a list— three real numbers that represent the **X** and **Y** and **Z** coordinates of the point picked. It's up to you to save that list in a variable so you can use it in the future. For example,

`(setq a (getpoint "\nPick first point: "))`

will produce the **X, Y** and **Z** coordinates of the point picked and will be saved in the variable **a**.

Type: `(setq b (getpoint "\nPick another point: ")) <RETURN>`

Now the value of the **X** and **Y** and **Z** coordinates of the second point are stored in the variable **b**. Don't disturb those values; you'll use them in the next section.

Another variation of **(getpoint...)** ties the point you pick to another known point.

Type: `(setq c (getpoint b "\nPick a 3rd point: ")) <RETURN>`

Notice how the AutoCAD "rubber-band" is tied to point **b**. This gives your program the same look and feel as AutoCAD.

1.15 (command)   AutoCAD Command

The above lets you use any valid AutoCAD command in an AutoLISP program. Variables that follow will be used in the command.

Type: `(command "line" a b) <RETURN>`

Since the **X, Y** and **Z** coordinates of one point are stored in the variable **a** and the **X, Y** and **Z** coordinates of the other point are stored in the variable **b**, the above statement should have drawn a 3D line from point **a** to point **b**. Move your cursor around the screen. Note that it left you in the **LINE** command with a rubber-band from the **ENDPOINT**. Cancel the **LINE** command and **erase** it from the screen.

Type: `(command "line" a b "") <RETURN>`

Notice this time the same line is drawn, but it doesn't leave you in the **LINE** command. The double quote is treated as a **CTRL-C** or **CANCEL** command.

`(command "line" a b c d "c")  <RETURN>`

In the above example, **(command...)** is followed by the AutoCAD command **line.** Note the AutoCAD command in quotes. If the AutoCAD command needs further information, then it simply follows the AutoCAD command. Any input needed (such as from point to point with the **LINE** command) first should be assigned to variables using **(setq...)** and **(getpoint...)** commands. Then the points are in the variables **a**, **b**, **c** and **d** that follow.

Other data may be supplied to the **LINE** command by putting them in quotes—just as you might type them from the keyboard. The **"c"** tells the **LINE** command to close the line.

In the above example, a four-sided figure could be drawn from points **a**, **b**, **c** and **d**, then **"c"**losed back to point **a**.

AutoLISP Program LES1.LSP

Now look at your first complete AutoLISP program, which illustrates the use of the commands you've just learned. The program, **LES1**, simply asks you for two points, then draws a line from the first point to the second. Actually, you've already written this program line by line in this chapter.

Copy this program from the *AutoLISP in Plain English Companion Disk*. *Note:* This procedure is used in all program lessons throughout the book. All lessons assume you're in AutoCAD's drawing editor when the program is loaded, and that **UNITS** and **LIMITS** are properly set.

If you have already changed the ACAD.PGP to the DOS EDIT—instead of EDLIN—as suggested at the beginning of this chapter, then from the AutoCAD Command: prompt line

Type: Edit <RETURN>

Response: File to edit: LES1.LSP

Type in the first line and continue to the end of the program. When you've finished, save the file and exit back to AutoCAD.

Copy all files to your hard disk. At this point, the file **LES1.LSP** should be on your disk, whether you typed it in or copied it from the disk. To load and run the first program,

Type: (load "les1") <RETURN>

Response: drawline

That displays the last function in the file that was loaded. To run the program,

Type: (drawline) <RETURN>

The program now will begin to run. Please refer to this section when doing lessons in future chapters. Below is **LES1.LSP**:

```
(defun drawline (/ pnt1 pnt2)
  (graphscr)
  (prompt "\nThis function is going to draw a line! ")
  (setq pnt1 (getpoint "\nPlease enter the first point: "))
  (setq pnt2 (getpoint "\nPlease enter the second point: "))
  (prompt "\nTHANK YOU! ")
  (command "line" pnt1 pnt2 "")
)
```

PURPOSE: To demonstrate an AutoLISP program in its simplest form.

TO LOAD:

Type: (load "les1")

Response: drawline

TO OPERATE:

Type: (drawline)

Response: This function is going to draw a line!

Please enter the first point:

Now pick a point on the screen.

Response: Please enter the second point:

Now pick a second point on the screen.

Response: THANK YOU!

The program will draw a line connecting the two points chosen. Let's go over the program item by item and see what it does.

(defun drawline (/ pnt1 pnt2)

(defun defines the function **drawline** and sets two local variables, **pnt1** and **pnt2**.

(graphscr)

makes sure the program begins on the drawing editor graphics screen.

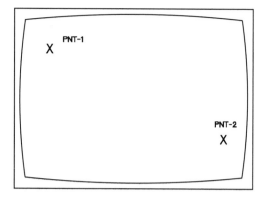

Figure 1-1: Pick two points on your screen.

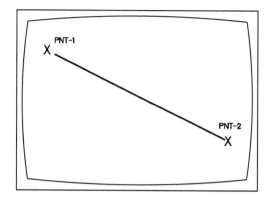

Figure 1-2: The line is drawn between the picked points.

```
(prompt "\nThis function is going to draw a line! ")
```

The **prompt** statement prints the message on the Command line.

```
(setq pnt1 (getpoint "\nPlease enter the first point: "))
```

(setq...) assigns the point secured by **(getpoint...)** to the variable **pnt1**. Remember, you may use a message following **(getpoint...)**.

```
(setq pnt2 (getpoint "\nPlease enter the second point: "))
```

The next **(setq...)**, like the first, assigns the point selected to the variable **(pnt2)**. Now **pnt1** contains the first point, and **pnt2** the **X, Y** and **Z** coordinates of the second point.

Note the space at the end of the text line **"\nPlease enter the second point: "** Normally, spaces are required only between commands and variables. AutoLISP doesn't care if you put too many spaces in, so if in doubt, use a space! In this case the spaces are inside the quotes, which are used to separate the prompts.

```
(command "line" pnt1 pnt2 "")
```

The above issues the command **"line"** to AutoCAD, where **pnt1** is the **from point** and **pnt2** is the **to point**. Note that the double quote is treated as a **CTRL-C**. If you didn't put it in, the line will continue prompting you for the next point.

```
)
```

Remember that **(defun** started with a left (parenthesis. The above is the right) closing parenthesis to end the function.

Moving On

You're now well on your way to understanding the basics of AutoLISP programming. In Chapter 2, "Managing Lists," you'll learn how to take a list apart, how to use **car**, **cdr** and **cadr**, and how to create a new list.

2
MANAGING LISTS

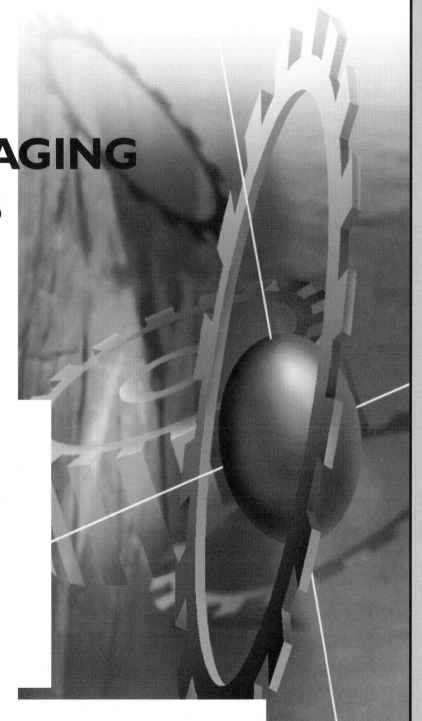

CHAPTER 2

Managing Lists

2.1 Taking a List Apart

When you used **(setq a (getpoint))** in Chapter 1, "Getting Started," you assigned the **X**, **Y** and **Z** coordinate numbers to a variable called **a**. That variable is now a list of three elements. If you want to look at the variable, AutoLISP gives you a convenient way to do so from the Command line.

```
!a
```

Placing the **!** in front of the variable will display the value or values of the variable. If you look at **a** after you assign the list, you might see the following:

```
(3.0  5.0  0.0)
```

That means you have a list of three values. **3** is the **X** coordinate, **5** the **Y** (**X** always comes first), and **0** is the **Z** coordinate. Combining the **X** coordinate of one point with the **Y** coordinate of another (to produce a third point) is useful in drawing rectangles, creating grids, deriving new beginning points for text and selecting objects. Therefore, you need a way to isolate a coordinate so you can assign it to a third variable.

2.2 (car...)   X Coordinate (1st Element)

Some AutoLISP commands don't easily translate into plain English—**(car...)** is certainly one such command. The primary command for taking a list apart, **(car...)** gives you the first element of the list. For example, if the value of **a** is a list of

```
(3.0  5.0  0.0)
```

then

```
(setq b (car a))
```

would assign to the variable **b** the value of the first element in **a**. Therefore, **b** would be the value **3**. Let's try one.

Type: `(setq a (getpoint "Pick a point: ")) <RETURN>`

Now pick a point.

`Type: !a`

As you can see, depending upon your AutoCAD release, the value of **a** is a list of either two or three numbers that represent the **X** and **Y** (and **Z**) coordinates of the point picked, enclosed in parentheses with only a space between them.

`Type:`   `(setq b (car a)) <RETURN>`
          `!b`

Note that the value of **b** is the same as the value of the **X** coordinate—not enclosed in parentheses—which means it's simply a number and not part of a list.

2.3 (cdr)   Second & Remaining

This is the secondary command for taking a list apart. **(cdr)** gives you the second element plus the remaining elements in the list. For example, if the variable **a** is a list of

`(3 5 7 9)`

then

`(setq b (cdr a))`

would assign to variable **b** the value of the second and remaining elements in **a**. Therefore, **b** would be the value

`(5 7 9)`

Although you'll put it to use in Chapter 7, "Managing Entities," **(cdr)** really serves no purpose in and of itself. Let's turn to something more practical.

2.4 (cadr)   Y Coordinate (2nd Element)

(cadr) is an abbreviation of a nested command. For example, let's assume list **a** contains

```
(3 5 7 9)
```

To pull just the second element from the list, you might write a sequence of commands like this:

```
(setq b (car (cdr a)))
```

which would assign to **b** the value of 5. **(cdr a)** is **(5 7 9)** and **(car (cdr a))** is the first of the rest of the elements, thus producing only the **5**.

That's the rough way to do it. AutoLISP has given us an abbreviation or *derived* command (cadr). Don't try to reason why or how this command was derived. Just use it.

(cadr), which may be used just as any other command, always produces the second item in the list. Assuming **a** still has the **X Y** coordinates,

Type: `(setq b (cadr a)) <RETURN>`
         `!b`

As you can see, that produces the **Y** coordinate. Simply stated, you use **(car)** to produce the **X** coordinate and **(cadr)** to produce the **Y** coordinate.

2.5 (caddr)   Z Coordinate (3rd Element)

Beginning with Release 10, all points and entities are expressed in **X,Y** and **Z** coordinates. **(caddr)** is the command that returns the third element (the **Z** coordinate). Let's assume that the variable **a** is a list of three elements (3 5 7).

To pull only the third element from the list,

Type: `(caddr a) <RETURN>`

This will isolate the **Z** coordinate.

2.6 (list)   Create a List

So far, you've assigned a different element of each list to a variable. But as you've seen, the resulting variable simply contains the single value of the **X** or **Y** coordinate and isn't a list.

But what if you want to create a new list? Let's say you want to assign the **X** coordinate of one point and the **Y** coordinate of another point to create a third point and assign it to a variable. Because the variable contains more than one value, it's a list. And you have to let AutoLISP know the new variable is going to be a list. To do that, precede the values with the command **(list)**.

Type: `(setq c (getpoint "\nPick a 2nd point: ")) <RETURN>`

Be sure to pick a point diagonally from the first point that you picked in variable **a**.

Type: `(setq b (list (car a) (cadr c))) <RETURN>`
        `(setq d (list (car c) (cadr a))) <RETURN>`

That command first sets up a variable **c** to accept the data. **(list)** tells you the values that follow are to be treated as a list, now assigned to the variable **c**. Those values are **(car a)**, the first element of **a**, and **(cadr c)**, the second element of **c**. Therefore, if **a** contains **(3 5)** and **c** contains **(7 9)**, then in

`(setq b (list (car a) (cadr c)))`

b would now contain a list of **(3 9)**.

You also created point **d**, which reversed the coordinates. Note the following example:

```
b (3 9)   c (7 9)
a (3 5)   d (7 5)
```

You started with **a (3 5)** and **c (7 9)**. You then derived **b** and **d**. **b** is a new list of the **(car a)** and the **(cadr c)**. **d** is a new list of the **(car c)** and the **(cadr a)**.

Type: `(command "line" a b c d "c") <RETURN>`

You now should have drawn a rectangle.

NOTE: The **"c"** above represents typing **C** (AutoCAD's **Close** command) from the keyboard while in the **LINE** command.

AutoLISP Program LES2a.LSP

Now try using **(car)**, **(cadr)** and **(list)** together to draw a rectangle. The program asks for two points at each corner of the rectangle, then draws the rectangle.

On the companion disk you'll find the program shown below. (For information on loading and saving programs, see Chapter 1, "Getting Started.")

If you have altered the ACAD.PGP file as suggested, from the Auto-CAD Command: prompt

Type: Edit <RETURN>

Response: File to edit:

Type: LES2a.LSP <RETURN>

Type the first line and continue to the end of the program. When you have typed the program completely, SAVE the file and EXIT.

At this point, the file **LES2a.LSP** should be on your disk, whether you typed it in or copied it from the disk. To load and run the first program, at the Command: prompt

Type: (load "les2a") <RETURN>

The screen will then display RECTAN, the last function in the file that was loaded. To run the program,

Type: (rectan) <RETURN>

The program now will begin to run.

NOTE: All other program lessons follow the above routine. Beginning with AutoLISP Program Lesson 3, we'll assume you have the hang of it.

LES2a.LSP

```
(defun rectan (/ pnt1 pnt2 pnt3 pnt4)
(graphscr)
(setq pnt1 (getpoint "\nFirst corner of rectangle: "))
(setq pnt3 (getpoint "\nSecond corner of rectangle: "))
(setq pnt2 (list (car pnt1) (cadr pnt3)))
(setq pnt4 (list (car pnt3) (cadr pnt1)))
(command "line" pnt1 pnt2 pnt3 pnt4 "c")
)
```

PURPOSE:	Draws a rectangle by pointing to two points.
TO LOAD:	

Type:	`(load "les2a")` `<RETURN>`
Response:	`rectan`

TO OPERATE:

Type:	`(rectan)` `<RETURN>`
Response:	`First corner of rectangle:`

Pick a point on the screen.

Response:	`Second corner of rectangle:`

Pick a second point on the screen, up and to the right of the first. The program will now draw a rectangle using those two points.

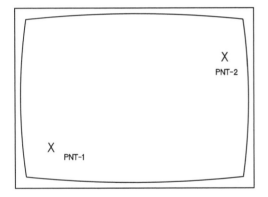

Figure 2-1: Pick two points onscreen.

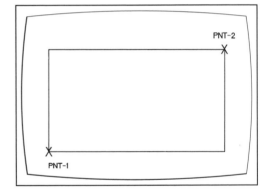

Figure 2-2: The rectangle will be drawn.

Let's look at the program line by line:

`(defun rectan (/ pnt1 pnt2 pnt3 pnt4)`

defines the function **rectangle** with four local variables to be used.

`(graphscr)`

makes sure you've switched to the graphics screen.

```
(setq pnt1 (getpoint "\nFirst corner of rectangle: "))
```

sets **pnt1** to the point selected. A message tells you which point is being selected.

```
(setq pnt3 (getpoint "\nSecond corner of rectangle: "))
```

sets **pnt3** to the point selected with the message.

```
(setq pnt2 (list (car pnt1) (cadr pnt3)))
(setq pnt4 (list (car pnt3) (cadr pnt1)))
```

secures the other two corners. **pnt2** will have the **X** of **pnt1** and the **Y** of **pnt3**. **pnt4** will have the **X** of **pnt3** and **Y** of **pnt1**. You now have the four points of the rectangle.

```
(command "line" pnt1 pnt2 pnt3 pnt4 "c")
```

executes the LINE command and draws a line from corner to corner using the variables of **pnt1, pnt2, pnt3** and **pnt4.** The **"c"** closes the line back to the start point of **pnt1** and ends the LINE command.

```
)
```

closes the function and lets it run as a valid AutoLISP program.

2.7 (getcorner)   Pick the Other Corner

(getcorner) works just like **(getpoint)**, except it assumes one point has already been chosen and assigned to a variable. You're now required to pick a second point, generally the other corner. It will produce, or return, the value of the point picked so that you may assign the point to a variable, just as with **(getpoint)**.

But **(getcorner)** adds one more dimension: As you move your cursor to the other corner, it creates a window effect (just as the **WINDOW** command does) to give you the look and feel of AutoCAD.

Type: `(setq pnt1 (getpoint "\nPick a point: ")) <RETURN>`

Pick any point

Type: `(setq pnt2 (getcorner pnt1 "\nPick another point "))<RETURN>`

Now move your cursor to pick the second point. Note the window it creates. When you pick a point, the window disappears; the point is selected and assigned to the variable.

Let's take the same program from **LES2a** and modify that one line to use **(getcorner)**. (This program is on the disk as **LES2b.LSP**.)

AutoLISP Program LES2b.LSP

```
(defun rectan (/ pnt1 pnt2 pnt3 pnt4)
  (graphscr)
  (setq pnt1 (getpoint "\nFirst corner of rectangle: "))
  (setq pnt3 (getcorner "\nSecond corner of rectangle: " pnt1))
  (setq pnt2 (list (car pnt1) (cadr pnt3)))
  (setq pnt4 (list (car pnt3) (cadr pnt1)))
  (command "line" pnt1 pnt2 pnt3 pnt4 "c")
)
```

PURPOSE: Same as LES2a, except this revision adds the command (getcorner), which dynamically drags the rectangle into position.

TO LOAD:

Type: `(load "les2b") <RETURN>`

Response: `rectan`

TO OPERATE:

Type: `(rectan) <RETURN>`

Response: `First corner of rectangle:`

Pick a point on the screen.

Response: `Second corner of rectangle:`

Pick a second point on the screen, up and to the right of the first.

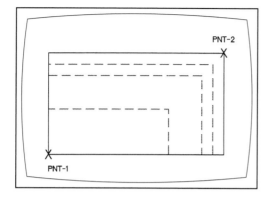

Figure 2-3: Pick two points onscreen and note the rubber-band effect of the program.

As you move the cursor to the second point, you'll see the image of the rectangle drag across the screen. The program now will draw a rectangle using those two points.

IMPORTANT NOTE: If you modified any of the Lesson 2 programs after running them, you must *reload* the programs before running the modified version to avoid making a very common mistake.

If you modify an existing program from inside AutoCAD and save it to your disk, don't run the program again or you'll be running the *original* version of that function that's still in AutoCAD's memory. You'll type

```
(load "les2a") <RETURN>
```

or

```
(load "les2b") <RETURN>
```

You must load the file again in order to bring the new version of the program into memory. Now rerun the *modified* version of the program and see what a difference that one change makes.

Moving On

You're well on your way to writing real programs. But you must control their flow and logic. This is what makes a computer a computer, not just a calculator. Chapter 3, "Controlling the Program," shows you the power of loops and how AutoLISP makes decisions.

3

CONTROLLING THE PROGRAM

Controlling the Program

3.1 Types of Data

AutoCAD and AutoLISP not only allow a wide variety of data types but also provide a number of ways to secure that data. Data types indicate kinds of variables. Major data types include

Real. A number that includes floating-point decimals. For example, **350.302** is a real number.

Integer. A counting number, positive or negative.

String. Usually text and known as a literal. Strings are set off by quotes. Numbers can be put in strings but lose their value as numbers unless they're converted to reals or integers.

List. A variable that contains more than one value or series of values.

Pickset. A table containing pointers to elements of the selection set created during **WINDOW, CROSSING, FENCE** or other selection set options.

Although several more exist, those are the major data types. Any variable can be tested to see what type it is by using the command **(type a)**, where **a** is the variable in question. That tells you the data type of variable **a**.

One interesting aspect of data types is that you don't need to know what type they are to work with them. Also, data types can be mixed. In BASIC, you would get an error if you input

```
a = "Hello how are you"
```

But AutoLISP lets you put all the following in the same program:

```
(setq a 5)
(setq a "Hello how are you")
```

Note that you didn't have to designate the data type in order to use it. In **BASIC**, you'd have to type **A$** in order to assign a string to the variable (as the variable **a** would simply be a numeric, single-precision real variable). AutoLISP doesn't care. You can mix, assign and reassign without regard to data types. The variable simply becomes the data type assigned to it and changes if a different data type is assigned.

3.2 nil   No Value

An AutoLISP variable with no value is said to be **nil**. Because **0** is a number, **nil** isn't the same as **0**. Therefore, if you print a variable that's empty, it will print **nil**. For example,

```
!a
nil
```

You can also empty a variable by assigning it to **nil**.

```
(setq a nil)
```

By assigning **nil** to a variable, you're assured that the variable begins without value. You also can test for **nil** in an **(if...)** statement.

3.3 (getreal)   Enter a Real Number From Keyboard

(**getreal**) secures a real number.

Type: `(setq a (getreal "\nEnter a number: "))  <RETURN>`

Type: `735 <RETURN>`

This assigns to **a** a real number entered through the keyboard. Resist the temptation to assign distances and angles with this command. If you do, your entry must be in the lowest units. When you use feet and inches, for example, you can enter only in inches from the keyboard. AutoLISP won't accept **'** or **"** for feet and inches. A better command would be **(getdist)**.

3.4 (getdist)   Enter a Real Number From Keyboard or Point to Distance

This command also secures a real number, except you can enter it from the keyboard or simply point to two points on the screen.

If you enter the number from the keyboard, all your AutoCAD options are present. You may enter your default units (such as feet and inches) as **3'4"**, or you may enter **40**, which represents **40** inches. If you enter **3'4"**, **(getdist)** will convert that to the real number **40**.

You also can pick two points, and the distance is produced, or returned, as a real number.

For the following example, be sure the AutoCAD **UNITS** command is set to **architectural** or **engineering feet** and **inches**. Type **UNITS** at the **Command** line, then choose **architectural** or **engineering**. Then press **<RETURN>** until you get back to the Command line.

Type: `(setq a (getdist "\nEnter height: ")) <RETURN>`

Let's try your three options.

Type: `3'4" <RETURN>`

Response: `40`

Type: `(setq a (getdist "\nEnter height: "))  <RETURN>`

Response: `Enter height:`

Now pick a point. The computer prompts you for the second point. Selecting both points produces the distance between the two points in the basic units.

Type: `(setq pnt1 (getpoint "\nPick a point: "))`

Response: `Pick a point:`

Now pick a point.

Type: `(setq a (getdist pnt1 "\nEnter height: "))  <RETURN>`

Response: `Enter height:`

In this example, the command supplies the first point—variable **pnt1**. Therefore, you have the first point picked and rubber-banded to the second point. When you pick the second point, it finds the distance between the two points as a real number, assigned to variable **a**.

3.5 (getstring)   Enter String (of Text) From Keyboard

The **(getstring)** command asks you to supply a string of text that can then be assigned to a variable. You may supply an optional flag, which means placing something after **(getstring)**. If the optional flag is anything except **nil** (such as a number), spaces are allowed in the string. If the optional flag is **nil**, no spaces are allowed in the string. If you leave the flag out, it's automatically set to **nil**. If you enter anything, it is not set to **nil**. For example,

Type: `(setq a (getstring 5 "\nEnter a line of text: ")) <RETURN>`

Now type any line of text followed by **<RETURN>**

Type: `!a <RETURN>`

You'll see the same line of text printed. Notice the **5** after **(getstring)**. That's the flag, set to **5**, allowing spaces in the string. There's no magic about the number **5**; it could have been **4** or **30**. If you leave it out, the flag is set to **nil** and no spaces are allowed.

That's important because you need to allow spaces if the string is to be text. On the other hand, you often may want to have the space bar to act as the **<RETURN>** key, which terminates the string input. If you don't allow spaces, the string may be terminated by the space bar or the **<RETURN>** key, as with AutoCAD commands.

Type: `(setq a (getstring "\nEnter text: "))  <RETURN>`

Now enter text, but notice what happens the first time you hit the space bar. It has the same effect as hitting **<RETURN>**.

Type: `!a <RETURN>`

That should print everything up to the time you hit the space bar. The difference is important, because most AutoCAD users are accustomed to hitting the space bar or the **<RETURN>** key as though they were one and the same. That will give your AutoLISP programs the same look and feel as AutoCAD.

3.6 (+ - * /)   Arithmetic Functions

The four arithmetic functions are

+	Add
-	Subtract
*	Multiply
/	Divide

Sequence is very important when using these functions.

`(+ a 3)`

If **a** started with the value **4**, the number **7** would be produced. Notice the + comes first, then the *to be added to* followed by *what will be added.* It reads "**Add to a, 3.**"

Note that in the above example the number **7** is produced only if **a=4**. The value of **a** hasn't changed. **3** hasn't really been added to the variable **a**. You must use **(setq)** to permanently assign any value to a variable. If you want to add **3** to **a** permanently, you'd use:

```
(setq a (+ a 3))
```

Note that **a** can be assigned to itself or to any other variable. In the above example, **a** now has the value of **7**.

Type: `(setq a 3)  <RETURN>`

Type: `!a  <RETURN>`

Notice that **a** has the value of **3**.

Type: `(+ a 2)  <RETURN>`

5, which is the value of **a + 2**, appears on the screen.

Type: `!a  <RETURN>`

But when you print **a**, it still has the original value of **3**.

Type: `(setq a (+ a 2))  <RETURN>`

Type: `!a  <RETURN>`

Now when you print **a**, it has the permanent value of **5** because you assigned it to **a**. A few more examples follow:

Type: `(setq a 6) <RETURN>`

Type: `(- a 5) <RETURN>`

Response: `1`

Type: `(* a 3) <RETURN>`

Response: `18`

Type: `(/ a 3) <RETURN>`

Response: `2`

3.7 (=)   The Equal Function

The **(=)** command isn't an assignment command, as it is in BASIC. You can't say

```
(= a b)
```

and assign the value of **b** to **a**. That can be done only with

```
(setq a b)
```

Remember that the only assignment statement is **(setq)**. The **(=)** command is simply used to test whether items are equal. It does not make them equal.

3.8 (if...)   If, Then, Else

(if...) is the standard **if-then-else** statement. Unlike other languages, in AutoLISP you may match only one **(if...)** statement with a **(then...)** statement. If you want to say

```
If xxxx
then do 1
   do 2
   do 3
else do 4
```

then you'll need the statement **(progn)**, which is covered later, in Chapter 7. For now, remember that you can match only one **(if...)** statement to one **(then...)** or **(else...)** statement. The format of the **(if...)** command is

```
(if (xxx1) (xxx2) (xxx3))
```

Following **(if...)** xxx1 is the item to be tested, which could demonstrate if **a=b** stated **(= a b)**. If the first expression is true, then **(xxx2)** is performed. If the first expression isn't true, then **(xxx3)** is performed. For example,

```
(if (= a b) (setq b 5) (setq b 6))
```

In the above example,
If **a** is equal to **b**
then **b** will be assigned the value of **5**
else **b** will be assigned the value of **6**
   Let's try it.

```
Type:    (setq a 5)  <RETURN>
         (setq b 6)  <RETURN>
         (if (= a b) (setq b "equal") (setq b "not equal"))  <RETURN>

Type:    !b  <RETURN>
```

Did you get **"equal"** or **"not equal"**? You should have gotten **"not equal."** The **(if...)** statement is one of AutoLISP's most important commands. It gives you the power to write real programs, rather than just macros.

3.9 (while)   Loop Statement

(while) is one of three loop control commands available in AutoLISP. A loop is necessary if you want to repeat a command. However, unless you have a way of controlling it, the program will loop indefinitely. The **(while)** loop in AutoLISP takes the form of

```
(while a)
```

where **a** is a variable. The loop continues as long as the variable **a** is not **nil**. If the variable **a** is **nil**, the program breaks out of the loop. What the program does while in the loop is defined between the parenthesis that begins the **(while)** and the parenthesis that closes the loop.

Therefore, you must set up the controlling variable with a value other than **nil**. When you want the loop to end, set the controlling variable to **nil** and the loop will break. For example,

```
(setq a "W")
```

sets up the controlling variable to a value other than **nil**. It doesn't matter what the value is.

```
(while a
```

the loop will continue, beginning with the commands that follow, until the variable **a** is set to **nil**.

```
(xxxxx)
   (xxxxx)
(xxxxx)
```

are the commands that will be performed during the loop.

```
(if (= c d)
(setq a nil))
```

evaluates whether **c** is equal to **d**, and if so, sets the loop controlling variable **a** to **nil**, so it will break out the next time through the loop.

```
)
```

The ending parenthesis closes the loop. When the loop breaks, it begins with the commands after this parenthesis.

3.10 (> < /=) Comparatives

The comparatives are

>   Greater than
<   Less than
/=   Not equal

You can use these in the **(if...)** statement exactly as you'd use the **(=)** statement. Below are some examples:

```
(if (< a b))
```

If **a** is less than **b**

```
(if (> a b))
```

If **a** is greater than **b**

```
(if (/= a b))
```

If **a** is not equal to **b**.

3.11 (and) (or) Logical Connectors

These *connectors* may be used with **(if...)** statements as long as your parentheses are placed properly.

```
(if (or (< a b) (> a 25)) (setq c 6))
```

This reads "if (a is less than b) or (a is greater than 25), then set c to 6.

AutoLISP Program LES3a.LSP

PURPOSE: AutoLISP Program Les3a asks you to supply the height of the text, then supply the number of text lines and line spacing. The program then writes the text.

Unless you constantly change system variables, AutoCAD fixes the distance between lines. This program gives you one additional adjustment so you can enter a series of text lines yet determine spacing between lines.

At this point, the file **LES3a.LSP** should be on your disk, whether you typed it in or copied it from the companion disk. *NOTE:* In this program you must be using a text style that has a zero height. To achieve a zero height, you must set height to 0 in the AutoCAD STYLE command.

To load and run the first program,

Type: (load "les3a") <RETURN>

Response: TEX

TEX is the last function in the file that was loaded. To run the program,

Type: (TEX) <RETURN>

The program will now begin to run. (If you need further information on creating and loading AutoLISP files, see AutoLISP Program Lesson 1.)

LES3a.LSP is written fully below.

```
(defun Tex (/ pnt1 a b c d e f)
(graphscr)
  (setq pnt1 (getpoint "\nStarting point: "))
  (setq a (getdist pnt1 "\nEnter Height: "))
  (setq b (getreal "\nNumber of text lines: "))
  (setq c (getdist pnt1 "\nLine Spacing: "))
  (setq d "T")
  (while d
  (setq e (getstring 1 "\nEnter Text: "))
  (setq b (- b 1))
  (if (= b 0) (setq d nil))
  (command "Text" pnt1 a "0" e)
  (setq pnt1 (list (car pnt1)(- (cadr pnt1) c)))
  )
)
```

PURPOSE: Lets you change the distance between multiple text lines. In addition to the standard starting point and height, you're asked to enter the distance between the text lines.

TO LOAD:

Type: `(load "les3a") <RETURN>`

Response: `Tex`

TO OPERATE:

Type: `(tex) <RETURN>`

Response: `Starting point:`

Pick a point on the screen for the starting point of the text.

Response: `Enter Height:`

Point to the distance of the text height. Or you can enter the height from the keyboard using your default units.

Response: `Number of text lines:`

Enter the number of text lines you wish to enter.

Response: `Line Spacing:`

Point to the desired distance between the text lines. You can enter the distance from the keyboard using your default units.

Response: `Enter Text:`

This prompt will occur for the number of text lines you specify. Enter the text followed by **<RETURN>**.

The program will print your text at the starting point, height and between-line spacing you specified.

The following is a line-by-line analysis of AutoLISP Program Les3a.lsp:

`(defun Tex (/ pnt1 a b c d e f)`

defines the function **Tex** with local variables.

`(graphscr)`

makes sure the program begins with the graphics screen.

`(setq pnt1 (getpoint "\nStarting point: "))`

asks for the starting point of the text and assigns the point coordinates to the variable **pnt1**.

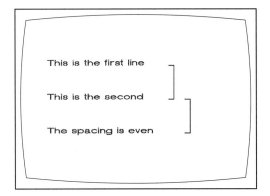

Figure 3-1: Pick the spacing for your text.

```
(setq a (getdist pnt1 "\nEnter Height: "))
```

asks you to give the height of the text by pointing. It uses the starting point of the text **(pnt1)** as the first point and then rubber-bands to the second point. When you specify the second point, it assigns a real number representing the distance from the first point to the second point. You can enter the distance from the keyboard.

```
setq b (getreal "\nNumber of text lines: "))
```

asks you to supply the number of text lines. This is a real number assigned to variable **b**, which also will be used in the loop to determine the number of lines to be typed in.

```
(setq c (getdist pnt1 "\nLine Spacing: "))
```

asks you to give the spacing of the lines by pointing. It uses the starting point of the text **(pnt1)** as the first point, then rubber-bands to the second point. When you specify the second point, it assigns a real number that represents the distance from the first to the second point. You could enter the distance from the keyboard.

```
(setq d "T")
```

sets up the loop control variable by setting the variable **d** to **T**. It simply sets it to something other than **nil**.

```
(while d
```

begins the loop for as long as **d** is anything but **nil**.

```
(setq e (getstring 1 "\nEnter Text: "))
```

The string typed in is assigned to the variable **e**. The 1 following (get-string) is the non-nil flag setting, indicating that spaces are allowed (otherwise, spaces would not be permitted and the space would be interpreted as a **<RETURN>**).

```
(setq b (- b 1))
```

The variable **b** started with the number of text lines you input. **1** will be subtracted from **b** each time through the loop. **b** is permanently assigned the new value.

```
(if (= b 0) (setq d nil))
```

This is the test to see if **b** has reached **0** yet. When it has, the variable **d** will be set to **nil**. Remember, variable **d** is the loop control variable. When set to **nil**, the loop ends and the program continues, following the parentheses closing the **(while....)**.

```
(command "Text" pnt1 a "0" e)
```

This is the AutoCAD command that starts the text. Text begins at **pnt1**, and variable **a** is the height. **"0"** is the angle, and variable **e** contains the line of text that was entered.

```
(setq pnt1 (list (car pnt1)(- (cadr pnt1) c)))
```

That's some line! Dissect it to see how much you've learned. The object is to print the next line a given distance below the previous line. Remember that the previous line's beginning point is in the variable **pnt1**. Now you need to set a new **pnt1** starting point for the next text line. Therefore, the new **pnt1** is the **(list)** of

```
(car pnt1)
```

the **X** coordinate of **pnt1**.

```
(- (cadr pnt1) c)
```

The **(cadr pnt1)** is the **Y** coordinate of **pnt1**. **c** is the space distance of the lines of text. The distance found in **c** is subtracted from the **Y** coordinate. Therefore,

```
(list (car pnt1)(- (cadr pnt1) c))
```

creates a new list of the **X** coordinate (car) of **pnt1** and the **Y** coordinate (cadr) of **pnt1** minus the variable **c** distance for the **Y** coordinate. Thus,

```
(setq pnt1 (list (car pnt1)(- (cadr pnt1) c)))
```

sets the new starting **pnt1** at the previous **X** coordinate and the previous **Y** coordinate minus the distance found in variable **c**.

```
  )
```

```
)
```

the next to last parenthesis closes the **(while)** loop. The final parenthesis completes the program.

AutoLISP Program LES3b.LSP (Revised)

This program has a degree of complexity. As you gain experience, you'll see what and how many variables you'll need from the start. Until then, the interactive capabilities of AutoLISP and AutoCAD let you program a few lines, then test them. You can correct, add variables and inputs (**get** statements), and rerun. Eventually, you'll be able to determine what's needed well in advance.

A group of specialized text programs should be among the first you write. If you have special text requirements, write a program that prompts for text in a predetermined style, height, spacing and so on. Small programs like those can save you many steps each time they're used. It's important to try not to put too much in any one program. Otherwise, you'll be answering so many questions that the program will no longer save you time.

The following program contains a simple modification to the preceding program, letting you type in as many lines as you want. When finished, press <RETURN> and the program terminates. We also added the **C:** prefix to the program name, permitting you to run the program from the AutoCAD Command: prompt without parentheses.

The following program is listed on the disk as **LES3b.LSP**.

```
(defun C:Tex2 (/ pnt1 a b c d e f)
   (graphscr)
   (setq pnt1 (getpoint "\nStarting point: "))
   (setq a (getdist pnt1 "\nEnter Height: "))
```

```
(setq c (getdist pnt1 "\nLine Spacing: "))
(setq d "T")
(while d
  (setq e (getstring 1 "\nEnter Text:   "))
  (if (= e "") (setq d nil))
  (command "Text" pnt1 a "0" e)
  (setq pnt1 (list (car pnt1) (- (cadr pnt1) c)))
  )
)
```

PURPOSE: Lets you change the distance between multiple text lines. In addition to the standard starting point and height, you're asked to enter the distance between text lines. Unlike Lesson 3a, you may enter as many lines as necessary.

To stop the program, press <RETURN>.

TO LOAD:

Type: (load "les3b") <RETURN>

Response: Tex2

TO OPERATE:

Type: tex2 <RETURN>

Response: Starting point:

Pick a point on the screen for the starting point of the text.

Response: Enter Height:

Point to the distance of the height of the text. You may enter the height from the keyboard using your default units.

Response: Line Spacing:

Point to the desired distance between the text lines. You may enter the distance from the keyboard using your default units.

Response: Enter Text:

This prompt will occur for each text line. Enter the text followed by **<RETURN>**.
You'll need one additional **<RETURN>** to end the program.

The program will print your text at the starting point, height and between-line spacing you specified. The following lines were eliminated:

```
(setq b (getreal "\nNumber of text lines: "))
(setq b (- b 1))
(if (= b 0) (setq d nil))
```

Those lines were used to control the number of text lines you were able to type. However, in the revised program you want to be able to type as many lines as needed. After the last line of text, press <RETURN> and the program will end.

```
(if (= e "") (setq d nil))
```

checks to see if you entered a blank <RETURN>. If that's the case, then **d** is set to **nil** and the loop stops.

Moving On

Not everything in AutoCAD is drawn with straight lines across the X Y grid. We can't imagine a world without angles. AutoLISP treats angles a little differently than you might think. Chapter 4, "Angles & Distances," introduces you to the world of angles and radians.

4

ANGLES & DISTANCES

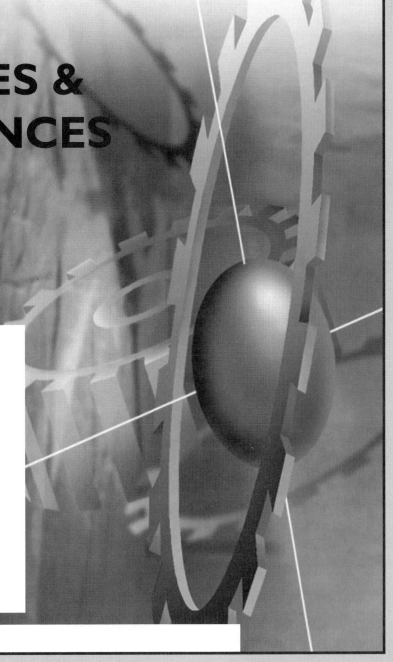

Angles & Distances

4.I ANGLES

Because all lines and entities aren't drawn at 90 degrees, angle processing is vital to any AutoLISP programming. Angles in AutoLISP are measured in radians, not degrees. Although the angle entry to AutoCAD is generally in decimal degrees, you'll often want angles displayed in degrees, minutes and seconds—or even by bearings.

It's important to emphasize the difference between an AutoLISP and an AutoCAD command. For example,

```
(angle)
```

is an AutoLISP command that's discussed in Section 4.3 of this chapter. Its purpose is to measure the angle of a line drawn between two known points. Thus, an AutoLISP command might be

```
(setq a (angle pnt1 pnt2))
```

The variable **a** would then contain the value of the angle. But since **(angle)** is an AutoLISP command, the value would be in radians.

If you want to use the value of **a** in an AutoCAD command, you might use this as an example:

```
(command "text" pt1 "40" a t)
```

This uses an AutoCAD **TEXT** command, where the text rotatation is the variable **a** from the previous example.

The above examples show that the AutoLISP **(angle)** command first measured the angle and assigned it to the variable **a**. Then the **(command "text" pt1 "40" a t)** used the angle in the variable **a** as an AutoCAD command.

The problem is that all AutoLISP commands use angles expressed in radians, and all AutoCAD commands use angles expressed in decimal degrees (if that is what your default UNITS are set to).

Therefore, you need a convenient way to convert radians to degrees and degrees to radians so you can go back and forth from AutoCAD entries to AutoLISP computations.

Two programs convert radians to degrees: **(dtr)** stands for **d**egrees **t**o **r**adians and **(rtd)** stands for **r**adians **t**o **d**egrees. These programs require no explanation. You'll know when to use them. **(rtd)** and **(dtr)** still aren't part of AutoLISP. But you can still use them as functions that you wrote and named.

4.2 ACAD.LSP

The **(dtr)** and the **(rtd)** commands are functions you'll use in nearly every program you write. As time goes on, you'll want to create your own favorite functions as if they were actually part of AutoLISP. It would be a waste of time to write those functions for every program you create—and AutoCAD provides a solution. The file **ACAD.LSP** is automatically loaded and remains resident each time the drawing editor is accessed. Often-used functions placed in this file are always available to any program you write.

NOTE: Releases 12 and 13 have added additional self-loading files. They are ACADR12.LSP and ACADR13.LSP, respectively. They are found in the \ACAD\SUPPORT directory.

The following page lists the **(dtr)** and **(rtd)** functions. Type those functions into a file called **ACAD.LSP** (available on the companion disk).

Think of **ACAD.LSP** as the **AUTOEXEC.BAT** file of AutoLISP. Any programs placed in the file are ready each time you bring up a drawing.

You'll want to add these two programs to your **ACAD.LSP** file:

```
; The dtr function converts degrees to radians
; The rtd function converts radians to degrees
(defun dtr (a)
(* pi (/ a 180.0))
  )
;
(defun rtd (a)
(/ (* a 180.0) pi)
  )
```

CAUTION: Some third-party software packages that use AutoLISP may already have their own **ACAD.LSP** file. If so, don't disturb the file, since functions used by the third-party software reside there. If you copy over that file or destroy it, your third-party software may not run.

Beginning with Release 13, Autodesk is suggesting to all third-party developers either not to use ACAD.LSP or at the very least not to protect the file. The ACAD.LSP file belongs to you the user, not the third-party developer. But not all developers are in compliance with this.

If you're using third-party software, check first to see if **ACAD.LSP** already exists. If it does and is available in source form, you can simply add the **(dtr)** and **(rtd)** functions. And always back up important files to a floppy disk!

ACAD.LSP is loaded automatically each time you enter AutoCAD's drawing editor. If you copied the **ACAD.LSP** file to your AutoCAD directory before entering the drawing editor, the **ACAD.LSP** file now should be fully loaded. However, if you created or changed the **ACAD.LSP** file with **Edit** while in the drawing editor, the file isn't currently loaded. The simplest way to load the file is to quit the current drawing and OPEN another drawing. As you load a new or existing drawing you'll see the message:

```
Loading acad.lsp
```

When you're in the drawing editor, all **ACAD.LSP** functions are immediately available to you and your programs.

Just as the **ACAD.LSP** file is loaded immediately as you enter the drawing editor, a feature introduced with Release 10 lets you set up what might be considered the equivalent of **AUTOEXEC.BAT** inside the **ACAD.LSP** file.

You may have defined in the **ACAD.LSP** file a function called **S::startup**. If it exists in the **ACAD.LSP** file at the time a drawing is loaded, **S::startup** will automatically begin executing.

The automatic feature of this function is available only within the ACAD.LSP file. Even though you may place this function in other files, it will not automatically execute when the file is loaded. Even in the ACAD.LSP file it will automatically execute only once, when loaded by the drawing editor.

4.3 (angle) Measure Angle of Two Points

The **(angle)** command measures the angle between two points in radians. If you want to use the angle as an input to an AutoCAD command, you'll need to convert it to degrees, using the **(rtd)** command. For example,

```
(setq a (rtd 3.017))
```

will convert **3.017** radians to **degrees**.

Type: ```
(setq pnt1 (getpoint "\nPick a point: ")) <RETURN>
(setq pnt2 (getpoint "\nPick 2nd point: ")) <RETURN>
(setq a (angle pnt1 pnt2)) <RETURN>
```

It assigns the radian angle from **pnt1** to **pnt2** to the variable **a**.

Type: ```
!a <RETURN>
```

Notice the value of the angle in **a** is expressed in radians. The order in which the angles are measured is very important. Let's set up an example:

Type: ```
(setq pnt1 (getpoint)) <RETURN>
```

Pick two points like the figure below.

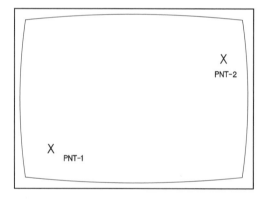

*Figure 4-1: Pick two points that look like this.*

Type: ```
(setq pnt2 (getpoint)) <RETURN>
(setq a (angle pnt1 pnt2)) <RETURN>
(setq a1 (angle pnt2 pnt1)) <RETURN>
(rtd a)    <RETURN>
(rtd a1)   <RETURN>
```

Even though the points are the same, the angle measured between them is different. Because of the way AutoCAD measures angles, they should differ by 180 degrees.

When writing your programs, you should either force AutoCAD to pick the points in a certain order so you can control which is **pnt1** and which is

pnt2, or you should test the number of degrees in the angle. If an angle command produces more than 180 degrees, you know the points were produced in one order. If the angle command produces less than or equal to 180 degrees, the points were produced in the other order.

4.4 (distance) Measure Distance Between Two Points

This command measures the distance from two known points.

Type: `(setq d (distance pnt1 pnt2)) <RETURN>`

Type: `!d <RETURN>`

Response: `The distance should be produced.`

It assigns the distance (from **pnt1** to **pnt2**) to variable **d**. If you maintained the values of **pnt1** and **pnt2** from the **(angle)** examples, then **d** should produce the distance between the points.

Unlike the angle command, the order of the points isn't significant.

4.5 (polar) Derive Point From Angle & Distance

(polar) is a fascinating command—without it you wouldn't be able to do 80 percent of the things you want to do with angles. It produces a point at an angle and distance from another point. For example, if you want a point to be 14 feet from another point at an angle of 272 degrees, then **(polar)** is the command to use. Remember, when using **(polar)**, the angle you supply must be measured in radians, not degrees. For example,

`(setq a (polar pnt1 ang1 dst1))`

If **pnt1** is a point, **ang1** is an angle and **dst1** is the distance, then the variable **a** is assigned a point **ang1 (angle)** and dst1 **(distance)** from **pnt1 (point)**.

That's particularly useful when producing parallel lines at an angle and distance plus or minus 90 degrees from each other.

Let's continue to use **pnt1** and **pnt2** from the previous examples and illustrate how **(polar)** is used to draw parallel lines.

Type: `(command "line" pnt1 pnt2 "") <RETURN>`

That draws a line between the two points.

Type: `(setq ang1 (angle pnt1 pnt2)) <RETURN>`

That measures the angle from **pnt1** to **pnt2**.

Type: `(setq pnt3 (polar pnt1 (+ ang1 (dtr 90)) 36)) <RETURN>`

(polar) creates a point **(pnt3)** 36 inches and the same angle plus 90 degrees from **pnt1**. Look at the angle part of the command.

`(+ ang1 (dtr 90))`

The **(+ ang1 (dtr 90))** adds 90 degrees to the existing angle **(ang1)**. Note that you cannot add 90 degrees directly because **ang1** is in radians. Use the **(dtr)** function to convert 90 to radians before it's added to **ang1**.

By creating two new points at the same angle plus 90 degrees and connecting the points, you'll draw a parallel line.

`(setq pnt4 (polar pnt2 (+ ang1 (dtr 90)) 36)) <RETURN>`

That's the same command except that **pnt4** is 36 inches plus 90 degrees from **pnt2**.

`(command "line" pnt3 pnt4 "") <RETURN>`

You should have drawn a line 36 inches to the left and parallel to the first line. Variations include subtracting, instead of adding, 90 degrees. That would put the parallel line to the right of the first. Also, by selecting your angle from **pnt2** to **pnt1** instead of **pnt1** to **pnt2**, you can reverse the side on which the parallel line is drawn.

4.6 Print Commands

AutoCAD has four print commands; most often you'll use two for printing to the screen. Those four commands are **(princ)**, **(prin1)**, **(print)** and **(prompt)**.

(princ) is the primary print command for printing to the screen.

(prin1) writes data to the screen or to a sequential file. It can print control characters to a particular file so they can be **(loaded)** back.

(print) is the same as **(princ)**, except it adds a line feed. Basically **(princ)** and **(print)** are used for the screen.

(prompt) is like **(princ)** or **(print)** but has the advantage of removing the quotation marks from literal string data. Since quotes often are confused with inches, **(prompt)** makes things easier visually.

If the variable **a** is assigned the list **(3 5 7 9)**, then **(princ a)** produces **(3 5 7 9)**.

4.7 (angtos) Angle Conversion

This command takes the angle (a real number in radians) and produces output in degrees, minutes and seconds, or your default units. It's important to remember that **(angtos)** is a string with no value.

```
(setq a (angtos b))
```

may produce an output such as

```
"14d22'33""
```

To get rid of the extra **" "** marks, use the **(prompt)** command:

```
(prompt (angtos b))
```

Let's try a few examples. (**Ang1** should already contain an angle expressed in radians from the previous example.)

Type: `(prompt (angtos ang1)) <RETURN>`

If your default units are in degrees, minutes and seconds, it should have produced the angle in that format.

Because angles may be produced in a variety of ways, **(angtos)** uses two flags. The first is used to determine the style of print and the second the precision (i.e., how many places in decimals, or minutes/seconds, are carried out).

    0   degrees
    1   degrees, minutes, seconds
    2   grads
    3   radians
    4   surveyor's units

Thus the command

```
(prompt (angtos a 1 5))
```

forces the output to be in degrees/minutes/seconds, even though the default units are in surveyor's units or decimal degrees.

Try each of these:

Type: (prompt (angtos ang1 0 5)) <RETURN>

Response: Result in degrees

Type: (prompt (angtos ang1 1 5)) <RETURN>

Response: Result in degrees/minutes/seconds

Type: (prompt (angtos ang1 2 5)) <RETURN>

Response: Result in grads

Type: (prompt (angtos ang1 3 5)) <RETURN>

Response: Result in radians

Type: (prompt (angtos ang1 4 5)) <RETURN>

Response: Result in surveyor's units

Note how you can force the output regardless of the default units.

4.8 (rtos)   Distance Conversion

(rtos) is to distance what **(angtos)** is to angles. Remember that all distances are stored in the basic units. For example, **3'4"** is stored as **40**. If the variable **a** is equal to **40**, and you'd like to print it as **3'4"**, give the command:

(prompt (rtos a))

That produces the output by using your default units of measurement. You also can force it as follows:

1   scientific
2   decimal
3   engineering
4   architectural
5   fractional

Thus,

(prompt (rtos a 3 4))

produces the output as a string in engineering feet and inches, with fractional inches expressed as decimals to four decimal places of precision. Remember, you don't have to use the flags if you want the output in the default units.

Let's try each of these. The variable **d** should already contain the distance from **pnt1** to **pnt2** in the prior example.

Type:	(prompt (rtos d 1 4)) <RETURN>
Response:	Result in scientific units
Type:	(prompt rtos d 2 4)) <RETURN>
Response:	Result in decimal units
Type:	(prompt rtos d 3 4)) <RETURN>
Response:	Result in engineering units
Type:	(prompt rtos d 4 4)) <RETURN>
Response:	Result in architectural units
Type:	(prompt rtos d 5 4)) <RETURN>
Response:	Result in fractional units

AutoLISP Program LES4.LSP

```
(defun C:para (/ pnt1 pnt2 pnt3 pnt4 a d d1)
  (graphscr)
  (setq pnt1 (getpoint "\nEnter first point: "))
  (setq pnt2 (getpoint "\nEnter second point: "))
  (setq d (getdist "\nEnter offset: "))
  (setq a (angle pnt1 pnt2))
  (setq d1 (distance pnt1 pnt2))
  (setq pnt3 (polar pnt1 (- a (dtr 90)) d))
  (setq pnt4 (polar pnt2 (- a (dtr 90)) d))
  (command "line" pnt1 pnt2 "")
  (command "line" pnt3 pnt4 "")
  (princ "\nThe distance of the line is: ") (princ d1)
  (princ "\nThe angle of the line is: ")
  (prompt (angtos  a 1 5))
)
```

PURPOSE: Draws two lines parallel to each other to illustrate the basic concepts of drawing parallel lines.

TO LOAD:

Type: (load "les4") <RETURN>

Response: para

TO OPERATE:

Type: para <RETURN>

Response: Enter first point:

Pick a point on the screen.

Response: Enter second point:

Pick a second point on the screen.

Response: Enter offset:

Point to the offset or enter from the keyboard using the default units.

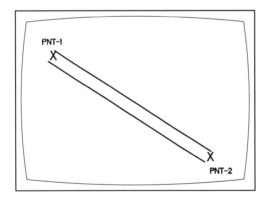

Figure 4-2: Pick two points on the screen as shown.

The program draws parallel lines between the two points for the **offset** chosen. When finished, it tells you the distance and the angle of the lines drawn.

The following is a line-by-line analysis of AutoLISP Program LES4.LSP

```
(defun C:para (/ pnt1 pnt2 pnt3 pnt4 a d d1)
```

defines the function C:para with local variables.

```
(graphscr)
```

begins the program on the graphics screen.

```
(setq pnt1 (getpoint "\nEnter first point: "))
```

asks you to choose a point, then assigns coordinates to **pnt1**.

```
(setq pnt2 (getpoint "\nEnter second point: "))
```

asks you to choose a second point, then assigns coordinates to **pnt2**.

```
(setq d (getdist "\nEnter offset: "))
```

asks you to choose the distance between the parallel lines. **(getdist)** lets you point or enter using default units such as feet and inches.

```
(setq a (angle pnt1 pnt2))
```

Variable **a** is assigned the angle in radians between the two points **pnt1** and **pnt2**.

```
(setq d1 (distance pnt1 pnt2))
```

Variable **d1** is assigned the real number, which is the distance between the two points **pnt1** and **pnt2**.

```
(setq pnt3 (polar pnt1 (- a (dtr 90)) d))
```

Let's begin to dissect this one. Remember,

> **a** is the angle in radians
> **pnt1** is the starting point
> **d** is the distance

Since you want to make the second line parallel (i.e., 90 degrees from the first), you must subtract 90 degrees from the angle line of the first two points. However, you cannot subtract 90 degrees from radians. Therefore, you must use **(dtr)** so you can subtract 90 degrees. Thus, **(- a (dtr 90))** is the angle less 90 degrees.

```
(setq pnt4 (polar pnt2 (- a (dtr 90)) d))
```

creates the fourth point, which is drawn parallel to the second point.

```
(command "line" pnt1 pnt2 "")
```

draws the first line from **pnt1** to **pnt2**, and **" "** terminates the **LINE** command.

```
(command "line" pnt3 pnt4 "")
```

draws the second line from **pnt3** to **pnt4**, and **" "** terminates the **LINE** command.

```
(princ "\nThe distance of the line is: ") (princ d1)
```

demonstrates the use of the **(princ)** command to combine, without a line feed, the literal **("\nThe distance of the line is: ")** and the variable **d1**.

```
(princ "\nThe angle of the line is: ") (prompt (angtos a 1 5))
```

The **1** and **5** determine the style of the print as degrees, minutes and seconds with **5** places of precision.

```
)
```

The final parenthesis closes the function.

Moving On

Many of the global functions of AutoCAD are buried in system variables. In Chapter 5, "System Variables," you're going to dig up a lot of power through the use of (getvar) and (setvar).

5

SYSTEM VARIABLES

System Variables

5.1 Controlling Your System Settings

AutoCAD lets you change a multitude of *system variables.* Unlike the AutoLISP variables that you've used so far, system variables basically control certain system settings. For example, you can control whether the text in a MIRROR command is mirrored. You can control commands such as DRAGMODE and BLIPMODE. Although a complete system variables listing appears in *The AutoCAD Reference Manual,* below are a few of the most important variables and how they work:

Aunits sets up your angular UNITS as follows: 0 = decimal degrees; 1 = degrees, minutes, seconds; 2 = grads; 3 = radians; 4 = surveyors (bearings). **(setvar "aunits" 1).**

Auprec sets up the precision of accuracy for angular UNITS. **(setvar "auprec" 4).**

Blipmode turns BLIPMODE on or off. 1 = on and 0 = off. **(setvar "blipmode" 0).**

Cmdecho determines if AutoLISP commands are **ECHO**ed to the screen. 1 = yes and 0 = no. **(setvar "cmdecho" 0).**

Coords determines how the coordinates are updated on the screen as follows. 0 = coordinates are updated only when points are picked; 1 = display of absolute coordinates are constantly updated as you move your pointing device; 2 = distance and angle from the last point are displayed. **(setvar "coords" 2).**

Dragmode turns **DRAG** on and off. 0 = off; 1 = on if requested; 2 = automatic. **(setvar "dragmode" 2).**

Gridmode turns **GRID** on and off. 0 = off and 1 = on. **(setvar "gridmode" 1).**

Highlight turns the object selection highlighting on and off. 0 = off and 1 = on. **(setvar "highlight" 1).**

Mirrtext determines if **TEXT** is mirrored. 0 = do not mirror text and 1 = yes, mirror text. **(setvar "mirrtext" 0).**

Orthomode turns **ORTHO** on or off. 0 = off and 1 = on. **(setvar "orthomode" 0).**

Osmode sets **OBJECT SNAP**. See Chapter 6, "Programming Techniques," for a full list of the **OBJECT SNAP** settings. **(setvar "osmode" 1).**

Snapmode sets **SNAP** on or off. 0 = off and 1 = on. **(setvar "snapmode" 0).**

5.2 (setvar) (getvar)   Set Variables/Get Variables

The AutoLISP command that sets system variables is **(setvar)**. The command that produces the current setting for the system variables is **(getvar)**.

```
(setvar "blipmode" 0)
```

    (setvar) is followed by the name of the system variable in quotes, followed by the variable setting. In the above example, **"blipmode"** is set to **0**, which eliminates blips from the screen. You must use the actual name of the system variable found in your AutoCAD manual.
    Use **(getvar)** to test for current settings.

```
(getvar "osmode")
```

will produce the current **OBJECT SNAP** mode.

5.3 (getorient) (getangle)   Find Angle

Both commands let you find an angle by pointing to two points.

Type: `(setq a (getangle "\nPick Angle: ")) <RETURN>`

    You may now point to the angle by picking two points. After you pick the first point, you'll be prompted for the second. The resulting angle is assigned to the variable **a** in radians.
    The result is different if one of the points is already known.

Type: `(setq pnt1 (getpoint)) <RETURN>`

Now pick a point.

Type: `(setq a (getangle "\nPick Angle: " pnt1)) <RETURN>`

    Note that you can rubber-band to your chosen angle. That's the usual way angle or rotation commands are produced in AutoCAD.

A final variation to the command is that the angle may be entered from the keyboard, using the default units.

Type: `(setq a (getangle "\nPick Angle: "))  <RETURN>`

Type: `14d15'22" <RETURN>`

Type: `!a <RETURN>`

Note that although entered as degrees, the angle is stored in variable **a** in radians. If you got an error message when you entered **14d15'22"**, be sure you included no spaces and that you typed it correctly. Then be certain your default units were in degrees, minutes and seconds. If they were in decimals or bearings, use decimal degrees or bearings.

(getorient) and **(getangle)** are very similar, except **(getangle)** maintains the current base and units. For example, if you've chosen **North** to be **0** degrees, then angles measured by **(getangle)** will use this orientation. On the other hand, **(getorient)** always uses **East** as **0** degrees.

Both commands let you point to a given angle from a first point to a second point. Or you can specify the start point and be prompted for the second point. Remember that although you can use current units, the answer always is returned in radians.

At this point, the file **LES5.LSP** should be on your disk, whether you typed it in or copied it from the disk. To load and run the first program,

Type: `(load "les5") <RETURN>`

Response: `anglelin`

The last function in the file that was loaded is displayed. To run the program,

Type: `anglelin  <RETURN>`

The program now begins to run.

AutoLISP Program LES5.LSP shows two different methods of getting angles and distances. The first is by pointing, and the second is through the keyboard.

The program asks you to start with a point, then asks for the direction in which you want the line to go and the distance. You may pick the distance, but it doesn't have to be in the eventual direction of the line.

This program allows you to draw a line the same distance as two other specified points in your drawing. That way you can measure the distance of your line by pointing to two points somewhere else in your drawing; yet you can draw the line from a given starting point and at your specified angle.

AutoLISP Program LES5.LSP

```
(defun C:anglelin (/ pnt1 pnt2 pnt3 a a1 d)
  (graphscr)
  (setvar "blipmode" 0)
  (setq pnt1 (getpoint "\nEnter beginning point: "))
  (setq a (getorient pnt1 "\nPoint direction of line: "))
  (setq d (getdist "\nPoint distance of line: "))
  (setq pnt2 (polar pnt1 a d))
  (command "line" pnt1 pnt2 "")
  (setq d (getreal "\nEnter distance from keyboard: "))
  (setq a1 (getreal "\nEnter decimal angle from keyboard: "))
  (setq a (dtr a1))
  (setq pnt3 (polar pnt2 a d))
  (command "line" pnt2 pnt3 "")
)
```

PURPOSE: You'll often need to draw a line the same length as another line in your drawing. This program lets you point to and measure the angle of the line to be drawn. You can then go to another point in your drawing and measure the length of the line to be drawn. The program draws the line at the first point picked, at the angle chosen for the distance measured.

TO LOAD:

Type: `(load "les5") <RETURN>`

Response: `anglelin`

TO OPERATE:

Type: `anglelin <RETURN>`

Response: `Enter beginning point:`

Pick the point where the line begins.

Response: `Point direction of line:`

Pick a point at the direction and angle you want. It doesn't have to be the length of the original line.

Response: `Point distance of line:`

At another point on the screen, pick two points to show the distance of the eventual line.

At that point, a line is drawn.

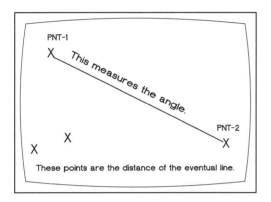

Figure 5-1: Pick start point and line direction.

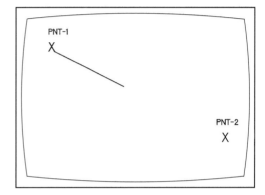

Figure 5-2: Pick line distance.

The following is a line-by-line analysis of LES5.LSP.

```
(defun C:anglelin (/ pnt1 pnt2 pnt3 a a1 d)
```

defines the function and local variables.

```
(graphscr)
```

sets the program to the graphics screen.

```
(setvar "blipmode" 0)
```

sets the system variable **"blipmode"** to **0**, eliminating blips from the screen.

```
(setq pnt1 (getpoint "\nEnter beginning point: "))
```

assigns the point picked to variable **pnt1**.

```
(setq a (getorient pnt1 "\nPoint direction of line: "))
```

pnt1 is used as the beginning point. The angle of the direction of the resulting rubber-band line is assigned to the variable **a**. Remember that **a** now contains the angle in radians.

```
(setq d (getdist "\nPoint distance of line: "))
```

measures the line's distance. That's done by pointing to two points some-where else in the drawing. The distance is entered (by pointing from the beginning point to the second point), then assigned to variable **d**.

Note that the distance doesn't necessarily have to measure itself in the direction of the eventual line. In fact, the length of an eventual line some-times is the same distance as an existing line going in another direction.

```
(setq pnt2 (polar pnt1 a d))
```

pnt2 is to be used as the second point in drawing the line. Remember that **(polar)** gives you a point a given distance and angle from another point. Therefore, **pnt2** is the angle and distance in variables **a** and **d** from **pnt1**.

```
(command "line" pnt1 pnt2 "")
```

draws the line.

```
)
```

closes **(defun**

Moving On

Learning how to program is not the same as learning programming. Chapter 6, "Programming Techniques," takes a breather to illustrate the process of programming by examining what it takes to put a complete program together from start to finish.

6

PROGRAMMING TECHNIQUES

Programming Techniques

6.1 Program Development

The AutoLISP commands you mastered in the first five chapters can create some very useful programs. Chapter 6 shows you how to develop basic AutoLISP programming skills so you can implement what you've learned so far. You'll learn two new commands; then you'll analyze a more complex program for technique.

As you will see, there's no one correct method of programming. Although textbooks would like you to follow their structured programming techniques, you'll find no substitute for hard work and good old trial and error.

Don't worry about creating the perfect program. You sometimes may be overwhelmed by the complexity of AutoLISP programs listed in periodicals and on bulletin boards. Remember, one programmer didn't instantly create them. They progressed from a series of small steps, tried and tested over time, overcoming initial problems as they developed. Some steps led to a dead end. Often, the programmer had to write a little program to cut through or go around a wall, which is why in other languages you see so many GOTO statements—efficient ways to get around a problem.

When a well-written program finally does its magic, even the programmer sometimes is astonished at the complexity and brilliance of the work! Of course, after the project is finished and the experience gained, a programmer sees with the benefit of hindsight that the program could have been more streamlined.

Although you can spend the rest of your life improving programs, most people use AutoLISP to make AutoCAD do the most work in the least amount of time. If a program works and saves time, use it and go on to another project.

6.2 (strcase)   String Case

(strcase) changes a string of text from lowercase to uppercase, leaving uppercase characters as they are. Its purpose is to test input. For example, when you answer a prompt **yes** or **no**, or provide any other input, you don't want to worry about whether the **CAPS LOCK** is on or off. When programs are tested to see if one set is equal to another, an exact match must be made. If some letters are uppercase and others lower, you'd have to test with an overwhelming number of (**if...**) or (**or...**) statements in order to get all the combinations. A better solution is to issue a command that ensures all the letters are uppercase.

This can be done two ways. First, you can test for just the function without permanently changing the actual variable. Or you might permanently reassign the variable with all-uppercase letters. Depending on the future use of the variable, either way is acceptable.

```
(strcase a)
```

This is the command format. When used in an (**if...**) statement, you can use one or both alternatives.

```
(setq a (strcase a))
(if (= a "Y") (. . .))
```

In this case, you first permanently change the variable **a** to uppercase, then test the variable.

The (**. . .**) represents the command that might follow the (**if...**) statement.

```
(if (= (strcase a) "Y") (. . .))
```

Here, you're directly testing variable **a**, which hasn't actually been changed. It reads: If the uppercase of **a** is equal to **"Y"** then . . . .

6.3 Object Snap Codes

```
(setvar "osmode" 1)
```

sets OBJECT SNAP to the ENDPOINT.

An integer is required when using the (setvar) command for "osmode" to set OBJECT SNAP system variables. The following is a table listing the integers for each OBJECT SNAP:

Center	4
Endpoint	1
Insert	64
Intersection	32
Midpoint	2

Nearest	512
Node	8
Perpend	128
Quadrant	16
Tangent	256
None	0

AutoLISP Program LES6.LSP

AutoLISP Program LES6.LSP inserts a part into a double wall and breaks the double wall around the block where both breaks are parallel. This AutoLISP program is one example of how that can be approached, but it isn't the last word on the subject! It's a simple, usable program that can be easily modified to accommodate even more variations. You may take many other approaches; after Lesson 6, you'll come up with a few yourself!

```
(defun C:ibreak (/ pnt1 pnt2 pnt3 pnt4 d a ip)
  (graphscr)
  (setq d (getdist "\nEnter wall thickness: "))
  (setq pnt1 (getpoint "\nPick a point on outer wall: "))
  (setq a (getangle pnt1 "\nSecond point (left or up): "))
  (setq fp (polar pnt1 (+ a (dtr 90)) d))
  (setq b (getstring "\nEnter block name: "))
  (setq ip (getpoint "\nInsertion point: "))
  (setq a1 a)
  (command "insert" b ip "1" "1" (- (rtd a1) 180))
  (setq os (getstring "\nEnter <E>nd point or <I>ntersection: "))
  (setq os (strcase os))
  (if (= os "E")
    (setvar "osmode" 1)
  )
  (if (= os "I")
    (setvar "osmode" 32)
  )
  (setq pnt2 (getpoint "\nEnter other point of object: "))
  (setvar "osmode" 0)
  (setq pnt3 (polar ip (+ a (dtr 90)) d))
```

```
(setq pnt4 (polar pnt2 (+ a (dtr 90)) d))
(command "break" pnt1 "f" ip pnt2)
(command "break" fp "f" pnt3 pnt4)
(command "line" ip pnt3 "")
(command "line" pnt2 pnt4 "")
)
```

PURPOSE: Lets you insert a door into parallel lines. The program breaks into the walls and inserts the door. Before using this program, you'll need to be in the sample drawing, LES6.DWG, or draw two parallel lines on your screen. A typical part, called door, is in the sample drawing.

TO LOAD:

Type: (load "les6") <RETURN>

Response: ibreak

TO OPERATE:

Type: ibreak <RETURN>

Response: Enter wall thickness:

Use the keyboard to enter the thickness of the wall, or pick the offset distance of the wall.

Response: Pick a point on outer wall:

Now pick a point to measure the angle of the wall. To pick the line for the future **BREAK** command, you might want to use **OBJECT SNAP, NEAREST**.

Response: Second point (left or up):

Pick a second point on the outer wall, to the left of or above the first. Note the direction you pick as it measures the angle of the wall.

Response: Enter block name:

If you're using **LES6.DWG**, type **DOOR**. Or enter your own door part name.

Response: Insertion point:

Pick a point along the outer wall. You might want to use **OBJECT SNAP, NEAREST**.

Response: `Enter <E>nd point or <I>ntersection:`

Enter **E** from the keyboard, which chooses **OBJECT SNAP, END POINT**. Depending on the way you drew your part, it might intersect the line. If that's the case, choose **I**. If you are using the sample drawing, choose **E**.

Response: `Enter other point of object:`

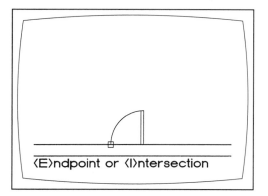

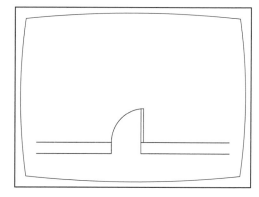

Figure 6-1: Choose end of door swing of outer wall.

Figure 6-2: Walls are broken and the door inserted.

Choose the endpoint of the door swing where it touches the line of the outer wall. The walls now are broken and the ends closed.

Now let's look at the logic behind the above program:

Problem Definition

If you have a drawing with parallel lines representing walls, you often need to insert doors, windows or other parts in the walls. After insertion, the parallel line cuts through your part, forcing you to break lines around the block.

One solution is to draw a phantom line at the endpoint of each of the first two breaks, then use **OBJECT SNAP INTERSECTION** to break the other line at the intersection of the two phantom lines. After the break, you erase the two phantom lines used for measurement. Obviously, that's a lot of steps for a common operation. Can you simplify this process and save some time? Absolutely!

Goal

The problem is listed above—now you must decide what to do about it! Your goal is to pick a point along the wall and tell AutoCAD the part name you want to insert. AutoCAD then inserts the part and automatically breaks the two walls exactly parallel at the insertion point and around the part.

Information Needed

When programming, you can't wave a magic wand and make things happen. You must tell the system, step by step, what to do, and you must work within the confines of AutoCAD. Start by listing the elementary pieces of information AutoCAD needs before it can do what you want.

Although you won't come up with a complete list at first, you'll add to it as you go through the program. Below is a list of elementary information you must furnish AutoCAD before it begins.

> **Wall Thickness**. The distance between the two parallel lines.
>
> **Block Name**. The name of the block at the point you use the **INSERT** command. AutoCAD has to know what to insert.
>
> **Insertion Point**. Where the block is to be inserted, oriented to its base (insertion) point.
>
> **Angle of Wall**. Your job would be much easier if every wall in which you inserted your block were exactly 90 degrees along your grid. Of course, you could measure the angle of the wall each time you performed that function, then **ROTATE** the grid. But that would be like turning the house to install the light bulb. Therefore, you must know the angle of the wall in order to adjust your part.

Those are just a few things you must know up front. You'll surely learn more as you progress with the program.

Writing the Program

Generally, the first place to start writing the program is with the information outlined above. You also should document a list of the variables you might need. Keep the list current so you can remember which variable contains which data.

Let's look at the first few lines of the program:

```
(defun C:ibreak (/ pnt1 pnt2 pnt3 pnt4 d a ip)
```

defines the program function as **ibreak**. Remember, when you start writing the program, don't put your variables in the following statement. Instead, insert **( )**.

```
(defun C:ibreak ( )
```

lets you examine the variables when the program crashes. Examining the variables can tell you a great deal about where the logic failed and crashed the program. For example, if you needed an insertion point and you found it was **nil**, that's obviously why it crashed. You then must return to the program and see why it didn't pick up the insertion point.

You might even have the variable printed on the screen to see if it ever had the point. Print statements like that scattered throughout the program can tell where and why a variable mysteriously loses or changes its data.

```
(graphscr)
```

changes to the graphics screen.

```
(setq d (getdist "\nEnter wall thickness: "))
```

Variable **d** contains the wall thickness. Remember, this is a real number that may be expressed in feet and inches. If you want to put it in feet and inches or point to the distance, use **(getdist)** instead of **(getreal)**, which must be represented in inches.

```
(setq pnt1 (getpoint "\nPick a point on outer wall: "))
```

This produces the wall angle, which requires two points to measure the wall's direction.

```
(setq a (getangle pnt1 "\nSecond point (left or up): "))
```

You'll use **(getangle)** to measure the angle, assigned to variable **a** and stored in radians. You used the previously defined **pnt1** as the beginning point to rubber-band to the second. (Later, you'll see why you should choose left or up as the direction of the line.) First, let's skip a couple of lines and look at three simpler lines.

```
(setq b (getstring "\nEnter block name: "))
```

Variable **b** will be assigned the block name to be inserted. You didn't use a flag—so no spaces are allowed. As in AutoCAD, the space is used as a **<RETURN>**.

```
(setq ip (getpoint "\nInsertion point: "))
```

Variable **ip** will be assigned the insertion point. You might ask why **pnt1** wasn't used as the insertion point as well as the first point in the measurement of the line. Actually, you used it at first then discovered you needed more information. When you use the **BREAK** command and you're confused about which line is to be broken, first pick the line, then use the **F** subcommand option to find the two points.

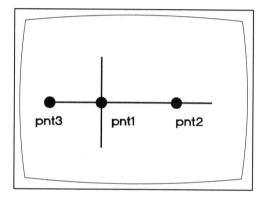

Figure 6-3: Pick points 1, 2 and 3 for the break command.

For example, if you wish to break the line above from **pnt1** to **pnt2**, you'd have to find a point along the line you want to break. That would be **pnt3**. You'd then issue an **F** command to break at the first point **pnt1** and the second point **pnt2**. Otherwise, there would be confusion at **pnt1** about which of the two lines is to be broken. In AutoLISP, the command would be

```
(command "break" p3 "f" p1 p2)
```

p3 chooses the line. **"f"** tells AutoCAD that the following two points, **p1** and **p2**, are to be broken on the specified line. Only if there's no confusion can you break the two points directly without using **"f."**

When working with a block inserted into a line, an error message somewhere along the line will say that you may not break a block. Therefore, you need a point that will choose the line to break so that you can use the **"f"** command. Since you needed the angle of the line anyway, you used **pnt1** as the point that chooses the line. Note that this point and the insertion point *must* not be the same point.

What's important here is the programming methodology and the mistake that made you realize you needed more information. You then rethink the logic and see where you can most efficiently get the data.

```
(setq a1 a )
```

derives the angle of rotation supplied to AutoCAD's **INSERT** command.

```
(command "insert" b ip "1" "1" (- (rtd a1) 180))
```

This line uses the command **"insert."** **b** is the block name. **ip** is the insertion point. You use **"1"** and **"1"** because AutoCAD's **INSERT** command is asking for scale X and scale Y. **a1** is the angle of insertion.

The block is inserted at this point in the program. You now must break the block. Do you have all the information you need? Let's make another list:

> **Second break point**. The first break point is **ip**—the insertion point. You know **pnt1** is the line to be broken, but you don't know where the second break point should be. You *do* know it should be where the other part of the block touches the line. One problem when testing the finished program on several kinds of parts is that **OBJECT SNAP** sometimes could be used for **ENDPOINT** and at other times **INTER-SECTION** could be used.
>
> **Line point for second line**. You need a point on the second parallel line that identifies the line to be broken.
>
> **First break point, second line**. You need the first break point on the second parallel line.
>
> **Second break point, second line.** You need the second break point on the second parallel line.
>
> **OBJECT SNAP alternatives**. If using **OBJECT SNAP** for the second point on the primary line, you must know what kind of **OBJECT SNAP** to use.

Now you can fill in the information gaps to complete the program. Let's go back and look at the lines you skipped.

```
(setq fp (polar pnt1 (+ a (dtr 90)) d))
```

chooses the point parallel to **pnt1** at the distance of the two wall lines in variable **d. fp** will be used for the second line, as **pnt1** is used in the **BREAK** command for the first line.

Now let's continue after the part has been inserted:

```
(setq os (getstring "\nEnter <E>nd point or <I>ntersection: "))
```

asks you to enter an **E** or an **I** depending on what type of **OBJECT SNAP** is to be used for the second break point. The answer is assigned to variable **os**. Note that a flag isn't used, so the space acts as a **<RETURN>**.

```
(setq os (strcase os))
```

changes variable **os** to uppercase so you can evaluate the answer more easily.

```
(if (= os "E")
   (setvar "osmode" 1)
)
```

If variable **os** is equal to "E," you set the system variable "osmode" to **1**. From the table presented earlier in this chapter, you can see that **1** is **ENDPOINT**. Note that the closing parenthesis is lined up with the opening parenthesis that begins the **"if"** statement. That's done for readability only. The **)** could just as well have been put at the end of the **(setvar "osmode" 1)** command.

```
(if (= os "I")
   (setvar "osmode" 32)
)
```

If **os** is equal to "I," set the system variable "osmode" to **32**. From the table, you can see that **32** is **INTERSECTION**.

By now, you may wonder what would happen if you entered something other than **E** or **I**. At this point, the program isn't error-checked and will crash. Well-written programs should add extensive code to protect against bad entries or anything else that could cause them to crash.

In fact, if you use commercial programs that crash when you enter incorrect information, the programmer either didn't go to the trouble of checking for errors or your error caused something the programmer never dreamed could happen.

NOTE: you could leave out this entire section by using (setvar "osmode" 33). Its the *sum-of -bits* 32 + 1 to make 33, the combination of ENDpoint and INTersection. For further details on sum-of-bits, see Section 15.22.

```
(setq pnt2 (getpoint "\nEnter other point of object: "))
```

With your **OBJECT SNAP** properly set, you should choose the **INTER-SECTION** or **ENDPOINT** of the other side of the object that touches the first line. That point is assigned to **pnt2**.

```
(setvar "osmode" 0)
```

Remember that **(setvar)** is a permanent change to the system variable, so **OBJECT SNAP** will remain that way until changed. That removes **OBJECT SNAP**.

```
(setq pnt3 (polar ip (+ a (dtr 90)) d))
```

pnt3 is the same point as **ip** (your insertion point), which is **90** degrees (parallel) and at **d** (distance of two lines) distance. **pnt3** is used in the same way as **ip** in breaking the second line.

```
(setq pnt4 (polar pnt2 (+ a (dtr 90)) d))
```

pnt4 is the same point as **pnt2** (your second break point), which is **90** degrees (parallel) and at **d** (distance of two lines). **pnt4** is used in the same way as **pnt2** in breaking the second line.

```
(command "break" pnt1 "f" ip pnt2)
```

issues the **BREAK** command, choosing **pnt1** as the line, with the **"f"** option from points **ip** to **pnt2**. This breaks the first line.

```
(command "break" fp "f" pnt3 pnt4)
```

issues the **BREAK** command, choosing **fp** as the line with the **"f"** option from points **pnt3** to **pnt4**. That breaks the second line.

```
(command "line" ip pnt3 "")
(command "line" pnt2 pnt4 "")
)
```

closes the function.

This optional set of commands closes off the parallel lines when you're inserting a door part.

Earlier, you learned why it's important to be able to measure the line left or up, rather than right or down. You got a different angle depending on which way you pointed to the line. The difference in the angles is 180 degrees, depending on which direction they're measured in.

In this exercise, you've gone through the basics to develop a working program. Each program and programmer are different, but the methodology is similar regardless of the labels you attach.

You've attempted to write a small program that could serve a large variety of data situations. An AutoLISP professional would test this program with every conceivable type of block. If you did that with this program, it would crash sooner or later. For example, what would happen if the block were shaped so the second part of it didn't cut through the first line, but *did* cut through the second? The program, of course, would crash. So write many small programs specific to each major part you plan to insert.

From a practical point of view, it might be easier to write an insert routine specifically for the types of blocks you use 99 percent of the time. They could be short programs for each block, set up in the macros of your menu or tablet, which did the whole operation without asking as many questions. It may not be the best programming, but it works. Remember, what you most want is to save time.

Important Techniques You've Learned in This Chapter

1. Identify the problem. This can be as simple as a sequence of commands that can be shortened to one or two.

2. Identify the steps necessary to solve the problem, using regular AutoCAD commands.

3. Gather the information that AutoCAD needs for each program line.

4. Write the code to gather the information and issue the program lines.

5. Test the program.

6. When the program crashes, try to identify why. Most often, it needed a missing piece of information. You'll never think of all

the necessary information at the outset, but it will come to you as you go along.

7. Modify the program to gather additional information, then re-test repeatedly until the program works to your satisfaction.

8. Final cleanup. This is mostly cosmetic, with prompts to make it run more smoothly and avoid misunderstandings. The amount of time you spend on this step depends on how "slick" you want the program to appear.

Moving On

In the last few pages, you picked up some important programming techniques. Chapter 7, "Managing Entities," is a culmination of all you've learned in the last six chapters. You'll realize AutoCAD power you never thought possible.

7

MANAGING
ENTITIES

CHAPTER 7

Managing Entities

In the last six chapters, you worked only in AutoCAD's drawing editor to create time-saving AutoLISP routines. Many of the programs could have been written using macros instead of AutoLISP, in fact. Your goal has been to reduce steps, eliminate repetitive drawing tasks and get the job done with less effort.

But AutoLISP's real power is its ability to go behind your drawing to the database where the drawing is stored and defined. You then can manage graphic and nongraphic information. Imagine being able to globally change text size within a window of crowded lines, circles and arcs, or to change general properties of groups of entities such as layers, line types or colors. When you're in control of AutoCAD's database, you'll find unlimited opportunities using the concepts taught in this chapter.

7.1 Entities

The purpose of this chapter is to show how entities are stored and referenced in the drawing database, and how they can be changed and manipulated using AutoLISP.

As you know, an entity is the smallest object you can place on your screen. The following are entities: **LINE**, **CIRCLE**, **ARC**, **TEXT**, **POLYLINE**, etc. You encounter these terms most frequently when AutoCAD tells you a **POLYLINE** or **BLOCK** is treated as a single entity. Individual entities are created when you **EXPLODE** a **BLOCK**.

Each entity has a massive definition in AutoCAD's database. For example, the data for a single line contains at least the following information:

> Entity type—**LINE**
> Layer
> Color
> Beginning **X Y** coordinate
> Ending **X Y** coordinate
> Line type

For each entity type, you can modify various aspects found in the drawing database. With **LINE**, for example, you can change the **COLOR**,

LAYER, **LINETYPE** and so on. For **TEXT**, you can change the same, as well as **HEIGHT** and **STYLE**. You also can secure information concerning the entities for use in other programs, without changing the entities themselves.

Using entities and AutoLISP, you control the drawing and its database. This far exceeds anything you can accomplish by writing simple macros.

7.2 Entity Hierarchy

Now let's see how entities are stored:

Selection set
Entity name
Entity list
Associative Codes (lists)
Sublists

When using entities, you usually aren't working with the entire drawing database. You want to choose several entities through any of the selection procedures, such as **WINDOW** and **CROSSING**. That creates a *selection set*, which contains all the entities you choose.

Each entity in the selection set has a name. It isn't a descriptive name such as **LINE** or **CIRCLE**. For example, the name of the first entity in a selection set might be

```
<Entity name: 60000014>
```

Not very descriptive, is it? However, like it or not, that's how you must reference individual entities.

Basically, the entity name is the header for the *entity list*—the list containing information about the individual entities.
Here's a sample entity list:

```
((-1 . <Entity name: 60000014) (0 . "CIRCLE") (8 . "LAYER1") (5 .
"1") (10   563.0   484.0   0.0) (40 . 60.0) (210   0.0   0.0   1.0))
```

Each item in the list is in two parts. The first item is an associative code number. The number informs us of the function of that entity. It's called *associative code* because it can be *isolated* with the **(assoc)** command. An associative code is referred to as a *dotted pair* list.

Listed below are a few associative code numbers for the entity **TEXT**:

1	Text verbiage
7	Text style
10	Insertion point X Y Z
40	Height
50	Rotation angle

The individual associative codes of an entity list might look like this:

```
(40 . 60.0)
(7 . "COMPLEX")
```

The second part of the item in the list differs according to the associative code. For example, following code **40**—the code for text height—is a real number, which is the actual height, in this case **60.0**. Following code **7**, **Text style**, is a string, which is the text style, **Complex**.

For more complicated lists, such as **BLOCKS** and **POLYLINES**, each entity can have subentities (which you won't use in this chapter).

Each entity in the selection set is referenced by an *index number*—its order in a selection set. Beside the index number is the entity name, a seemingly meaningless number. But the entity name is required to secure the entity itself. However, the name can be secured if you know its index number.

For example, the first entity is index **0**, the second is index **1**, the third is index **2**, etc. Using that information, you can create a loop to page through the entities until you find the one you want.

AutoLISP even gives you a command that tells you ahead of time how many entities are in a given selection set so you can set your loop counter. Of course, even without that you can page through until you reach a **nil**.

Now let's look at what you'll need to pull out a specific entity and change it.

(ssget)	selects the entities for the selection set. The command creates the selection set.
(entsel)	selects the name of a single entity.
(entlast)	selects the name of the single last entity.
(sslength)	gives the number of entities in the selection set.
(ssname)	gives the name of the entity—the long number. You'll need it later.
(entget)	sets the entity list.

(assoc)	gives you the ability to rapidly search for a desired associative code.
(subst)	lets you substitute one associative code for another. Note that you must know the current value in order to use this function. That's why you need **(assoc)**, which gives you the current value.
(cons)	lets you construct a new associative code list. Remember, the elements in the associative code lists are in two parts, which means they're lists in themselves. Thus, you must be able to take them apart and construct a new list of that code alone.
(entmod)	lets you take the newly modified entity list and write it back to the database to update the drawing.

AutoLISP has more functions, but the ones above let you change values in the database. Let's examine them one at a time. Then you can run through a simple exercise on accessing and extracting entities. You might not understand the following at first, but it will become apparent as you proceed through the chapter.

7.3 (ssget), (entsel), (entlast) Select Entities

The (ssget), (entsel) and (entlast) commands select entities. **(entsel)** selects only one entity at a time. You may not use **WINDOW** or **CROSSING** to select entities. However, (ssget) lets you use **WINDOW** or **CROSSING** as well as other selection techniques. You'll mostly be using (ssget). **(entlast)** selects the last entity created.

```
(setq a (ssget))
```

When you use **(ssget)** this way, you may enter **W** or **C** or any other selection option, or point to your entities. Each chosen entity is added to the selection set, and the name of the selection set is assigned to variable **a**.

```
(setq a (ssget "W" pnt1 pnt2))
```

lets you choose the **WINDOW** area. **CROSSING** can be used the same way with "**C**," of course.

Remember, you've created a selection set with a specific name, **<Selection set: 1>**, assigned to variable **a.**

If you use **(entsel)** instead of **(ssget)** you can select only one entity at a time. You may not use the **WINDOW** or **CROSSING** options to select entities. **(entsel)** is a much more efficient command when you want to select only one entity, of course. The **(entsel)** command returns the entity name and the beginning **X, Y, Z** coordinates immediately so you don't need to secure the entity name with the **(ssname)** command.

A shortcut to pulling up an entity list for only one entity is

```
(setq b (entget (car (entsel))))
```

After you select the object, the entity list is immediately returned to the variable **b.** Since **(entsel)** returns not only the entity name but also the beginning **X, Y, Z** coordinates of the chosen point when you picked the entity, you need **(car (entsel))** to isolate the entity name.

Just as **(entsel)** is a shortcut to securing the entity list when only one object is to be selected, **(entlast)** is a shortcut if the entity is the last entity created.

```
(setq b (entget (entlast)))
```

(entlast) returns the name of the last entity created. **(entget)** returns the entity list assigned to the variable **b.** Notice that **(entlast)** doesn't require the **(car)** command, because **(entlast)** returns only the entity name and not additional coordinates.

Remember, in every case your objective is to secure the entity name because **(entget)** requires the entity name to call up the entity list.

7.3A (ssget) With Filter Option

You can search the entire database for certain entities or codes. The syntax for this is

```
Type:      (ssget "x" '((0 . "TEXT")))
```

Response: `<SELECTION SET: 1>`

Any text in your database now is captured in the selection set. WINDOW or CROSSING are no longer necessary. More than one search criterion may be included. The following are valid search codes in the entity list:

    0   Entity type
    2   Block
    6   Linetype

7	Text style
8	Layer
38	Elevation
39	Thickness
62	Color
66	Attributes
210	3D extrusion direction vector

7.4 (sslength) Selection Set Length

This command lets you determine the number of entity names in a selection set. Assume variable **a** contains the name of the selection set,

```
(setq n (sslength a))
```

assigns to variable **n** the number of entities in selection set **a**.

7.5 (ssname) Get Entity Name

(ssname) lets you secure the name of the entity from the selection set. Remember, the name of the entity is really a hexadecimal number. Don't expect the entity name to look like line, circle, etc. For example, the name of the first entity might be **60000014**.

Assume variable **a** is the selection set and variable **i** is set to **0**.

```
(setq na (ssname a i)
```

That assigns variable **na** the entity name found in selection set **a** at index number **i**. Remember that a selection set may contain more than one entity name. You can point to each entity by using its relative number in the selection set. For example, entity **#1** is index **0**, entity **#2** is index **1**, etc.

7.6 (entget) Get Entity List

This command actually pulls out the entity list. The entity list can be assigned to a variable. Assume variable **na** is the entity name.

```
(setq b (entget na))
```

That assigns to **b** the entire entity list for that entity name. You can now examine the list to see what's inside by typing **!b**, which prints the list on your screen. Parentheses surround each element pair. With each element, you'll see the code number. For example, **TEXT** with **HEIGHT** of **.5** would be

```
(40 . 0.50)
```

Note that a dot separates the **40** from **HEIGHT 0.50**. (Autodesk refers to this as a dotted pair.) If you assigned that element to variable **c**, you'd now have the following list in **c**:

```
(40 . 0.50)
```

You could look at both parts of the list with **(car c)**, which would give you **40**, or with **(cdr c)**, which would give you **0.50**.

7.7 (assoc)   Associative

Often used with **(subst)**, this command lets you search an entity list for a specific associative code list, then assign that code to a variable.

Assume variable **b** is the entity list, and you're looking for code number **40**, which describes **TEXT HEIGHT**. You want to pull out the entire associative code list and assign it to variable **c**.

```
(setq c (assoc 40 b))
```

That assigns the associative code list containing the **40** in list **b** to variable **c**. Now variable **c** is a list that might contain **(40 . 0.50)**.

7.8 (subst)   Substitute New for Old

Use **(subst)** if you now want to use **.25** as the **HEIGHT** instead of **.5**. Always substitute the new associative code list for the old one (not vice versa).

Assume variable **b** is the name of the list and variable **c** contains the current value of the associative code, as described above:

```
(40 . 0.50)
```

The apostrophe (') serves a special function in AutoLISP. A group of items preceded by an apostrophe is treated as a list.

```
(setq b1 (subst '(40 . 0.25) c b))
```

b1 is now the new list. **'(40 . 0.25)** is the new element substituted for the old element **c** found in list **b**.

CAUTION: You can use the previous example *only* when using constants. For example, assume you place the new height in variable **h**. You use the following, but instead of using the constant **0.25**, you want to use **h**, which represents the value.

```
(setq b1 (subst '(40 . h) c b ))
```

It appears to work, but it doesn't. The new associative code list will look like this:

```
(40 . h)
```

In the above example, **(subst)** cannot interpret variables. You need to construct a new variable containing the entire code list, then use the new variable in the **(subst)** command. See **(cons)** below for details.

7.9 (cons)   Construct New List

(cons) constructs a new associative code list with the new code number placed at the beginning. Assume variable **c** contains the following list:

```
(40 . 0.50)
```

Also, assume variable **h** contains the real number **0.25**. Then,

```
(setq d (cons (car c) h))
```

Remember, **(car c)** gives you **40**. Therefore, **(car c)** is the new first element, followed by the value **h**. Thus, the expression produces **(40 . 0.25)**.

Now that **d** contains the entire associative code list, you may use the **(subst)** command.

```
(setq b1  (subst d c b))
```

substitutes the new list found in variable **d** for the old list found in variable **c** (in the entity list found in variable **b**) and assigns the new list to **b1**.

7.10 (entmod)   Entity Modification

Now that you have a new entity list in the variable **b1**, you want to make **b1** the permanent entity list in your drawing database. **(entmod)** writes the new entity list back.

```
(entmod b1)
```

At this point, you'll see the change appear on the screen.

7.11 (progn)   Group Commands as One

In the section on **(if...)** commands in Chapter 3, "Controlling the Program," you learned that each **(if...)** command can have only one **(then...)** statement following it. Alternately, you can use the **(else...)** statement instead of the **(then...)** statement. However, you might want to have more than one statement occur should the **(if...)** prove to be true.

To permit that, AutoLISP sets off multiple commands with the command **(progn**, which also must be enclosed in parentheses.

```
(if (= a b)
(progn
  (xxx)
  (xxx)
  (xxx)
 )
)
```

In the above example you started with an **(if...)** statement, which says if **a** is equal to **b**, then...

That's followed by the command **(progn**. Notice that the **(progn** is not enclosed in parentheses. Three commands follow in the above example, but there could be as many as you need.

(progn is enclosed in parentheses when commands that depend on the **(if...)** statement being there end. The **(if...)** statement is finally closed. You can also use the **(progn** command to group multiple **(else...)** statements, as well as multiple **(then...)** statements.

7.12 (repeat) Loop **X** Number of Times

With this alternate method of controlling loops, you simply tell AutoLISP how many times you want the loop repeated. It's important to note that the number *must* be an integer. If it's a real number, it won't work.

```
(repeat 5
(xxx)
(xxx)
(xxx)
)
```

In the above example, the commands **(xxx)** are repeated five times. **(repeat)** must be followed by an integer, which must be followed by the commands you want repeated. You must close the end of the loop with a parenthesis **)**.

Now that you've examined the component parts, let's take a look at AutoLISP Program Lesson 7, which lets you **WINDOW** an area and globally change **TEXT** size for any text in the window.

Place a few lines of text in your drawing, as well as your choice of circles, lines, arcs, etc. The program asks you to put a **WINDOW** around all entities. It then changes the size of only the text found within the window.

AutoLISP Program LES7a.LSP

```
(defun C:chtext (/ a ts n index b1 b c d b2)
  (setq a (ssget))
  (setq ts (getdist "\nEnter new text size: "))
  (setq n (sslength a))
  (setq index 0)
  (repeat n
    (setq b1 (entget (ssname a index)))
    (setq index (+ index 1))
    (setq b (assoc 0 b1))
    (if (= "TEXT" (cdr b))
      (progn
        (setq c (assoc 40 b1))
        (setq d (cons (car c) ts))
```

```
                    (setq b2 (subst d c b1))
                    (entmod b2)
                )
            )
        )
    )
```

PURPOSE: Lets you globally change the size of the text within a **selection set** without affecting other entities. You can use the sample drawing **LES7.DWG**.

TO LOAD:

Type: (load "les7a") <RETURN>

Response: chtext

TO OPERATE:

Type: chtext <RETURN>

Response: Select objects:

Type: w <RETURN>

Put a **WINDOW** around the text and other objects on the screen and confirm the selection.

Response: Enter new text size:

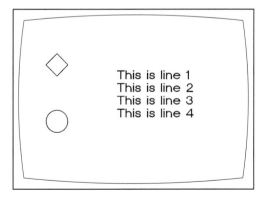

Figure 7-1: Place some text onscreen.

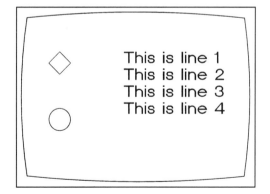

Figure 7-2: Change the size of the text.

Enter the new text size. At this point only the text will change to the new text size.

Let's look at the program line by line:

```
(defun C:chtext (/ a ts n index b1 b c d b2)
```

defines the function **(chtext)** and local variables.

```
(setq a (ssget))
```

lets you use **W** or **C** for **WINDOW** or **CROSSING** or other selection set options, then assigns the name of the selection set to variable **a**.

```
(setq ts (getdist "\nEnter new text size: "))
```

assigns the real number of units for the new text size to variable **ts**.

```
(setq n (sslength a))
```

assigns the number of entities found in variable **a** to variable **n**.

```
(setq index 0)
```

sets the variable **index** to an initial value of **0**. Remember, the selection set contains several entities. (You know how many from the **(sslength)** command.) You now need to increase your index by one to step through the selection set, which extracts your entities one by one.

```
(repeat n
```

That's the beginning of your loop. Variable **n** is the number of entities in your selection set. You cannot use the variable **n** as your index for two reasons. First, it doesn't begin at **0**. Second, it doesn't change as it does in other languages. Note that **(repeat n** isn't closed with a parenthesis. That's done at the end of the loop.

```
(setq b1 (entget (ssname a index)))
```

This combination of commands saves steps. **(ssname a index)** produces the entity name in selection set **a** for **index**, which begins at **0**. **(entget)** extracts this entity and assigns its list to variable **b1**. **b1** now contains your first entity.

```
(setq index (+ index 1))
```

The command increases the variable **index** by one, then assigns the value to itself **(index)**. It's a simple counter. The first time through the loop, **index** has value **0** because you initialized it that way. The second time through the loop, its value is **1**, then **2** and so on.

```
(setq b (assoc 0 b1))
```

Here, you're looking for the associative code **0**, which identifies the entity type. When the **(assoc)** command finds a code beginning with **0** in list **b1**, it assigns the entire code list to variable **b**. It should look like this:

```
(0 . "TEXT") or
(0 . "LINE")
```

As you see, you can have more than one type of entity within your **selection set**.

```
(if (= "TEXT" (cdr b))
```

That's your initial text question. You want to see if you have found a **"TEXT"** entity. **(cdr b)** should produce **"TEXT"** or **"LINE"** or **"CIRCLE"**, etc.

```
(progn
```

If your text question passes and you indeed do have a **"TEXT"** entity, you want to perform more than one operation.

```
(setq c (assoc 40 b1))
```

You're now looking for the associative code that controls **TEXT HEIGHT**. When you find it, assign the code list to **c**, which will become the old code list you'll use in the **(subst)** command.

```
(setq d (cons (car c) ts))
```

Remember, **ts** is the new **HEIGHT**. **(car c)** captures the **(40 .)** portion of the code list and places it in front of variable **ts**, which contains the new height. That newly constructed code list is assigned to variable **d**. You now have your new code list **d** and your old code list **c** for entity list **b1**.

```
(setq b2 (subst d c b1))
```

You now create a new entity list, substituting the new code list **d** for the old code list **c** in entity list **b1**, then assigning it to the new entity list **b2**.

```
(entmod b2)
```

That command writes the new entity list **b2** to the drawing database. At this time, you should see the change appear on the screen.

```
      )
```

closes **(progn**

)

closes **(if**

)

closes (repeat n

)

closes **(defun**.

NOTE: This is a single-purpose program that makes only one change: **TEXT HEIGHT**. In practice, changing only **TEXT HEIGHT** may not be enough. For example, if you have multiple lines of text, each line will begin at a given **X Y Z** coordinate. If you make the text larger, individual lines will still begin at the same place—and may even overlap.

AutoLISP Program LES7b.LSP   (Revised, using Filters)

This program illustrates (ssget) with the filter option.

```
(defun C:chtext2 (/ a ts n index b1 b c d b2)
  (setq a  (ssget "x" '((0 . "TEXT"))))
  (setq ts (getdist "\nEnter new text size: "))
  (setq n (sslength a))
  (setq index 0)
  (repeat n
    (setq b1 (entget (ssname a index)))
    (setq index (+ index 1))
    (setq c (assoc 40 b1))
    (setq d (cons (car c) ts))
    (setq b2 (subst d c b1))
    (entmod b2)
  )
)
```

The filter option lets you write global search and replace programs with elegance. As illustrated in the revised program, the filter option eliminates as many as three separate steps: searching, replacing and bringing in only those entities sought in the list.

The "Recipe" for Selecting & Changing Entities

Although entity access and manipulation are fairly complex subjects, they can be divided into component parts in a way that's less difficult to master. Each time you want to pull out an entity and change it, you need to follow a simple recipe, step by step.

The following steps let you select and change entities.

1. **(setq a (ssget))** defines a selection set.

2. **(setq n (sslength a))**   Optional step. You need to secure the number of entities captured in the selection set only when you might possibly capture more than one. In such a case, you need to know how many were captured in order to set up a loop counter to page through the index.

3. **(setq na (ssname a i))** secures the entity name from the relative position in the index of the selection set. **a** is the selection set and **i** is the index number.

4. **(setq b (entget na))** produces the entity list and assigns it to variable **b**. **na** is the entity name.

5. **(setq d (assoc 40 b))** searches the entity list **(b)** for the associative code number **(40)** and produces the code list assigned to **d**. Therefore, **d** would look something like **(40 . 60.0)**.

6. **(setq b1 (subst '(40 . 30.0) d b))** substitutes the new code list **(40 . 30.0)** for the old code list **d**, found in entity list **b**.

    Note: When you use a variable instead of a constant, use **6a** and **6b** instead of **6**. See below.

6a. **(setq d1 (cons (car d) h))** constructs a new associative code list assigned to **d1** with the two elements **(car d)**—the first element of the old code list and the variable **h**.

6b. **(setq b1 (subst d1 d b)** substitutes the new code list **d1** for the old code list **d** found in entity list **b**.

7. **(entmod b1)** updates the database and changes the entity.

You must use this recipe for each entity you want to change. If you write a master routine following the above examples, you need only to insert the different component parts. Although it's a long procedure, you'll find that with practice it's not as difficult as it appears. Begin by experimenting with different entities and examining the lists they produce.

Now let's try one more simple example using the above revised program. First, clear your drawing screen and draw a simple **CIRCLE** with a 5-foot radius. Using the recipe, change the size of the circle to a 30-inch radius.

Type: `(setq a (ssget))` `<RETURN>`

Pick the CIRCLE through any selection method such as WINDOW, CROSSING, selection, etc. Confirm your selection.

Type: `(setq n (sslength a))` `<RETURN>`

This isn't really needed because you know you have only one entity in your selection set. It's only important if you might have captured multiple entities.

`(setq na (ssname a 0))` `<RETURN>`

secures the entity name found in selection set **a** and index number **0**. In this case, **0** is the first and only entity in the selection set.

`(setq b (entget na))` `<RETURN>`

produces the entity list and assigns it to variable **b**. The entity list should look like this:

`((-1 . <Entity name: 60000014>) (0 . "CIRCLE")`
`(10 563.0 484.0) (40 . 60.0)`

Your entity name may be different. Type **0** should say **"CIRCLE."** Type **8** designates **LAYER** and will probably be layer **0**. Your starting point will be different from the above. The center point of the circle will be the coordinates designated as associative code **10**. Code **40** is the radius and should be 60 inches, as shown here.

`(setq d (assoc 40 b))` `<RETURN>`

pulls out the code list designated as associative code **40** and assigns it to variable **d**.

`(setq b1 (subst '(40 . 30.0) d b))` `<RETURN>`

Now substitute a new code list of **(40 . 30.0)** for every occurrence of the old code list found in variable **d** (from the old entity list **b**). The new entity list is assigned to variable **b1**. Notice the apostrophe, which designates that everything in the parentheses should be treated as a single list. When printed, your new list should look like this:

```
((-1 . <Entity name: 60000014) (0. "CIRCLE") (8 . "0")
(10 563.0 484.0) (40 . 30.0)
```

Note that the only change, **(40 . 60.0),** is **(40 . 30.0)**—the radius of your circle.

```
(entmod b1) <RETURN>
```

At this point, the size of the circle should change from a radius of **60** to **30** inches. If you want the old circle back, remember that its definition is found in variable **b**.

```
(entmod b) <RETURN>
```

The original circle should have returned. Actually, you can toggle back and forth by storing the definition of any entity to a variable and using **(entmod)**.

This "recipe" can be used for any entity or entities in the database. Although the steps appear complicated, the routine becomes second nature with use. Practice other single entities and groups of entities.

The real power of AutoLISP lies in entity selection and change, which let you secure total information about your database and use it in other programs. There's literally no limit to what you can accomplish.

Moving On

Congratulations! You have completed the basic tutorial of AutoLISP programming. With the information you have so far you can begin building exciting programs that not only save you time but let you manipulate AutoCAD in ways you never thought possible. But don't stop here.

Learning is an ongoing process. After you've written some programs, you'll be ready for Advanced AutoLISP. The next few chapters provide you the information you need to become an advanced AutoLISP programmer. And don't let the "Advanced AutoLISP," title fool you. You don't have to be an advanced programmer to learn advanced concepts. In fact, you're ready now!

8

ADVANCED
AUTOLISP

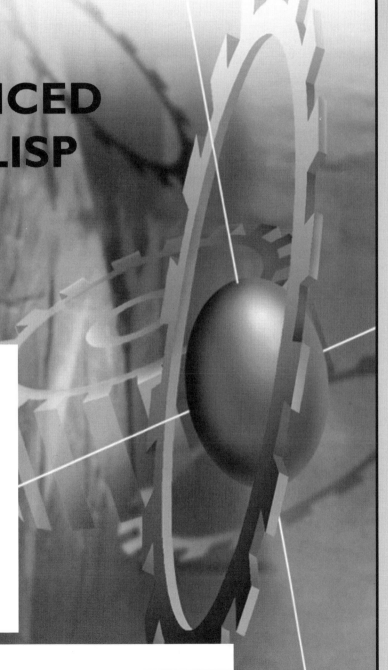

CHAPTER 8

Advanced AutoLISP

AutoLISP Files

Programmers generally work with two major groups of files: **random access** and **sequential**. The random access file lets the programmer select information from anywhere in the file, change it and then replace the information in the original file. AutoLISP only supports sequential files, which must be read in and written to the file item by item.

This means you can't skip around in the file. One piece of data after another must be read in. For example, let's say you wanted to look at the fiftieth item in a file. You must read 50 items until you get to the one you want, after which you can stop reading from the file. But if you want to change the fiftieth item, it gets a little more difficult.

To change a sequential file, you must read the entire file and write it back to disk. But you can't write it to the same file from which it's being read. So you must open two files: you'll read from one file and write to the other. If you want to change the fiftieth item in the file, you read sequentially all items until you arrive at the fiftieth. Each time you read an item, you're immediately writing that item back to the write file. When you read the fiftieth item, you then change it and write it to the write file. But you must continue to read in and write out the remainder of the file, or you'll lose it.

The sequential file isn't the most efficient file structure available, but it's the only type AutoLISP supports. It's adequate for relatively small files and offers a convenient way for AutoLISP to communicate with the outside world and other programs. It also gives you the ability to output to a printer. Let's take a quick look at how to write to a file.

Type: `(setq f (open "temp" "w"))  <RETURN>`

Type: `(print "I wrote this to the file" f)  <RETURN>`

Type: `(close f)  <RETURN>`

You have now successfully written "**I wrote this to the file**" to a file called "**temp.**" To prove this, type out the file.

Type: `type  <RETURN>`

Response: File to list:

Type: temp   <RETURN>

Response: I wrote this to the file

If the type command doesn't ask you for a file to list, you can shell out and enter **TYPE TEMP <RETURN>**.

NOTE: The type command is dependent on being set up in the **ACAD.PGP** file. See Appendix B, "Editing the ACAD.PGP file."

Before a file can be used, it must first be opened. The AutoLISP **(OPEN)** command returns what is called a file handle, which must be assigned to a variable. The next item in quotes is the name of the file you want to open. In the above example, the file name is **"temp."** The file name can have a complete **drive:\path\filespec** including extension. For example, it might have been

```
(setq f (open "c:/datadir/temp.ext" "w"))
```

NOTE: AutoLISP uses forward slashes, not backslashes. Also note that AutoCAD lets you use either / or \\ for directory descriptors.

The **"w"** in quotes tells AutoLISP that this file is being opened for the purpose of writing to it. Here, it's important to note that when the file is opened with a **"w,"** the contents of any file by that same name is first destroyed. Therefore, if you opened with a **"w"** file then closed it, even though you didn't write anything to it, any previous file by the same name would be destroyed and you would be left with an empty file.

Options other than **"w"** are available when opening a file. You may open a file as **"r,"** which lets you read from the file. You might also open a file as **"a,"** which appends any data you write to the end of the file. This lets you add to the file.

It's important to note that AutoLISP requires the **"w," "r"** or **"a"** be in lowercase. If it's not, the file won't open.

When the file is opened, it returns a file handle. It might look something like **<File: #228c8>**. The file handle should be assigned to a variable. In the above example, the variable **f** was chosen. While the file is open, you tell AutoLISP which file you're working with by telling it the file handle.

Let's look at a simple program to see how writing to a file can be used. This program is called **REMEMBER**. The program's purpose is to record to a file the four points you pick to form a rectangle. Later, you'll use a program called **REPLAY** that will read in those four points and redraw the same rectangle.

AutoLISP Program LES8a.LSP

```
(defun C:remember ( )
  (setq fi (getstring "\nEnter file name: "))
  (setq f (open fi "w"))
  (prompt "\nNow draw 4 points of a rectangle: ")
  (setq p1 (getpoint "\nFirst point: "))
  (print p1 f)
  (setq p2 (getpoint "\nSecond point: "))
  (print p2 f)
  (setq p3 (getpoint "\nThird point: "))
  (print p3 f)
  (setq p4 (getpoint "\nFourth point: "))
  (print p4 f)
  (close f)
  (command "line" p1 p2 p3 p4 "c")
)
```

PURPOSE: This program records the four pick points of a rectangle.

TO LOAD:

Type: (load "les8a") <RETURN>

Response: remember

TO OPERATE:

Type: remember <RETURN>

Response: Enter file name:

Type: temp <RETURN>

Response: Now draw 4 points of a rectangle:
First point: (pick the first point)
Second point:(pick the second point)
Third point: (pick the third point)
Fourth point:(pick the fourth point)

The program now draws a rectangle and saves the coordinates to a file called **temp**.

The following is a line-by-line analysis of AutoLISP Program Les8a.lsp:

```
(defun C:remember ( )
```

defines the function **remember**. With the **C:** in front of **remember**, it may be used without **( )**.

```
(setq fi (getstring "\nEnter file name: "))
```

asks you for the file name and assigns it as a string to the variable **fi**.

```
(setq f (open fi "w"))
```

opens a file named in the string variable **fi**. The "w" indicates the file is open for writing. The file handle is returned and assigned to the variable **f**. This is later used to identify the file in other commands.

```
(prompt "\nNow draw 4 points of a rectangle: ")
```

tells the user to draw four points of a rectangle.

The next series of lines are similar for **p1**, **p2**, **p3** and **p4**.

```
(setq p1 (getpoint "\nFirst point: "))
```

asks the user to pick a first point and assigns the coordinates of that point to the variable **p1**.

```
(print p1 f)
```

writes the coordinates found in the variable **p1** to the file referred to by the file handle found in **f**. Notice that you identify the file in all file-related commands with the variable containing the file handle.

Now each point is identified and immediately written to the file with a **(print)** statement.

```
(close f)
```

closes the file. The file isn't actually written to until it's closed. The information may be stored in the buffer.

```
(command "line" p1 p2 p3 p4 "c")
```

draws the rectangle.

```
)
```

ends the function.

Now let's look at how you can replay the rectangle that you drew. First erase the rectangle from the screen and run the following program. The program called **REPLAY** reads the coordinates you wrote to the file and draws the rectangle.

AutoLISP Program LES8b.LSP

```
(defun C:replay ( )
  (setq fi (getstring "\nEnter file to replay: "))
  (setq f (open fi "r"))
  (read-line f)
  (setq p1 (read-line f))
  (setq p2 (read-line f))
  (setq p3 (read-line f))
  (setq p4 (read-line f))
  (close f)
  (setq p1 (read p1))
  (setq p2 (read p2))
  (setq p3 (read p3))
  (setq p4 (read p4))
  (command "line" p1 p2 p3 p4 "c")
)
```

PURPOSE: This program reads from a user-selectable file the four coordinate points of a rectangle that were written to the file by **REMEMBER** then redraws the rectangle from those coordinates.

TO LOAD:

Type: `(load "les8b")   <RETURN>`

Response: `replay`

TO OPERATE:

Type: `replay   <RETURN>`

Response: `Enter file to replay:`

Type: `temp   <RETURN>`

The program now draws the original rectangle.

The following is a line-by-line analysis of the program:

```
(defun C:replay ( )
```

defines the function.

```
(setq fi (getstring "\nEnter file to replay: "))
```

asks you for the file name and assigns it as a string to the variable **fi**.

```
(setq f (open fi "r"))
```

opens a file named in the string variable **fi**. The file is opened for read-only as indicated by the **"r."** The file handle is returned and assigned to the variable **f**. This file handle is used to identify the file in other commands.

```
(read-line f)
```

Something interesting is happening here. The command **(read-line)** reads a line in from the file identified by the file handle in the variable **f**. Notice that you're not assigning the value to anything, because you first must read in a blank line. This is because the **(print)** command that wrote the coordinates to the file always precedes the print with a line feed. As a result, the first print to the file is always a blank line. Therefore, you should enter one blank line before the data begins.

```
(setq p1 (read-line f))
(setq p2 (read-line f))
(setq p3 (read-line f))
(setq p4 (read-line f))
```

reads in the next four lines and assigns each group of coordinates to its respective variable, **p1**, **p2**, **p3** and **p4**.

```
(close f)
```

closes the file.

```
(setq p1 (read p1))
(setq p2 (read p2))
(setq p3 (read p3))
(setq p4 (read p4))
```

These lines are there because the command **(read-line)** is used to read in string information from a file. In fact, when data are stored in a file, they are always read in as a string. A number must be converted to a number. A list must be stripped of the " ". The easiest way to do that is with the **(read)** command.

```
(command "line" p1 p2 p3 p4 "c")
```

draws the rectangle.

```
)
```

ends the function.

Other commands are utilized in reading and writing to files. **(write-line)** writes a string to a file. **(write-char)** writes to a file character by character. **(read-line)** reads a string from a file. **(read-char)** reads character by character from a file. Notice how many times **(write-line)** and **(print)** may either be used if strings are applied. In the first program, this wasn't the case since the coordinates were in the form of a list.

The next program is an adaptation of the first and illustrates how you can send a hard-copy printout to your printer using the same techniques.

AutoLISP Program LES8c.LSP

```
(defun C:remember2 ( )
(setq fi "prn")
  (setq f (open fi "w"))
  (prompt "\Now draw 4 points of a rectangle: ")
  (setq p1 (getpoint "\nFirst point: "))
  (print p1 f)
  (setq p2 (getpoint "\nSecond point: "))
  (print p2 f)
  (setq p3 (getpoint "\nThird point: "))
  (print p3 f)
  (setq p4 (getpoint "\nFourth point: "))
  (print p4 f)
  (close f)
  (command "line" p1 p2 p3 p4 "c")
)
```

Notice the only difference between this program and the first is that the name of the file is **"prn."** In fact, you could keep the programs the same and simply give the name of the file as **prn**, and the output would go to the printer instead of the file.

If you want to send a file to your printer, just open the printer as though it were a file and print to that file. Rather than going to your hard disk, the data will print. When using DOS, **prn** is the name of the printer device attached to **lptl:**.

Moving On

Not everything you need is in the AutoCAD entity database or system variables. Much of what AutoCAD knows about a drawing is found in a part of AutoCAD known as the tables. Chapter 9, "Working With Tables," shows you how to access the many tables that AutoCAD maintains and get vital information to make your program work.

9

WORKING WITH TABLES

Working With Tables

9.1 What Are Tables?

The AutoCAD database consists not only of the entities that you know thus far. The AutoCAD drawing includes several sections, such as the Table Section. Tables are not entities. They store information about entities which are maintained globally in the drawing. When you insert a block, for example, how does AutoCAD know what that block looks like? The definition of that block is stored in the block table. In this table are the actual entities that make up that block. When an entity is to display its color by layer, AutoCAD draws upon a layer table that knows everything about a layer. These tables hold lots of information, which you can access through AutoLISP.

This example shows how information in a table can help you in an AutoLISP program. Assume that you need to create a layer. You have to know whether that layer already exists. If you try to create a layer that already exists, you'll get an error message in your program. Therefore, you search the layer table to see if the layer exists. Then you write an **(if...)** statement to create the layer only if it doesn't exist. In another example, you often need to check on the current text style and whether that text style has a fixed height for the text or if the text height within the style is set to 0. This is important when you write your own text programs.

Example 1:

```
(command "text" pt1 ht rot tx)
```

Example 2:

```
(command "text" pt1 rot tx)
```

Unlike Example 1, Example 2 doesn't give the variable for height. If the current text style does not have a fixed height, you have to use example 1 to create text. If on the other hand the current text style does have a fixed height, then AutoCAD doesn't ask you for the height of the text since it already knows it. In that case you can't include the height as one of your variables in a command expression.

The only way for you to know which one to use is to evaluate the table.

There are nine tables that you can access:

Layer Table	"LAYER"
Linetype Table	"LTYPE"
Named View Table	"VIEW"
Text Style Table	"STYLE"
Block Table	"BLOCK"
Named UCS Table	"UCS"
Named Application ID Table	"APPID"
Named Dimension Style Table	"DIMSTYLE"
Vport Configuration Table	"VPORT"

A table has two parts: the **names** of the entries in the table and the **details** of each entry. Using the layer table as an example, the name of the entries would be the names of the layers that exist. The details of an individual layer would be color, linetype, on, off, frozen, thawed, locked, unlocked or current.

9.2 (tblsearch)   Accessing Tables

This command is one of the commands used to access a table. You'll use the command if you already know the table's name. If you didn't know the name of the table and you needed a list of the table entries, you'd use **(tblnext)**.

Assume you wanted to know if a layer called DIMN existed. Create the layer DIMN, then

Type: `(setq t (tblsearch "LAYER" "DIMN"))`

The entity list of that layer would be returned.

Response: `((0 . "LAYER") (2 . "DIMN") (70 . 64) (62 . 7) (6 . "CONTINUOUS"))`

Look at the entry list above and pay attention to the numbers. As you can see, this is a standard entity list. The first part of the entry list is **"0"**, indicating Associative 0. In this case it's an entry in the **"LAYER"** table. Associative 2 indicates the name of the layer. Here it's called "DIMN." Associative 70 is the state of the entity. 1, for example, is Frozen, 2 is Frozen on new paper space view ports and 4 is locked. These numbers are added to 64, which means that the layer has been referenced at least one time during this editing session. In this case the layer is neither frozen nor locked. Associative 62 is the color of the layer. In this case it is white, which is color number 7. If the color number is a negative number then the layer is off. Associative 6 is the linetype of the layer, and **"CONTINU-OUS"** is the current type.

If the (tblsearch) command had not found the layer DIMN then the command would have returned **nil** and you would know that the layer did not exist.

9.3 (tblnext)   Next Layer or Block

There are times you don't know the name of the layer or block but you need a list of them. Use the command (**tblnext**). Assume that four layers exist in your drawing.

They are layers 0, DIMN, MECH and TXT.

Type: `(tblnext "LAYER")  <RETURN>`

Response: `((0 . "LAYER") (2 . "0") (70 . 0) (62.7) (6 . "CONTINUOUS"))`

Continue to type the same (**tblnext "LAYER"**) command four additional times. You will get a new entity list for each of the three additional layers. The last time that you type the command the program will return *nil* because there are no additional layers. In this way you can page through the layer table to see what layers exist and their status. Below is the loop that you would use.

```
(setq f 1)
  (while (setq t (tblnext "LAYER" f))
  (setq f nil)
  (setq b (assoc 2 t))
  (princ b)
)
```

In the above code segment you search the layer table for all layers. Notice that the variable **f** is added at the end of the (**tblnext**) command. If this variable is non-nil, the pointer will be set to the top of the table. If the variable is nil then each time the (**tblnext**) command is issued it will be advanced one item down the table. Therefore, in this case we begin by setting it to 1, a non-nil value and begin a (**while...**) loop.

The expression following the while loop will return a non-nil value as long as it keeps finding layers. When it finds no more layers, the expression will return nil and the loop will terminate. Immediately after the first layer is found, the variable **f** is set to nil so that the pointer will not return to the top of the layer table. The variable **b** secures the name of the layer found, which is Associative 2 of the layer entity list. Finally, it's printed.

9.4 Using Tables
AutoLISP Program LES9a.LSP

```
(defun C:playoff ()
  (setq f 1)
    (while (setq t (tblnext "LAYER" f))
    (setq f nil)
    (setq b (assoc 62 t))
    (if (< (cdr b) 0)
      (progn
        (setq b (cdr (assoc 2 t)))
        (terpri)
        (princ b)
      )
    )
  )
(princ)
)
```

PURPOSE:　This program prints only the layers that are OFF.

TO LOAD:

　Type:　(load "les9a")　<RETURN>

Response:　PLAYOFF

TO OPERATE:

　Type:　playoff　<RETURN>

The program prints the names of the layers that are turned off. Let's look at the program line-by-line.

(defun C:playoff ()

defines the function.

(setq f 1)

sets the flag to non nil.

```
(while (setq t (tblnext "LAYER" f))
```

begins the (while) loop using the **(tblnext)** command as the loop expression.

```
(setq f nil)
```

sets the flag to non-nil so that the **(tblnext)** pointer does not go to the top of the table.

```
(setq b (assoc 62 t))
```

assigns the color integer to the variable b. Remember that the layer is **on** or **off** depending on whether the color is a positive or negative value.

```
(if (<  (cdr b) 0)
  (progn
```

begins the **(if…)** statement to test whether the integer color number is less than 0.

```
(setq b (cdr (assoc 2 t)))
(terpri)
(princ b)
```

This section the program makes an evaluation for you. If the **(if…)** statement passes and the color integer is less than **0**, it is negative and the layer must be **off**. When this is the case, the name of the layer is assigned to the variable **b**, and the layer name is printed.

```
)
```

This closes the (while… statement.

```
)
```

This closes the (if… statement.

```
)
```

This closes the (progn… statement.

```
(princ)
```

This prevents *nil* being written onscreen at startup.

```
)
```

This closes the (defun… statement and the program.

AutoLISP Program LES9b.LSP

```
(defun C:clayer ()
  (setq na (getstring "\nEnter layer name to be created:  "))
  (setq b (tblsearch "LAYER" na))
  (if (= b nil) (command "layer" "n" na ""))
  (if (/= b nil)(prompt "\nLayer already exists:  "))
  (princ)
)
```

PURPOSE: This program rapidly creates layers or informs you if a layer already exists.

TO LOAD:

Type: `(load "les9b")  <RETURN>`

Response: `CLAYER`

TO OPERATE:

Type: `clayer <RETURN>`

Response: `Enter layer name to be created:`

Type: `mech1  <RETURN>`

The layer is created. If that layer already exists it responds **"Layer already exists."**

Let's look at the program line-by-line.

```
(defun C:clayer ()
```

defines the function

```
(setq na (getstring "\nEnter layer name to be created:  "))
```

asks you for a layer name and assigns the layer name to the variable **na**.

```
(setq b (tblsearch "LAYER" na))
```

If the layer exists in the table, the list is assigned to the variable **b**. If the layer does not exist, then nil is returned to the variable **b**.

```
(if (= b nil) (command "layer" "n" na ""))
(if (/= b nil)(prompt "\nLayer already exists: "))
```

If the layer does not exist in the table, the AutoCAD command "layer" makes a new layer. If the layer exists in the table, the program prompts the user.

```
(pinc)
```

This prevents *nil* being written onscreen at start-up.

```
)
```

This closes the (defun… statement and the program.

AutoLISP Program LES9c.LSP

```
(defun C:pblkct ()
    (setq f 1)
    (while (setq t (tblnext "BLOCK" f))
      (setq f nil)
      (setq na (cdr (assoc 2 t)))
      (setq b  (assoc 2 t))
      (setq c (ssget "x" (list '(0 . "INSERT") b)))
      (if (/= c nil)
        (progn
          (setq n (sslength c))
          (terpri)
          (princ na)(prompt "  ")(princ n)
        )
      )
    )
  (princ)
)
```

PURPOSE: This program counts all the referenced blocks in the drawing.

TO LOAD:

Type: (load "les9c") <RETURN>

Response: PBLKCT

TO OPERATE:

Type: pblkct <RETURN>

The program runs automatically and prints the name of each referenced block in the drawing and how many of each.

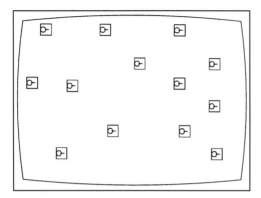

Fig. 9-1: The program prints your references blocks.

Let's look at the program line-by-line.

```
(defun C:pblkct ()
```

defines the function

```
(setq f 1)
```

sets the flag to non-nil.

```
(while (setq t (tblnext "BLOCK" f))
```

begins the **(while…)** loop using the **(tblnext)** command as the loop expression.

```
(setq f nil)
```

sets the flag to non-nil so that the **(tblnext)** pointer does not go to the top of the table.

```
(setq na (cdr (assoc 2 t)))
(setq b  (assoc 2 the))
```

These two lines are similar. The first uses **(cdr)** to secure only the name of the block and assign it to the variable **na**. The second secures the entire Associative 2 list that will be used next in the **(ssget)** filter command.

```
(setq c (ssget "x" (list '(0 . "INSERT") b)))
```

filters in only those entities whose entity type is an **INSERT** and block name is the list found in **b**.

```
(if (/= c nil)
(progn
(setq n (sslength c))
(terpri)
(princ na)(prompt "   ")(princ n)
```

If the selection **c** is not nil, the length of the selection set (the number of entities captured) is assigned to **n**. Finally, the name of the block and the count are printed.

```
)
```

This closes the (while… statement.

```
)
```

This closes the (if… statement.

```
)
```

This closes the (progn… statement.

```
(princ
```

The prevents *nil* being written onscreen at startup.

```
)
```

This closes the (defun… statement and ends the program.

Moving On

Accessing tables is no more difficult than accessing other entities and takes you deep into the heart of the AutoCAD database so you can gather the information you need to prevent errors from happening and control the global parameters of AutoCAD. Errors happen; and as an amateur AutoLISP programmer, you need to know how to check and trap errors to create a smoothly running program. Chapter 10, "Error-Checking" will guide you in keeping your programs error free.

10

ERROR-CHECKING

CHAPTER 10

Error-Checking

10.1 Why Error-Check & Error-Trap?

Programs do not always run as the programmer intended. Obviously, when you write a program, you check it for bugs and make certain that the program does what you intended it to. But you can't check for every mistake the user can make. Controlling the program when mistakes occur is what error-checking and error-trapping are all about.

As you learned in Chapter 6, you write your program for an intended user. If the program is strictly for your use and mistakes occur while you're running it, who cares? If the program crashes, just begin it again and do it right the next time. It's your program.

As you write programs for other users, you'll want to pay more attention to error-checking and error-trapping.

10.2 Types of Errors

There are basically three types of errors you need to check for:

syntax error
machine error
logical error

The first error is the most common. It is either a syntax error or an error of input or data. A syntax error might be

```
(setq a (getstrin "\nEnter text: ")).
```

You will see this flaw the first time you run the program because **(get-string)** is misspelled.

```
(setq pt1 (getpoint "\nPick a point: "))
```

might produce an error from time to time if the user fails to pick a point but instead presses <RETURN>. Later in the program if pt1 is nil, the program will crash.

The second type of error is a machine error. This can occur when disk drives and printers are not ready or files are not found. AutoCAD considers even **Ctrl C** an error and will stop the program.

The third type of mistake is a logical error. This type of error will not cause the program to crash, but you might get an incorrect answer if formulas are wrong. This can be devastating since many users believe without question what a computer says.

An example of a "logic error" might be program lines using the wrong pick point to measure the length of a line. The program won't stop, but the user doesn't know that the program is measuring from the wrong place.

10.3 Error-Checking

There are two basic methods of error-checking. You **test** or you **trap**.

You either anticipate the possible errors that might occur and write the code to "test" for those errors or you can "trap" the error. You use an error trap to identify any possible errors that might occur, and the trap in turn logs the error result and sends it to a routine that can handle it. The log informs the user where the error is happening.

Anticipated error-checking in AutoLISP is very cumbersome. It is generally done with an **(if...)** statement. In the previous chapter we used error-checking in program LES9c.LSP. The following is a segment of that code:

```
(if (/= c nil)
  (progn
  (setq n (sslength c))
  (terpri)
  (princ na)(prompt "")(princ n)
  )
)
```

In this program, the variable **c** is a selection set. What do you think would happen if the value of **c** were **nil**, meaning that no selection set were created? By the way, this will occur quite normally in this program since there are no references to the block that is being searched.

(sslength c) will generate an error, **"bad argument type,"** and crash the program if this happens. In this example of LES9c.LSP, we check for this fatal possibility and only permit the program to use **(sslength)** if the value of **c** is not **nil**. This is a prime example of anticipating an error and taking care of the possibility before it happens.

Another common example occurs when the user makes a mistake. You need to anticipate that mistake, but, moreover, you should give the user the opportunity to try again. This scenario occurs many, many times.

```
(setq pt1 (getpoint "\nPick a point: "))
(if (= pt1 nil) ...
```

Then what? Obviously, you want the user to return to the **(setq pt1 (getpoint))** expression and try again until a point is picked. But there is no **GOBACK** command in AutoLISP. The generally accepted method of doing this is to place the entire **(getpoint)** routine in a loop that will repeat over and over until the point is picked. Here's how it's done:

```
(setq lct 1)
(while lct
(setq pt1 (getpoint "\nPick a point: "))
(if (= pt1 nil)(princ "\nBad point!  Pick again: "))
(if (/= pt1 nil)(setq lct nil))
)
```

This looks like a lot of code just to have someone pick a point. The variable **lct** is a loop controller. If **pt1** is **nil**, an error message is printed and the loop continues permitting the user to pick again. If **pt1** is not **nil**, the loop controller, **lct**, is set to **nil**; and thus the **(while...)** loop terminates and the program continues.

10.4 Using (initget) & (getkword)

Not all error-checking in AutoLISP is cumbersome. A built-in function helps you restrict the user's choices. This is especially useful when the answer must be **Y** or **N**, not maybe.

```
(initget  1  "  Y  N  y  n")
(setq a (getkword "\nEnter Y or N "))
```

AutoLISP controls the error loop for you. If you enter anything other than the options listed in **(initget)** then AutoLISP tells you that is an invalid keyword and cycles you back. You may still have to use **(strcase)** to convert the answer to all uppercase depending on the needs of your program.

Notice that the 1 in **(initget)** is the flag field and uses the *sum of the bits* technique to error-check, meaning they are added together to combine options. Thus a flag of 40 is the sum of 8+32, which does not check drawing limits and uses dashed lines when drawing a rubber-band rectangle. The following are the possible flag options:

1	Disallow null input
2	Disallow zero values
4	Disallow negative values
8	Do not check drawing limits, even if LIMCHECK is On
16	(Not currently used)
32	Use dashed lines when drawing rubber-band line or box
64	Disallow input of a Z coordinate (getdist only)
128	Returns arbitrary keyboard input

(initget) is an error-checking function that can be used with a variety of commands. The valid commands available with **(initget)** and their possible flags are:

(getint)	1, 2, 4, 128
(getreal)	1, 2, 4, 128
(getdist)	1, 2, 4, 32, 64, 128
(getangle)	1, 2, 32, 128
(getorient)	1, 2, 32, 128
(getpoint)	1, 8, 32, 128
(getcorner)	1, 8, 32, 128
(getkword)	1, 128
(getstring)	NONE
(entsel)	NONE
(nentsel)	NONE
(nentselp)	NONE

All the above commands permit keyword limits except **(getstring)**. Each must immediately follow the **(initget)** command.

10.5 File Handling

You'll crash the program if you try to open an existing file that doesn't really exist. There are two ways to prevent this from happening. The first is with the **(findfile)** command. This command returns the path spec of the file if it exists. If the file does not exist then it returns **nil**.

```
(setq f (findfile "acad.lsp"))
```

A more elegant method to allow the user to choose a file is to bring up the built-in file dialogue box. This is done with the command **(getfiled).**

```
(setq f (getfiled "LISP FILES" "" "LSP" 1))
```

The expression returns the name of the file chosen by the user and is assigned to the variable **f**. The first string in quotes, **"LISP FILES,"** is the title of the dialogue box. The second string is a default file name you want to start with. In our example it's **" "** because we don't want to use a default name. But the position *cannot* be left blank. The third position is the extension that is searched, and the fourth position is the flag.

Possible flags are **1, 2, 4** and **8**. These are *sum of the bits,* meaning that they're *added* together to combine options. Let's look at what the flags mean.

1   User will be warned about overwriting an existing file.
2   The "type it" button will be disabled.
4   The user is permitted to change the extension.
8   AutoCAD uses its search path and only the name of the file, not the path spec. If it's not set, then the entire path spec will be returned.

10.6 Error-Trapping

The error-trapping mechanism allows AutoLISP to intercept an error and send the program to another function of your choice. In this way you control what happens when an unexpected error occurs.

The error-trap function is very specific and has a very specific name:

```
*error*
```

Here's an example of how you might be able to use it in a program:

```
(defun *error* (errmsg)
  (princ "\nAn error has occurred in the program  ")
  (terpri)
```

```
    (prompt errmsg)
    (princ)
)
```

First, the error-trap function must be called ***error***. It also must have an argument passing variable. In our example the variable is **errmsg**. It doesn't matter what you call this variable. Then you may put whatever you like inside the body of the function.

To test the error trap, place the above ***error*** function in a **.LSP** file and load the file. The function is now loaded. Then begin running any program you want. In the middle of the program do a Ctrl C. Remember that AutoLISP interprets this as an error. Control will be transferred to the error-trap function.

10.7 Saving an Error Trap

You can have one and only one ***error*** function. But it's possible to load more than one error trap even though you can use only one at a time. Let's assume you have three trap routines:

```
(defun trap1 (errmsg)
(defun trap2 (errmsg)
(defun trap3 (errmsg)
```

Each of the above functions (they are only the beginning segment) can treat errors differently. None of the above functions can be the error trap until it is the ***error*** function. Fortunately, one function can be assigned to another function simply with a **(setq)** command.

```
(setq *error* trap1)
```

This command assigns the entire function **(trap1)** to ***error***. **(trap1)** has not changed. One by one, you can place different error traps in your program, but remember, only use one at a time.

In any program you should be courteous to people who might be using other programs or have existing settings. You should never change a user setting, including an existing error trap, without first saving it as a variable and then replacing it at the end of the program.

But remember to place the replacement of the original error trap in your error trap routine as well since you have no guarantee that your program will come to a normal conclusion.

AutoLISP Program LES10.LSP

A complete error-trap example appears below:

```
(defun C:clayer2 ( )
  (setq temperr *error*)
  (setq *error* trap1)
  (setq os (getvar "osmode"))
  (command "undo" "m")
  (setq na (getstring "\nEnter layer name to be created: "))
  (setq b (tblsearch "LAYER" na))
  (if (= b nil) (command "layer" "n" na ""))
  (if (/= b nil)(prompt "\nLayer already exists: "))
  (setvar "osmode" os)
  (setq *error* temperr)
  (princ)
  )

(defun trap1 (errmsg)
  (command "undo" "b")
  (setvar "osmode" os)
  (setq *error* temperr)
  )
```

In the above example the existing ***error*** error trap is saved to the variable **temperr. *error*** is then assigned your error trap, which is called **trap1**. Any system variables such as object snaps are then saved. In this case the original OSNAP is assigned to the variable **os** and an **UNDO MARK** is put in place. If there is an error, your drawing is reset back to it's original settings.

```
(setvar "osmode" os)
(setq *error* temperr)
```

The error trap first performs an **UNDO BACK**. At the end of the program the saved items and error trap are placed back the way you found them.

Finally, if you want an error trap to be turned off, use the simple command

```
(setq *error* nil).
```

Moving On

LISP stands for List Processing. One of the real powers of any LISP-based programming language is how it handles lists. The first part of the book introduced lists with some simple list-handling techniques.

Chapter 11, "Advanced List Concepts," shows you how to work with large amounts of data and gives you several useful utilities to help you handle various elements of a list effectively.

11

ADVANCED LIST CONCEPTS

Advanced List Concepts

11.1 Why Use Lists

After all, LISP stands for list processing. And therein lies its strength. A list lets you manipulate large amounts of data easily. This ability makes AutoLISP unique among programming languages.

LISP is the basis of AutoCAD's programming language because of this unique aspect. Look at something as simple as expressing coordinates picked from the screen, for example.

```
(setq pt1 (getpoint "\nPick a point: ")).
```

Once you pick the point, it's stored as three values: the X, Y and Z in a single variable. The three coordinates are stored in a list that can be manipulated, taken apart and put back together.

There is virtually no limit to the complexity of the lists that can be created. In fact, the entire entity database is expressed in AutoLISP as a list called the entity list. This allows the entire entity to be expressed as a single variable. Even within the entity list are smaller nested lists, such as associatives that describe various aspects of the entity such as type, color, layer, size and coordinates.

11.2 How to Create a List

For users who are more accustomed to BASIC or other high-level languages, data manipulation through a list is foreign. You might be more familiar with the concept of an array. This is a structure with data ordered as subscripts and allowed random access. The data, for example, might be expressed in a variable as A(4), which is the fourth element of the array.

The array is not an efficient method since memory and space must be set aside whether it is used or not. A list, on the other hand, only uses data as it needs it.

Lists are created in two ways. First, there are commands which by their very nature create lists. These are commands such as **(getpoint)** and **(entget)**. Whenever you use these commands, a list is created.

The second way to create a list is directly with two commands. You use these commands when you have a series of data that you want to make into a list. This can be done directly. Try this example:

Type: `(setq a (list 2 4 6 8 10))  <RETURN>`

Type: `!a <RETURN>`

When you look inside the variable **a**, this is what you see:

Response: `(2 4 6 8 10)`

Notice how the numbers are within parentheses. A list is always within parentheses, and the elements of a list are separated with a space.

Type: `(type a) <RETURN>`

Response: `LIST`

When you ask AutoLISP what data type the variable **a** is, AutoLISP tells you that it's a list. Therefore, the command **(list)** is one way to create a list from a series of elements. But there is another way.

Type: `(setq b '(2 4 6 8 10))`

This method does the same thing. Regardless of which method you used, the elements are now part of a list. Either method works.

There is one other command for creating a list: it's the **(cons)** command. This is a special command that creates *associative lists* used within the entity list. If you wanted to create an **Associative 8** list for the description of a layer called **MECH** so that you can use it within a substitute command, you would use the **(cons)** command.

Type: `(setq d (con 8 "MECH"))`

This creates a dotted pair Associative 8 list.

`(8 . "MECH")`

11.3 (nth)   Isolate Single Element Within List

In the first section of the book you learned how to use CAR, CADR, CDR and CADDR to isolate the first, second, third and remaining elements of a list. This is all well and good for coordinate points, but it becomes very cumbersome if the list is extremely long. The command that can isolate any single element within a list is the **(nth)** command. Let's use the list in the variable **a** as an example.

```
(2 4 6 8 10)
```

To isolate the third element of a list, use the command **(nth 2 a)**. It's a **2** rather than a **3** because the first element of the list is counted as a **0**.

To help you understand further, at the end of the chapter you'll find a series of example AutoLISP programs that are list utilities. The AutoLISP program LISP11a.LSP, for example, is a program that subtracts 1 from your item number; so you can think in terms of first, second and third elements of a list instead of being confused with 0, 1 and 2 elements.

11.4 (subst)   Change All Occurrences of a List

Again, begin with the list of variable **a** (2 4 6 8 10). The need here is to change every occurrence of an **8** in the list to a **6**.

In this case the **4th** item in the list is an **8**; you therefore want your list to end as **(2 4 6 6 10)**. You'll use the **(subst...)** to achieve this. For example,

```
(setq a (subst 6 8 a))
```

This command was used in a previous chapter. You'll remember the **(subst)** command for substituting Associative lists within an entity list. This command substitutes all occurrences of one value for another. The new value always comes first. In order to make the list, the new permanent value has to be set to itself.

11.5 Change the Value of an Element of the List

Here, your object is to change only the fourth element of the list. From the last example, the list should now be (2 4 6 6 10) because you changed the 8 to a 6. If you used the previous example to change the 6 back to an 8, you would change both 6's to 8's. This is not what you want to do. You only want to change the fourth element of a list back to an 8. Therefore, you need a different technique.

This technique is substantially more complex. You must split the list into two separate lists, the first ending before the item you want to change and the second beginning after the item you want to change. If the list is

(1 2 3 4 5 6 7 8 9 10) and you want to change the fourth item to a 9, you split the list into (1 2 3) and (5 6 7 8 9 10). Then you append the first list plus the new value plus the second list. That then gives you (1 2 3 9 5 6 7 8 9 10).

Obviously, this technique can't be performed as a simple one- or two-line program. In the list utility programs, you'll find LES11b.LSP is a program that does just this with a complete explanation.

11.6 (member)   Change Only First Occurrence

If you wanted to change every occurrence of a value in a list, you use the **(subst)** command. Use this list as an example (1 2 3 4 8 6 7 8 9 10). In this example there is more than one 8. You want to change only the first occurrence of the 8 to a 5, but you don't know where in the list this first occurrence is going to be. In order to make this work, you must first know the item number of the first occurrence of your target element.

The command **(member)** in AutoLISP finds the first occurrence for you and returns a list that is that occurrence and the remainder of the list. By subtracting from the length of the original list the length of the **(member)** list, you have the position of the target element. By adding **1** to this number, you get around the fact that lists begin their numbering with **0**.

In the following code segment, **n** represents the position number in the list, **a** is the list variable and **8** is the target occurrence.

```
(setq n (+ (- (length a)(length (member 8 a))) 1))
```

The length of **(member 8 a)**, which is the target occurrence and the remainder of the list, is subtracted from the length of the list as a whole; and 1 is added. This number is assigned to the value of n. Once you have this number, you can use the program discussed in the previous section to change the single occurrence. A complete program for this change method is found at the end of this chapter as LES11c.LSP.

11.7 (append)   Add an Element to a List

This is a simple concept. Just use the **(append)** command. The only tricky thing about this command is that you can only append lists together. But that's easy to get around.

```
(setq a '(1 2 3 4 5))
```

The following will add **6** to list **a**.

```
(setq a (append a (list 6)))
```

Assume that you have three lists.

```
(setq a '(1 2 3))
(setq b '(4 5 6))
(setq c '(7 8 9 10))
(setq d (append a b c))
```

puts all three lists together.

11.8 (mapcar) & (lambda)   Handling Large Lists

(mapcar) and **(lamda)** are two of the most powerful commands in Auto-LISP for handling large lists. They have unusual names, but they really are not too difficult to understand. And they work nicely together.

Let's start with **(mapcar)**. **(mapcar)** performs a function on each of the elements of the list. The simplest example is to add 1 to each element of a list.

Lets try a simple one first.

Type: `(setq a 1)`

Type: `(mapcar '1+ (list a))`

Response: `(2)`

See how **(mapcar...** adds 1 to the **(list a)** to make **(2)**
Let's try a longer list.

Type: `(setq  a  '(1 2 3 4 5 6 7 8 9 10))`

Type: `(mapcar    '1+   a)`

Response: `(2 3 4 5 6 7 8 9 10 11).`

You might be asking why there is an **(')** apostrophe in front of the **1+**. This is really shorthand for the **(quote)** command. The **(quote)** command maintains everything within the quote as a literal that is unevaluated.

The example below shows why this is important. We'll start with a function called **(cat)**.

```
(defun cat ( ) (prompt "\nHello")).
```

Obviously, **(cat)** is a function; and if you use **(cat)** in an AutoLISP program it will say **Hello.** But there are times you don't want **(cat)** to execute the function directly. You want it simply to return **(cat)**, not perform the function. That is when you'd use **(' (cat))** or **(quote (cat))**. It would then return **(cat)**. Remember, the **(')** apostrophe is AutoLISP shorthand for **(quote)**.

The following **(mapcar)** function would work just as well:

```
(mapcar (quote 1+) a)
```

But what if you wanted to add **5** to each of the elements within the list? That's where **(lambda)** comes in. **(lambda)** lets you write an in-line function without having to create a defun command. Look at the following example:

```
(defun addit (x) (+ x 5))
```

(addit) is a function that adds **5** to whatever value is sent to it.

```
(mapcar (quote addit) a)
```

This expression will run the **(addit)** function against each element of list **a.** The value of each element is passed to the **(addit)** function.

(lambda) permits you to write the **(addit)** function in-line within the **(mapcar)** expression without having to define a separate function.

```
(mapcar (quote (lambda (x) (+ x 5))) a)
```

The above expression adds **5** to each element of list **a.**

(lambda (x) (+ x 5)) is the same as (defun addit (x) (+ x 5)) when you use the (addit) function.

In reality, **(lambda)** can be used anywhere you need a speedy function and you don't want the trouble of writing and making sure a **(defun)** function is loaded.

11.9 (foreach) Reading Lists From Files

Program LES11d.LSP is an AutoLISP program that writes a list to a sequential file. Whereas, LES11e.LSP reads from a sequential file and creates a list. Both of these programs use the **(foreach)** command. The **(foreach)** command performs a function on each of the elements of a list. In LES11d.LSP the function is to write each element to a file.

The syntax for the **(foreach)** command is **(foreach variable list)**. If you're going to print all the elements of list **a**, use

```
(foreach n a (princ n)(terpri))
```

This expression prints vertically.

```
1
2
3
4
5
6
7
8
9
10
```

Once a list is written to disk, the program may not read back the elements of the list as they once were. The program reads them back as strings. This may not be as you want it. For example,

```
(1 2 3 4 5 6 7 8 9 10)
```

may now look like

```
("1" "2" "3" "4" "5" "6" "7" "8" "9" "10")
```

You can use **(mapcar)** to go from one to the other.

Type: `(setq a '(1 2 3 4 5 6 7 8 9 10)) <RETURN>`

This creates a list of (1 2 3 4 5 6 7 8 9 10)

Type: `(setq b (mapcar (quote itoa) a))` `<RETURN>`

Your list **b** is now ("1" "2" "3" "4" "5" "6" "7" "8" "9" "10").

Type: `(setq b (mapcar (quote atoi) b))` `<RETURN>`

This sets **b** back to integers of (1 2 3 4 5 6 7 8 9 10).

11.10 List Utility Programs

AutoLISP Program LES11a.LSP

```
(defun nthlist (item lst)
  (setq item (1- item))
  (nth item lst)
)
```

PURPOSE: Finds any element of a list.

TO LOAD:

Type: `(load "les11a")` `<RETURN>`

TO OPERATE:

In this example, you begin with list **a** of

`(setq a '(1 2 3 4 5 6 7))`.

But, to let you find the fourth element of the list,

Type: `(nthlist 4 a)` `<RETURN>`

The fourth element of the list is returned.

AutoLISP Program LESIIb.LSP

```
(defun chnitem (value num lst)
  (setq num (- num 1))
  (setq tmplt (list nil))
  (setq tmplt2 (list nil))
  (setq counter 0)
  (repeat num
    (setq tmplt (append tmplt (list (nth counter lst))))
    (setq counter (+ counter 1))
  )
  (setq counter (+ counter 1))
  (repeat (- (length lst) (+ num 1))
    (setq tmplt2 (append tmplt2 (list (nth counter lst))))
    (setq counter (+ counter 1))
  )
  (setq tmplt (cdr tmplt))
  (setq tmplt2 (cdr tmplt2))
  (setq lst (append tmplt (list value) tmplt2))
)
```

PURPOSE: Changes any single element of a list.

TO LOAD:

Type: `(load "les11b") <RETURN>`

TO OPERATE:

In this example, begin with list **a** of

`(setq a '(1 2 3 4 4 6 7))`.

To change the fifth element of the list to an 8,

Type: `(setq a (chnitem 8 5 a)) <RETURN>`

Response: `(1 2 3 4 8 6 7)`

The fifth item in the list was changed to an 8.

AutoLISP Program LES11c.LSP

```
(defun chfitem (oldval newval lst)
  (setq numb (+ (- (length lst)(length (member oldval lst))) 1))
  (chlitem newval numb lst)
)
```

PURPOSE: Changes only the first occurrence of an item.

TO LOAD:

Type: `(load "les11c") <RETURN>`

TO OPERATE:

In this example, begin with list **a** of

Type: `(setq a '(1 2 3 4 4 6 7)).`

To change the first occurrence of 4 to an 8 without changing any others,

Type: `(setq a (chfitem 4 8 a)) <RETURN>`

Response: `(1 2 3 8 4 6 7)`

The first occurrence of the 4 was changed to an 8, but the second occurrence was not. In order for LES11c.LSP (chfitem) to run, it is necessary to make certain that LES11b.LSP is also loaded since (chfitem) uses (chnitem) as one of its functions.

AutoLISP Program LES11d.LSP

```
(defun savelist (lst filnam)
  (setq fn (open filnam "w"))
  (foreach n lst (princ n fn)(princ "\n" fn))
  (close fn)
  (princ)
)
```

PURPOSE: Saves a list to a file.

TO LOAD:

Type: `(load "les11d") <RETURN>`

TO OPERATE:

In this example, begin with list **a** of

`(setq a '(1 2 3 4 4 6 7))`.

To save this list to a file,

Type: `(savelist a "tempfile") <RETURN>`

The list is saved to a file called tempfile. You may use any valid file-name or path spec you wish, of course. Make sure that the name of the file is a string variable or is in quotes.

AutoLISP Program LES11e.LSP

```
(defun readlist (filnam / tmplst x)
  (setq tmplst nil)
  (setq fn (open filnam "r"))
  (while (setq x (read-line fn))
  (setq tmplst (append tmplst (list x)))
  )
  (close fn)
  (setq tmplst tmplst)
)
```

PURPOSE: Reads a file and assigns it to a list.

TO LOAD:

Type: `(load "les11e") <RETURN>`

TO OPERATE:

In this example, begin with a saved file called "tempfile." This may be created using LES11d.LSP.

Type: `(setq b (readlist "tempfile")) <RETURN>`

The file is saved as a list assigned to the variable **b**. You may use any valid filename or path spec you wish. Make sure the name of the file is a string variable or is in quotes.

Moving On

Now that you have a firm understanding of how to work with lists, Chapter 12, "Advanced Entity Manipulation," will show you how to get the most out of selection sets and entities.

12

ADVANCED
ENTITY
MANIPULATION

Advanced Entity Manipulation

In Chapter 7, "Managing Entities," you learned how to create a selection set, select individual entities, secure information from the entities and modify entities in the database. But there are many more options in creating selection sets and working with entities.

12.1 (ssget) The Basic Selection Set Filter

A selection set places all the entities you need in one place and works on them as a group. The basic command to create the selection set is **(ssget)**.

```
(setq a (ssget))
```

The above expression lets you begin the basic select objects routine in AutoCAD. It gives the user the ability to choose any selection set method available, such as Window, Crossing, Fence, WPoly, CPoly. The only problem with this basic command is that the user has no control over the kind of entity being selected.

AutoCAD, therefore, lets you create selection set filters. Here's how the basic filter works:

```
(setq a (ssget "x"))
```

This expression automatically chooses every entity in the database and doesn't ask questions. All the entities are assigned to the variable **a**. The beginning of this basic filter is the **"x"** following the **(ssget...)**. This is the same as using the **ALL** option when selecting entities.

By only using the **"x"** you have no control over the kind of entities that are automatically being selected, however. You can limit the kind of entities by following the **"x"** with a list of Associative codes. Each Associative code limits the selection of all entities to entities that match the Associative codes.

For example, create layer MECH and place an arc, a line and a circle of any size on it, then

Type: `(setq a (ssget "x" '((8 . "MECH"))))`

Response: `<Selection set: 1>`

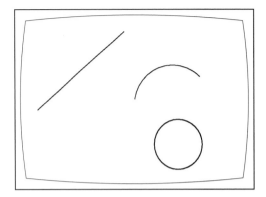

Figure 12-1: Create a line, an arc and a circle on layer MECH.

The above expression brings into the selection set only those entities that are on the MECH layer. Associative code 8 refers to layer, and you have limited the selection set to only those entities that are on that **"MECH"** layer.

Look at the apostrophe and all those parentheses just for one Associative code. This is a little confusing, but it will become clear. You can use more than one Associative code when limiting the entities. But these codes must be placed in a list following the **"x."** Look at the next example:

```
(setq a (ssget "x" '((0 . "CIRCLE")(8 . "MECH")))))

     '((0 . "CIRCLE")  (8 . "MECH"))
```

Notice how Associative 0 and Associative 8 are both used in the example. Each is a list, but they must be combined into a single larger list; thus the two outer parentheses. Since it's to be treated as a list, you place the apostrophe at the beginning. AutoLISP has no way of knowing how many of these Associative codes you'll be using; therefore it uses the same rules for all.

```
     '((8 . "MECH"))
```

This example is the same as the one above except that the (0 . "CIRCLE") has been removed. It's still a list within a list. That's why you need the extra parentheses.

You may add as many Associatives to limit the entities as you want, but remember that each of these is an **AND**. In other words, the entities selected must meet all the criteria, not just one of them.

12.2 Filters Within a User Selection Set

As useful as the **"x"** option of **(ssget...)** is, it has limitations. It collects all the entities in the entire database that meet the filtered criteria. At times you want the user to select a Window or Crossing and choose a group of entities, but within the entities you want to include only selected ones. In other words, you want to use a filter within a user selection set.

```
(setq a (ssget '((0 . "CIRCLE"))))
```

The example above looks the same as the previous examples except there is no **"x."** It's a straight **(ssget...)** with a filter added. This permits the user to select objects, but no matter what the user selects, only circles are added to the selection set in the example.

12.3 How to Use an <OR...>

When you add Associate codes within an **(ssget...)**, you connect them with an implied **AND**. This means that the entities selected must meet all the criteria. There is a way to turn those into an **<OR...** so you can select entities that meet any one of the criteria. To use the **OR,** you must tell AutoLISP that it's coming up. A very special Associative code does this.
    The code is **-4**. And it must be used as a pair.

```
'((-4 . "<OR") -------------------- (-4 . "OR>"))
```

The example above is not yet complete, as the dashed line represents the Associative codes that go between as typical choices. The first **-4 <OR** opens the **OR** and the last one closes it. Notice the direction of the less than and greater than signs at the beginning and end.
    Below is a more complete example. Assume you want to select only entities on the "MECH" layer OR the "DIMN" layer.

```
(setq a (ssget '((-4 . "<OR")(8 . "MECH")(8 . "DIMN")(-4 ."OR>"))))
```

    It's also permissible to use **(-4 . "<AND")** -------- **(-4 . "AND>")** groups and nest them with the **OR...** groups.

12.4 How to Use Prompts With (ssget)

You can't directly do this. The following is not permitted:

```
(setq a (ssget "w" "\nSelect by Window: "))
```

You'll get an error every time.

You can make it appear that's what you're doing, however, by having the user pick the points of the window first using the standard prompts of **(getpoint)** and **(getcorner)**. You may then return these coordinates to the **(ssget...)** command. Here's an example:

```
(prompt "\nSelect the entities by Crossing Window: ")
(setq pt1 (getpoint "\nFirst corner:  "))
(setq pt2 (getcorner pt1 "\nOther corner: "))
(setq a (ssget "c" pt1 pt2)
)
```

For all practical purposes it appears you added prompts to the **(ssget...)** command.

12.5 Other Options With (ssget...)

There are several other options with **(ssget...)**. You can force a previous selection set if one with **(setq a (ssget "P"))** exists. The **"P"** stands for previous. You may do the same with **"L"** for last. **(setq a (ssget "L"))**. This creates a selection set with the last entity created.

Another option is the ability to create a selection set of any entities chosen and captured in the last implied window. An implied window or crossing window, for example, is activated when you pick an area that is blank and either you create a window or a crossing. This in turn is terminated by picking the other corner.

If you pick from left to right, it's an implied window. If you pick from right to left it's an implied crossing. Thus the entities captured are in the implied selection set. They may be sent to a real selection set as

```
(setq a (ssget "I")).
```

12.6 (ssadd..) (ssdel..) Add & Delete Entities in a Selection Set

Adding and deleting entities from a selection set is easy. AutoLISP uses **(ssadd...)** to add and **(ssdel...)** to delete. The syntax of both of these commands is the same:

```
(ssadd ename ss)
(ssdel ename ss)
```

The entity name and selection set are optional for **(ssadd...)**. If one entity is included with **(ssadd...)**, but without a selection set, then a selection set of one entity is created.

If the selection set is included with the entity name, the entity is added to the selection set. You can't have **(ssadd...)** with a selection set but no entity name. All three must be included with **(ssdel...)**.

This example shows how **(ssadd...)** can be used.

```
(setq a (ssget))
(setq e (car (entsel)); (car (entsel) returns the entity name
(setq a (ssadd e a))
```

The above example adds the additional entity to selection set **a**. Use the option below if you want to delete the chosen entity from the selection set.

```
(setq a (ssdel e a))
```

The problem is, you can't directly add an entire selection set to another selection set and thus combine the two. But you can place the second selection set in a loop and add the entities one-by-one each time through the loop. Here's how that's done:

Create two selection sets called **a** and **b**. The following code segment adds each of the entities in selection set **b** to selection set **a**.

```
(setq ct 0)
  (repeat (sslength b)
  (ssadd (ssname b ct) a)
  (setq ct (+ ct 1))
)
```

12.7 Working With Polylines

What does a **PLINE** entity look like? PLINEs are complex entities that have a parent/child relationship. When you use the **(entget)** command on a complex entity, you only get the parent entity list.

Try one. Draw three joined polylines. Then

Type: `(setq e (entget (car (entsel))))`   `<RETURN>`

Pick the polyline you just created. Here's what it may look like:

```
((-1 . <Entity name: 600002ec>)(0 . "POLYLINE")(8 . "0")(66 . 1)(10 0.0 0.0 0.0)

(70 . 0)(40 . 0.0)(41 . 0.0)(210 0.0 0.0 1.0)(71 . 0)(72 . 0)(73 . 0)(74 . 0)(75 . 0))
```

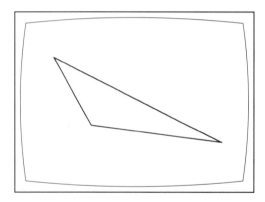

Figure 12-2: Create three joined polylines.

Of course, yours will be slightly different, but the principle is the same. It doesn't look much like polylines. There are no coordinates; and where does AutoCAD get the coordinates for all the vertices? This is the parent entity. That's why. Look at the children to see the rest of the polyline. To do that, you use the **(entnext)** command. **(entnext)** requires the entity name of the entity before it.

Look at the following code segment:

```
(setq e (entget (car (entsel))))
(setq e1 (entget (entnext (cdr (car e)))))
(setq e2 (entget (entnext (cdr (car e1)))))
(setq e3 (entget (entnext (cdr (car e2)))))
```

```
(setq e4 (entget (entnext (cdr (car e3)))))
(setq e5 (entget (entnext (cdr (car e4)))))
```

The **(cdr (car e))** returns the entity name of entity list **e**. In each one of these we are using the **(entnext ename)** of the entity that preceded it. Look at the entity type of each one of these:

```
e    (0 . "POLYLINE")
e1   (0 . "VERTEX")
e2   (0 . "VERTEX")
e3   (0 . "VERTEX")
e4   (0 . "VERTEX")
e5   (0 . "SEQEND")
```

As you can see, a three-line polyline consists of a parent list, four vertex entities and an end-of-sequence list. As you can imagine, the code can get a little tricky depending on what you are trying to do.

Following is a sample code that prints the coordinates for each of the vertices. Notice the sequence of the loop and how the loop tests for the SEQEND to know that the polyline has no more vertices.

```
(setq e (entget (car (entsel))))
  (setq r 1)
  (while r
  (setq e (entget (entnext (cdr (car e)))))
  (if (/= (cdr (assoc 0 e)) "SEQEND")
    (progn
      (terpri)
      (princ (cdr (assoc 10 e)))
    )
  )
  (if (= (cdr (assoc 0 e)) "SEQEND")(setq r nil))
)
```

First, you pick the polyline entity in this example. It runs as follows:

A counter variable, **r**, for the **(while)** loop is set to **non-nil**. The **(while)** loop begins. Each time through the loop you use **(entget (entnext))** of entity **e** and set it to itself. If it's not a **SEQEND** then you print Associative 10. If the entity is a **SEQEND,** the variable **r** is set to **nil** to stop the loop.

Obviously, there are many other variations to this type of loop depending on what you're trying to do with complex entities.

12.8 You Can Create Your Own Entities

The easiest way to draw a line in AutoLISP is

```
(command "line" pt1 pt2 "")
```

If you want, you may create your own entities directly.

Type: `(setq e '((0 . "LINE")(8 . "0")(10 2.0 2.0 0.0)(11 4.0 4.0 0.0)))` `<RETURN>`

Type: `(entmake e)` `<RETURN>`

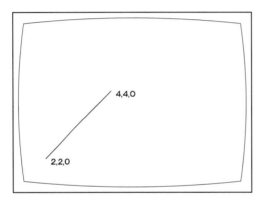

Figure 12-3: A line appears at the coordinates you indicated from 2,2,0 to 4,4,0.

A line appears on your screen at those coordinates. If there is an error in the entity list, it returns **nil** so that you can test for an unsuccessful **(entmake)**.

12.9 (nentsel)   Getting Right to a Block or a Polyline

If you don't like having to use **(entnext)** to find a vertex of a polyline, this next command is for you.

(nentsel) gives you the ability to select any entity and return the name of that entity so you can get it even if the entity belongs to a block or a polyline. If the entity selected doesn't belong to a block or a polyline, it works just like **(entsel)**.

Begin by drawing three joined polylines.

Type: `(setq e (entget (car (nentsel))))` `<RETURN>`

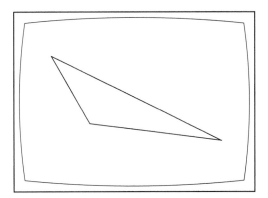

Figure 12-4: Create three joined polylines.

Notice that the syntax is exactly like **(entsel)**. When you pick one of the segments of the polyline, you get the entity record of that vertex.

Let's try it with a block.

Create a block of two lines and a circle. Block it and then insert the block in your drawing.

Type: (setq e (entget (car (nentsel))))   <RETURN>

Incredible! If you pick the circle, you get the circle even though it's part of a block. What happens if you change the radius of the circle? Let's revisit Chapter 7 and try it, only this time use **(nentsel)**. This example will assume that your existing circle in your block is a 1.0 radius. And you're going to change it to a 2.0 radius.

Type: (setq e (entget (car (nentsel))))   <RETURN>

Pick the circle.

Type: (setq d (assoc 40 e))   <RETURN>

Type: (setq e1 (subst '(40 . 2.0) d e))   <RETURN>

Type: (entmod e1)   <RETURN>

This is the standard routine for changing the radius of a circle. But this isn't really a circle; it's a block. So what happened? The block on your screen changed, but it also redefined the block definition and thus changed every block with the same name. You may have to use **REGEN** to see the change.

Type: REGEN

Response: You'll see the circle changed to a new radius of 2.0

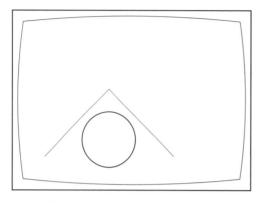

Figure 12-5: Your block—of two lines and a circle—is updated.

Moving On

 AutoLISP is rich in data types. The string is the one data type that causes problems for programmers in any language if they don't know how to work with them effectively.

In Chapter 13, "Working With Strings," you'll learn all the AutoLISP functions that work with strings. You'll also create a couple of new ones to make your life easier.

13

WORKING
WITH
STRINGS

Working With Strings

13.1 Basic String Review

Working effectively with strings is one of the keys to programming in any language. AutoLISP is no exception. First, let's define a string. It gets its name from the manner in which data is stored in computer memory. The computer views text data as simply one letter after another without any rhyme or reason. It requires a program to format that endless series of letters into words. Since data is stored as a continuous string of letters, text data is traditionally called "strings." Therefore, a string data type is ordinary text, as opposed to numeric data types, which are integers and real numbers.

Strings are among the most accurate data types you can have. Numbers when stored as strings leave no doubt as to their eventual value. They are what they say, whereas numbers may require conversion in many systems. Many times in AutoLISP you'll want to store information as strings and then take the strings apart as the need arises. Strings are the only way you can work with files. So they are useful to know.

The basic input statement you learned in section one is **(getstring)**. It asks the user for input and stores the input as a string. **(getstring)** when used by itself does not permit spaces. Input of a space acts as a delimiter. If a **non-nil** flag such as a **1** is added and you write **(getstring 1)**, spaces would be allowed.

The other basic string command you learned in the first section was **(strcase)**. It's primarily used to test for uppercase input. **(strcase)** converts all letters in the string to uppercase for consistency. If you add a **non-nil** flag to **(strcase),** such as **(strcase a 1)**, the **1** in this case causes **(strcase)** to convert all letters to lowercase.

13.2 (strcat)   Putting Strings Together

Strings can be joined. The technical name for this is concatenation. The command used in AutoLISP for this function is **(strcat)**.

Type: `(setq a (getstring 1 "\nType string 1: "))  <RETURN>`

Now type a few letters, **abc**.

Type: `(setq b (getstring 1 "\nType string 2: "))  <RETURN>`

Now type some different letters, **def**.

Type: `(setq c (strcat a b))  <RETURN>`

Type: `!c  <RETURN>`

Response: `"abcdef"`

If the variable **a** had a value of **ABC** and the variable **b** had a value of **DEF**, then variable **c** now has a value of **ABCDEF**.

13.3 (substr)   Taking Strings Apart

Begin with a string **"abcdef,"** which is assigned to the variable **a**. If you wanted two strings as **"abc"** assigned to **b** and **"def"** assigned to **c**, **(substr)** is the command you use. The command secures a substring of the string. The syntax is

`(substr  string  start  length)`

Therefore, **(setq b (substr a 1 3))** returns to **b** the substring beginning at the first letter and continues for three letters including the first.

`(setq c (substr a 4 3))`

begins with the fourth letter and continues for three letters returning the **"def."**

If the start position is at a position beyond the length of the string, the **(substr)** commands returns "" *non-nil*. If the length parameter is greater than the rest of the string, then **(substr)** returns from the start to the end of the string. No error will result.

What if you wanted to insert a string within another string? Here's how it's done. Begin with **(setq a "abcdef")**. Assume you want to insert **x y z** after the **c** and before the **d**. You'd use

```
(setq temp1 (substr a 1 3))
(setq temp2 (substr a 4 3))
(setq a (strcat temp1 "xyz" temp2))
```

The variable **a** is now **"abcxyzdef."**

13.4 Substituting Strings

AutoLISP doesn't have a command that will substitute one substring for another substring. Here's what this means:

```
(setq a "abcxyzghi")
```

In this example you want to change the **"xyz"** substring to **"def."** LES13.LSP is a program called **(instr)** that will do it for you.

The program is written to find the length of the old string, the new string and the existing string.

AutoLISP Program LES 13.LSP

```
(defun instr (olds news estr)
  (setq temp1 nil)
  (setq temp2 nil)
  (setq nold (strlen olds))
  (setq nnew (strlen news))
  (setq nest (strlen estr))
  (setq ct 1)
  (setq e 1)
  (while e
    (setq tststr (substr estr ct nold))
    (setq ct (+ ct 1))
    (if (= tststr "")(setq e nil))
    (if (= (strcase tststr) (strcase olds))
      (progn
        (setq e nil)
        (setq ct (- ct 1))
        (setq temp1 (substr estr 1 (-ct1)))
        (setq temp2 (substr estr (+ ct nold) nest))
```

```
                       (setq estr (strcat temp1 news temp2))
                       )
                    )
                 )
             )
```

PURPOSE: To substitute a substring for another.
TO LOAD:

Type: `(load "les13a")  <RETURN>`

TO OPERATE:

The syntax for this function is

`(instr oldstring newstring existingstring)`

Begin with a string.

Type: `(setq a "abcxyzghi")  <RETURN>`

Type: `(setq a (instr "xyz" "def" a)  <RETURN>`

Response: `"abcdefghi"`

Program Objective

The objective of the program is to find the length of the old string, the new string and the existing string. The loop begins and the program evaluates each group of letters, beginning with the first letter of the existing string for the length of the new string and tested against the old string until it is found. Once it is found, the string is taken apart as in section 13.3, "Taking Strings Apart," and then put back together using **(strcat)**. That's all there is to it.

13.5 Reading & Writing to Strings & Files

 Since AutoLISP has only one file format **(the sequential file)**, everything in AutoLISP is written as a regular text file. This means it's read back in as a string.

Two commands write to a file: **(write-char) (write-line).** And two commands **(read-char) (read-line)** read from a file.

You'll use the **(read-char)** command if you're reading one character at a time. Look at the following sequence:

```
(setq fn (open "/autoexec.bat" "r"))
(setq a (read-char fn))
(close fn)
```

What did you get? If your **AUTOEXEC.BAT** file begins with **@ECHO OFF,** then **a** would have the value of **64**. That's because the **(read-char)** command doesn't actually return the letter; it returns the ASCII character code of the letter. If you want to see the letter, you'll have to convert it.

```
(setq a (chr a))
```

The **(chr)** command converts an ASCII code into the printable string letter.

```
(write-char)
```

The **(write-char)** command writes a single letter at a time to a file. The only problem is that the character must be in ASCII code format for the letter. You can convert the string letter to its ASCII counterpart with the (ascii) command.

```
(setq fn (open "test.txt" "w"))
(write-char (ascii "a") fn)
(close fn)
```

Remember, both the **(read-char)** and the **(write-char)** work with only one letter at a time. This generally is not the most practical or most efficient way to read from or write to a file.

(read-line) and **(write-line)** are the two most common read and write commands for a file. They are much easier to use.

```
(setq fn (open "test.txt" "w"))
(write-line "This is line 1" fn)
(write-line "This is line 2" fn)
(close fn)
(setq fn (open "test.txt" "r"))
(setq a (read-line fn))
(setq b (read-line fn))
(close fn)
```

As you can see, the **(read-line)** command and the **(write-line)** command are very straightforward. The important thing you have to remember about the **(write-line)** command is that it will *only* work with strings. You can't write integers and real numbers to a file with the **(write-line)** command. If that's the type of data you want to write to a file, you should either convert the numbers to strings and then use **(write-line)** or use the **(princ)** command. **(read-line)** will read anything from a text file since its format is a string.

13.6 String Conversions

You've already reviewed three conversion commands without knowing them as conversion commands. You'll remember them as **(strcase),** which converts the case of the string; **(chr),** which converts ASCII code to a recognizable letter of the alphabet; and **(ascii),** which converts a letter to the ASCII code.

Three other conversion commands work with strings:

(rtos)
(angtos)
(distof)

The first section of the book discussed **(rtos)** and **(angtos)**. **(rtos)** converts a real number representing a distance to a string using either the default units of measurement or any unit of measurement and precision you choose.

(angtos) converts a real number representing an angle to either the default angular units of measurement or any angular unit of measurement and precision you choose.

(distof) is an interesting command. If you have a string in the distance format of architectural units, you can convert it to a real number by using **(distof)**.

```
(setq a "14'3-3/4")
(setq b (distof a 4))
```

This returns 171.75. Notice the 4 at the end of the command follows the same format as the units command flags below:

1   Scientific
2   Decimal

3 Engineering (feet and decimal inches)
4 Architectural (feet and fractional inches)
5 Fractional (angtof)

This is to **(angtos)** as **(distof)** is to **(rtos)**. In other words, **(angtof)** will convert a string in angular format back to its real number as expressed in radians.

```
(setq a '45d22'")
(setq b (angtof a 1))
```

This returns .791798.

This is the real number expressed in radians. Mode flags are as follows:

0 Degrees
1 Degrees/minutes/seconds
2 Grads
3 Radians
4 Surveyor units

The last three conversion commands are

(atof), which converts a string to a real number;
(atoi), which converts a string to an integer number;
(itoa), which converts an integer to a string.

Moving On

For years, AutoCAD users have made attributes the primary way to store intelligent information within a drawing. The problem with this method is that it's generally restricted to blocks. But there's a more powerful way. Extended entity data attaches the information to the entities themselves.

The amount of data you can attach to any given entity is quite large. Also, different applications have the ability to attach their individual data information to the same entity. AutoCAD can keep them straight. Chapter 14, "Extended Entity Data," will show you the in's and out's of this powerful concept.

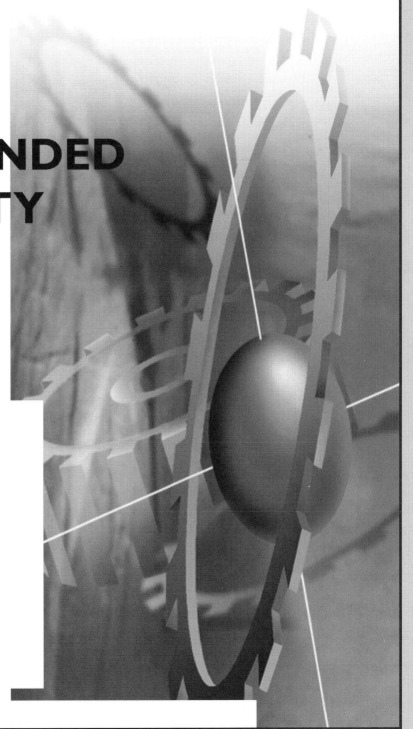

14

EXTENDED
ENTITY
DATA

CHAPTER 14

Extended Entity Data

14.1 What Is It?

From AutoCAD's earliest days, users have had the ability to add information to a drawing through attributes. Attributes let you set up fields called tags and add information to blocks when they are inserted. This lets users produce a "bill of materials" and in many ways create "intelligent" drawings.

Attributes have always had their own inherent limitations. They have never been extremely easy to use and have generally required that the vehicle to which they are attached be a block, even though the attribute itself could be the block. They are also limited to the kind of information they can relate.

Third-party developers needed individual entities within a drawing to communicate more information than the entity data base could provide.

Autodesk, therefore, devised a way to attach an enormous amount of information to the individual entity. This new concept, called Extended Entity Data, let's you add up to 16k of information to each and every entity in the drawing. You also have the ability to keep the information you add to an entity totally separate from the information added by other programs.

Extended Entity Data becomes part of the entity list and is attached to the individual entity—not to blocks, although blocks are not excluded. The easiest way to access Extended Entity Data is through AutoLISP or ADS.

14.2 Sample Exercise

The simplest way to show how Extended Entity Data works is to attach some information to an entity. Begin by drawing a simple line on your screen. Then

Type: `(regapp "MYNAME705")  <RETURN>`

Type: `(setq e (entget (car (entsel))))  <RETURN>`

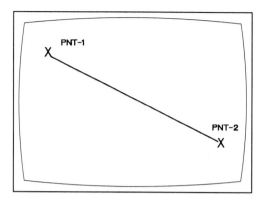

Figure 14-1: Create a line onscreen.

Pick the line you've just drawn.

Type: `(setq edata '((-3 ("MYNAME705" (1000 . "This is data 1"))))`

Type: `(setq el (append e edata))  <RETURN>`

Type: `(entmod el)  <RETURN>`

At this point the Extended Entity Data has been attached to the entity. The following lines will recall the entity with its Extended Entity Data.

Type: `(setq e (entget (car (entsel)) '("MYNAME705")))  <RETURN>`

Response: `((-1 . <Entity name:60000022>)(0 . "line")(8 . "0")`
`(5 . "1")(10 2.44 5.70 0.0) (11 9.06 4.88 0.0)(210 0.0 0.0 0.0`
`1.0)) (-3 ("MYNAME705" (1000 . "This is data 1"))))`

Your response will be different. Notice the Extended Entity Data at the end of the entity list.

`((-3 ("MYNAME705" (1000 . "This is data 1"))))`

Now let's take a detailed look.

14.3 Registering the Application

Any program can write Extended Entity Data to any entity in your drawing. AutoCAD needed a way to prevent different programs from bumping into each other. Generally, a program is only interested in the Extended Entity Data that it has written to an entity, not the data that might have been written by another program.

Each program can register its unique name and use this name as a unique identifier for its own Extended Entity Data. Beginning with Release 13, Autodesk has permitted third-party developers to register a unique four-character name that is uniquely theirs. This is not to be confused with the registration of the name found in the drawing, although developers will, of course, use their unique Autodesk-registered name whenever they use Extended Entity Data.

If you're not a third-party developer, you don't need to register your name with Autodesk. You do have to make sure that the name you use within the AutoCAD drawing is unusual enough that other third-party software you may be using will not step on your identifier. One way you can do that is to use names with more than four letters. You might also use a number suffix to minimize any chance that someone else could be using your name.

Before you can add any Extended Entity Data to an entity in your drawing, you must tell that particular drawing your unique entity data name. You do this by registering the name with the drawing. The command is **(regapp)**.

Type:
```
(regapp "MYNAME705") <RETURN>
```

If the name is successfully registered with the drawing, it will return the name you used. If the name can't be registered but is still a valid name, then **(regapp)** will return **nil**. It does no harm to register a name that has already been registered. **(regapp)** simply returns **nil** if that is the case. If you want to check to see if the name already exists, use the **(tblsearch)** command. The table you are Searching is called **"appid."**

```
(tblsearch "appid" "MYNAME705")
```

If this command returns *nil*, then that name has not yet been registered. If it *has* been registered, it will return the table list.

```
((0 . "APPID")(2 . "MYNAME705")(70 . 0))
```

Remember that this list is *read only*. You can't register a name by trying to update this list. You must use the **(regapp)** command.

14.4 The Extended Entity Data List

The Extended Entity Data that you attach to an entity is really nothing but a super Associative list. The Associative code number is **-3**. Items following the **-3** are the parameters of this Associative code. The following is the minimum amount of information that has to be in the Extended Entity Data Associative list:

```
((-3 ("MYNAME705" (1000 . "This is data 1"))))
```

Just look at what follows the Associative **-3**:

```
(registeredname associative1 associative2 associative3)
```

It begins by identifying the registered name you're using. This is followed by other nested Associative codes and their parameters for your Extended Entity Data.

Notice that the registered name begins a list with each of the additional Associatives (which is the actual data) making up its parameters. That's why ("MYNAME705" begins with a parenthesis but does not immediately close. Then, each of the Associatives, which are dotted-pair Associatives are enclosed within parentheses. Finally, the registered name list is closed, and the **-3** Associative is closed with parentheses.

Just remember that the registered name list is really the parameter of the **-3** and that the interior Associative lists (the actual Extended Entity Data) are collectively the parameters of the registered name list.

As with any list, it can be built on the fly by placing an apostrophe in front of the parentheses. Since your program is the one controlling the data, this is the easiest way.

```
'((-3 ("MYNAME705" (1000 . "This is data 1")(1000 . "This is data
2"))))
```

Important: Use the model that is presented here. The number of parentheses and their placement is vital in working with Extended Entity Data.

14.5 Extended Entity Data Associative Codes

One of the confusing things about working with Extended Entity Data Associative codes is that you can have more than one of the same Associative codes in the Extended Entity Data. This is not true when you work with regular Associative codes.

In a regular entity list, for example, you can't have more than one Associative 10 or Associative 40. If you do, **(entmod)** will fail to modify the entity. That is not the case with Extended Entity Data Associative codes that make up the actual Extended Entity Data itself for your registered name.

It's important to recognize that you can have only one Associative **-3** in an entity list. Even though two or more applications might have Extended Entity Data on the same entity, AutoCAD sees the entity list as having only one **-3** Associative. You, as the application programmer for your application, should access your entity data exclusively, not other applications' Extended Entity Data. If you access other application's Extended Entity Data and blindly append yours to theirs and then **(entmod)** the entity, you might harm their Extended Entity Data with your Extended Entity Data. If on the other hand you have not accessed another applications' Extended Entity Data but only the basic entity list, then appending your data will not harm other Extended Entity Data on the list.

The following sections describe the kind of data you can include in your Extended Entity Data and the Associative code you must use for each kind of data. The Associative codes listed and explained below are **1000, 1001, 1003, 1010, 1040, 1070, 1071, 1002, 1011, 1012, 1013, 1041 and 1042.**

Associative Code 1000

The **1000** Associative code is used any time your data is string data. Any given string is limited to **255** characters. This is what we've been using in our examples. Remember, you can have more than one of any of these Associative codes in your data.

Since you are the exclusive author of the data attached to an entity by your application, you know the order of the data. Therefore, you access your own data, not by **(assoc)**, as you'd use with other entity lists, but by the position of the Associative **1000** in your own data. That's why you can have more than one. Look at the following example:

```
'((-3 ("MYNAME705" (1000 . "This is data 1")(1000 . "This is data
2"))))
```

Associative Code 1001

The Associative code **1001** is used when your data is an application name. And it's in string format. Don't confuse this with your application name. If your application needed to store another application name as part of your Extended Entity Data, this is the Associative Code to use.

This code might be used if your own program stored more than one kind of data on an entity and for some reason you wanted to register more than one application name with the drawing. In that case, AutoCAD would keep the two Extended Entity Data names separate. But you still want one name to know about the other. Therefore, the logic of your program might store the other application name as an Associative data field within its own Extended Entity Data. This is the Associative code you would use: 1003.

Associative Code 1003

Use the Associative code of 1003 when your data is a layer name. This doesn't mean that your entity, to which the Extended Entity Data is attached must be on that layer. It simply means that you want to store a layer name in the Extended Entity Data for your own reasons. In order for AutoCAD to identify this information as a layer name rather than just some string data, use 1003 as the Associative code. Remember, the layer must exist before the entity is updated.

Associative Code 1005

The 1005 Associative code is used to store entity handles. This doesn't mean it's the entity handle of the entity to which the Extended Entity Data is attached. It can be an entity handle of another entity in your drawing.

Associative Code 1010

The 1010 Associative code stores 3D coordinate values. You store a point there.

Associative Code 1040

This Associative code stores real numbers.

Associative Code 1070

The 1070 Associative code stores integer numbers up to a 16-bit signed or unsigned integer.

Associative Code 1071

The Associative code 1071 stores long integer numbers. Only ADS recognizes this Associative code. AutoLISP returns the value as a real number and doesn't recognize the Associative code. When you're using **(entmake)** to create a 1071 Associative code, you may use either an integer or a real number.

Associative Code 1002

The 1002 Associative code is used as a control code to set off nested lists that can be keyed on by your program. Let's look at a nested list example.

Assume you need to organize data as a list with multiple Associative codes within the list. But you also want the lists to be grouped as a single list so you'll be able to pull them out together. You could use

```
(1002 . "{")(1000 . "LINE")(1003 . "MECH")(1070 . 5)(1002 . "}")
```

From the opening **(1002 . "{")** to the last **(1002 . "})**, your application may treat all the Associative codes in between as a group. It's important to note that AutoLISP doesn't treat them as a group. AutoLISP will check to see if the braces are balanced before it updates an entity. It's up to your program to key in on the opening brace and the closing brace so that your program can group information. In this way you can add and delete information from the group without having to redo the logic of your program.

Associative Code 1011

This Associative code is used as a 3D coordinate point that will be moved, scaled, rotated, stretched and mirrored with the entity to which it is attached.

Associative Code 1012

This Associative code is used as a 3D coordinate point that is scaled, rotated or mirrored along with the entity to which it is attached. It can't be stretched, however.

Associative Code 1013

This Associative code is used as a 3D point that is rotated or mirrored along with the entity to which it is attached. It cannot be scaled, stretched or moved.

Associative Code 1041

This Associative code is used as a real value that is scaled along with the entity to which it's attached. It's used for distance.

Associative Code 1042

As with Associative Code 1041, this Associative code is used as a real value that is scaled along with the entity to which it's attached. It's used for a scale factor.

14.6 How to Add an Initial Extended Entity Data

Let's start with the assumption that Extended Entity Data have never been attached to an entity for your registered application. Remember that the first thing you have to do is register your application. Begin with a new line.

Type: `(regapp "MYNAME705")  <RETURN>`

If the application name has not been registered, the name is returned; otherwise, **nil** is returned.

Type: `(setq e (entget (car (entsel)) '("MYNAME705")))  <RETURN>`

Notice the positioning of the parentheses. If you add the parameter of **'("MYNAME705")** to **(car (entsel))**, AutoLISP will include the Extended Entity Data for that application name. It's important to know if the Extended Entity Data for that application name already exist. If they do exist and you attempt to overwrite it, the entity will not **(entmod)**.

In this example, you'll see that no Extended Entity Data currently exist. You can test for this as

`(assoc -3 e)`

If the expression returns **nil**, no Extended Entity Data exist for the entity in this application. But, if it returns the Extended Entity Data list, you'll need to use the next section, 14.7, for substituting data rather than appending to the list.

If you've determined that Extended Entity Data *do not* exist, then you're ready to create a list of Extended Entity Data to append to the entity list.

Type: `(setq d '((-3 ("MYNAME705" (1000 . "Text 1")(1040 . 7.0)))))`
       `<RETURN>`

The variable **d** now contains the complete list of Extended Entity Data, including the Associative code **-3**. You're now ready to append this to the entity list, which is found in variable **e**.

Type: `(setq e1 (append e e1))  <RETURN>`

The variable **e1** now contains the completed entity list.

Type: `(entmod e1)  <RETURN>`

The entity list is now updated.

14.7 How to Replace Existing Extended Entity Data

In this case, you want to replace the existing Extended Entity Data list with a new one you've created. You don't care what is in the old Extended Entity Data list. You simply want the new one to replace it. We'll start, for this example, with the entity updated in Section 14.6. Its current entity data is

```
(-3 ("MYNAME705" (1000 . "Text 1")(1040 . 7.0)))
```

Type: `(regapp "MYNAME705")  <RETURN>`

If the application name has not been registered, the name is returned; otherwise, **nil** is returned.

Type: `(setq e (entget (car (entsel)) '("MYNAME705")))  <RETURN>`

The variable **e** now contains the entire entity list for the entity and the Extended Entity Data for this application.

Type: `(setq d (assoc -3 e))  <RETURN>`

This pulls the Extended Entity Data out of the application list and assigns it to the variable **d**.

Type: `(setq d1 '((-3 ("MYNAME705" (1000 . "Text 2")(1040 . 7.0)))))`
          `<RETURN>`

The variable **d1** is the new Extended Entity Data list you want to replace. Notice that the only difference between **d** and **d1** is that in **d1** the string says **"Text 2"** rather than **"Text 1."**

Type: `(setq e1 (subst d1 d e))  <RETURN>`

This is a simple substitute of Associative statements you've used all along. It substitutes the entire new Extended Entity Data list **(d1)** for the old Extended Entity Data list **(d)** found in entity list **e**.

Type: `(entmod e1)  <RETURN>`

The entity is now updated with the replacement data.

14.8 How to Isolate Associative Fields Within Extended Entity Data

Attaching Extended Entity Data to an entity would not do you much good if you couldn't get to the individual parts of the list.
  In the list created in Section 14.7, the Extended Entity Data list is

```
(-3 ("MYNAME705" (1000 . "Text 2")(1040 . 7.0)))
```

The object here is to isolate the (1040 . 7.0). This is the data you created. You organized it and you know the order in which it was created in the entity list. It's your program's responsibility to keep track of this information. In this case, you know that following the name of the registered application, the (1040 . 70), is the second list. Begin by securing the basic entity list then isolate the Extended Entity Data list.

Type: `(regapp "MYNAME705")` `<RETURN>`

If the application name has not been registered, the name is returned; otherwise, **nil** is returned.

Type: `(setq e (entget (car (entsel)) '("MYNAME705")))` `<RETURN>`

The variable **e** now contains the entire entity list for the entity and the Extended Entity Data for this application.

Type: `(setq d (assoc -3 e))` `<RETURN>`

This pulls the Extended Entity Data out of the application list and assigns it to the variable **d**. Here is what **d** should look like:

Type: `!d` `<RETURN>`

Response: `(-3 ("MYNAME705" (1000 . "Text  2")(1040 . 7.0)))`

Type: `(setq d1 (car (cdr d)))` `<RETURN>`

Response: `("MYNAME705" (1000 . "Text 2")(1040 . 7.0))`

You'll always use **(setq d1 (car (cdr d)))** to get to the basic list and strip the outer **-3** list groups away. Now that **d1** contains an ordinary list, to see which part of the list you want, type the following:

Type: `(nth 0 d1)` `<RETURN>`

Response: `"MYNAME705"`

Type: `(nth 1 d1)` `<RETURN>`

Response: `(1000 . "Text 2")`

Type: `(nth 2 d1)` `<RETURN>`

Response: `(1040 . 7.0)`

Now that it's an ordinary list, you can use it to isolate any part you need.

14.9 Changing an Existing Extended Entity Data Associative Value

The challenge here is to change the value of an existing Associative code within an Extended Entity Data list. It's not as straightforward as you might think. That's because you can have more than one Associative code by the same code and even the same value. You may only want to change the second one and not the first. Start with the Extended Entity Data from Sections 14.8 and 14.7.

Type: `(regapp "MYNAME705")` `<RETURN>`

If the application name has not been registered, the name is returned; otherwise, **nil** is returned.

Type: `(setq e (entget (car (entsel)) '("MYNAME705")))` `<RETURN>`

The variable **e** now contains the entire entity list for the entity and the Extended Entity Data for this application.

Type: `(setq d (assoc -3 e))` `<RETURN>`

This pulls the Extended Entity Data out of the application's list and assigns it to the variable **d**. Here is what **d** should look like:

Type: `!d` `<RETURN>`

Response: `(-3 ("MYNAME705" (1000 . "Text 2")(1040 . 7.0)))`

Type: `(setq d1 (car (cdr d)))` `<RETURN>`

Response: `("MYNAME705" (1000 . "Text 2")(1040 . 7.0))`

The variable **d1** is now a basic list. But you have a problem here. You want to change the second element of **d1** to **(1000 . "Text 3")**. Look back at Chapter 11, "Advanced List Concepts," Section 11.5. Changing a given element of a list is not easy. That's why an AutoLISP utility function was written to help do it.

It's imperative that you maintain a library of functions so you don't have to reinvent the wheel. You'll use that function here. You'll find it in program **LES11b.LSP;** the name of the function is **(chnitem)**.

It requires three parameters: *(chnitem value itemnumber list)*. Assuming the function is loaded,

Type: `(setq d2 (chnitem '(1000 . "Text 3") 2 d1))` `<RETURN>`

Response: `("MYNAME705" (1000 . "Text 3")(1040 . 7.0))`

Now you can do a simple substitution within **d**. **d2** is the new basic list you'll substitute for **d1**, the old basic list within the more complex list **d**.

Type: `(setq d3 (subst d2 d1 d))  <RETURN>`

d3 is now your entire new Extended Entity Data list. **d** is the old entire Extended Entity Data list. You may now substitute the new **d3** for the old **d** in the entity list **e** itself.

Type: `(setq e1 (subst d3 d e))  <RETURN>`

Type: `(entmod e1)  <RETURN>`

Your entity list is now changed and updated. This is a common situation, and the AutoLISP function **LES14a.LSP** is another program you can add to your utility library. Since the **(eesub)** function uses the **(chnitem)** function from Chapter 11, it's included in the file. If the file is already loaded it doesn't have to be included here. If it's not loaded, you'll get a null function error.

AutoLISP Program LES14a.LSP

```
(defun eesub (nl item lst)
  (setq d (assoc -3 e))
  (setq d1 (car (cdr d)))
  (setq d2 (chnitem nl item d1))
  (setq d3 (subst d2 d1 d))
  (setq e1 (subst d3 d e))
)
  (defun chnitem (value num)
    (setq num (- num 1))
    (setq tmplt (list nil))
    (setq tmplt2 (list nil))
    (setq counter 0)
    (repeat num
      (setq tmplt (append tmplt (list (nth counter lst))))
      (setq counter (+ counter 1))
    )
  (setq counter (+ counter 1))
  (repeat (- (length lst) (+ num 1))
    (setq tmplt2 (append tmplt2 (list (nth counter lst))))
```

```
      (setq counter (+ counter 1))
    )
    (setq tmplt (cdr tmplt))
    (setq tmplt2 (cdr tmplt2))
    (setq lst (append tmplt (list value) tmplt2))
  )
```

PURPOSE: Changes the value of an Associative code of the Extended Entity Data list.

TO LOAD:

Type: (load "les14a")   <RETURN>

TO OPERATE:

This function passes three variables: the new Associative code list, the item number within the Extended Entity Data list and the entity list. The function returns the new entity list which you may use in an (entmod) command to update the entity.

```
(eesub  value  number  list)
```

14.10 How to Add an Extended Entity Data Associative

 You may need to add an Associative code to an existing Extended Entity Data list. You can't simply use the **(append)** command because that will append it to the end of the entity list. It must be appended to the proper place within the Extended Entity Data list.

Start with the entity list from Section 14.9.

Type: (regapp "MYNAME705")   <RETURN>

If the application name has not been registered, then the name is returned; otherwise, **nil** is returned.

Type: (setq e (entget (car (entsel)) '("MYNAME705")))   <RETURN>

The variable **e** now contains the entire entity list for the entity and the Extended Entity Data for this application.

Type: (setq d (assoc -3 e))   <RETURN>

This pulls out of the list the Extended Entity Data for the application and assigns it to the variable **d**. Here is what **d** should look like:

Type: !d   <RETURN>

Response: `(-3 ("MYNAME705" (1000 . "Text 2")(1040 . 7.0)))`

Type: `(setq d1 (car (cdr d)))  <RETURN>`

Response: `("MYNAME705" (1000 . "Text 3")(1040 . 7.0))`

The variable **d1** is now a basic list. You want to add another text string to the Extended Entity Data. Now that you have the basic list you may use the **(append)** command. Notice how you must also use the command **(list)**. This places it at the correct position at the end of the list with the one additional parentheses around the entire list.

Type: `(setq d2 (append d1 (list '(1000 . "Text 4"))))  <RETURN>`

Response: `("MYNAME705" (1000 . "Text 3")(1040 . 7.0)(1000 . Text 4"))`

Now you can do a simple substitution within **d**. **d2** is the new basic list which you will substitute for **d1**, the old basic list within the more complex list **d**.

Type: `(setq d3 (subst d2 d1 d))  <RETURN>`

d3 now is your entire new Extended Entity Data list. **d** is the old entire Extended Entity Data list. You may now substitute the new **d3** for the old **d** in the entity list **e** itself.

Type: `(setq e1 (subst d3 d e))  <RETURN>`

Type: `(entmod e1)  <RETURN>`

Your entity list is now changed and updated. Since this is a common situation, the AutoLISP program **LES14b.LSP** is a solution you can create and add to your utility library.

AutoLISP Program LES14b.LSP

```
(defun eeadd (nl lst)
  (setq d (assoc -3 e))
  (setq d1 (car (cdr d)))
  (setq d2 (append d1 (list nl)))
  (setq d3 (subst d2 d1 d))
  (setq e1 (subst d3 d e))
)
```

PURPOSE: Adds an Associative code list to an existing Extended Entity Data list.

TO LOAD:

Type: `(load "les14b") <RETURN>`

TO OPERATE:

The function passes two variables: the new Associative code list and the entity list. The function returns the new entity list, which you may use in an **(entmod)** command to update the entity.

`(eeadd  value list)`

14.11 Using Selection Set Filters With Extended Entity Data

Filtering all the entities that have Extended Entity Data attached to them is as follows:

`(setq a (ssget "x" '(( -3 ("MYNAME705")))))`

As you can see, you use Associative code **-3** and the registered application name. All the entities in the selection set have this registered Extended Entity Data. You may add registered names for those entities. This is an **AND**; thus the entities must have Extended Entity Data for all applications.

14.12 Write Extended Entity Data to Files

Working with Extended Entity Data and writing it to files through Auto-LISP is much easier than working with attributes. The procedure is to secure a selection set, as in Section 14.11, with entities that contain Extended Entity Data. Loop through the selection set for each of the entities selected. One by one, reduce the Extended Entity Data list to the basic list. Now you can write the data to a sequential file. Notice that in this scenario you don't have to set up attribute templates ahead of time. This makes Extended Entity Data ideal for bills-of-material programs.

Many times you would like the file to be in a comma-delimited format ASCII file with each of the items on the same line separated by commas. This is useful if you are porting the file to a spreadsheet or database.

The following is a sample program you may use as a basis for a more customized program. It asks for a file name and then proceeds to write all Extended Entity Data to a (CDF) comma-delimited-format ASCII file.

To test the program, begin with three or four entities that contain Extended Entity Data. The easiest way to do that is to create an entity such as the one you created in 14.10. Then copy the entity and its data several times. You might want to change a couple of Associatives in order to see the difference between entities.

The program uses the registered name of "MYNAME705."

AutoLISP Program LES14c.LSP

```
(defun C:eewrite ( )
  (setq fname (getstring "\nEnter file name: "))
  (setq fn (open fname "w"))
  (setq a (ssget "x" '((-3 ("MYNAME705")))))
  (setq i 0)
  (repeat (sslength a)
    (setq e (entget (ssname a i) '("MYNAME705")))
    (setq i (+ i 1))
    (setq d (assoc -3 e))
    (setq d1 (cdr (car (cdr d))))
    (foreach n d1 (princ (cdr n) fn)(princ "," fn))
    (princ "\n" fn)
  )
  (close fn)
  (princ)
)
```

PURPOSE: Writes Extended Entity Data to an ASCII file in (CDF) comma-delimited-format.

TO LOAD:

Type: `(load "les14c")  <RETURN>`

TO OPERATE:

Type: `eewrite  <RETURN>`

Response: `File name:`

Type: Test1

All of the entity data belonging to registered name "MYNAME705" are written to the file. The file is now ready to be brought into a spreadsheet or database. When working in the spreadsheet or database, make certain you choose delimited, not fixed, format.

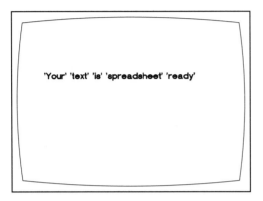

'Your' 'text' 'is' 'spreadsheet' 'ready'

Figure 14-2: Your CDF extended entity data is ready for a spreadsheet.

Obviously, this program is only a model that brings in entity data from one registered application. It should be used as a model and modified according to your data and the needs of your target program. Some programs may need quotation marks around the text data.

The key to the program is the use of the **(foreach)** command to step through the list and the **(princ "," fn)**, which adds a comma after each of the fields. The **(princ "\n" fn)** on a line by itself separates each entity on a different line in the file.

Moving On

The tasks you'll want to do in AutoLISP are virtually infinite. And there is no way a single book can cover them all. Chapter 15 is a collection of tips and tricks to give you a head start.

15

TIPS & TRICKS

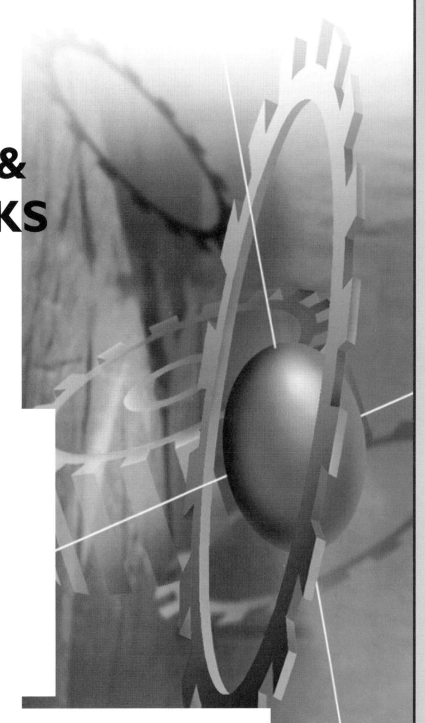

Tips & Tricks

As with any new endeavor, there's always a hard way and an easy way to do it. With work and practice, AutoLISP professionals have found valuable shortcuts that free up time for the truly creative part of programming.

This chapter lists valuable tips and techniques that will save you time in creating, revising and debugging your programs. Many of the techniques were stated or implied in the previous fourteen chapters. By consolidating the important points in one concise list, this chapter should help you work more efficiently, with as few problems as possible.

At the end of this chapter, you'll find an additional section of tips and techniques specifically dedicated to debugging.

Now for some programming tips and tricks...

15.1 Write many little programs rather than one large program.

Many beginners try to make a program do too much, forcing the user to make too many decisions and answer too many questions, resulting in little time-savings.

15.2 Make all your programs part of the menu system.

Don't call up your programs from AutoCAD's **Command** line. Instead, make them part of your tablet or screen menu. Remember, you're writing programs for ease and efficiency.

15.3 Don't load the ACAD.LSP file with all your programs.

Many programmers try to pack all their functions into the ACAD.LSP file so the functions will be available all the time.

There is a better way to do that—by creating a single library file listing the programs you wish to load. Then call only that file.

The larger the ACAD.LSP file, the longer the delay in calling up each drawing. The best way to use the ACAD.LSP file is to call up your single library file as discussed later in this chapter in Section 15.24. At the end of Chapter 17 you'll find an example on creating a single library file.

15.4 Use the (if not...) command when you attach your functions to a menu system.

For example,

```
(if (not rectan) (load "les2"))
```

Include the above command before the command **(rectan)** is given in the macro of your menu command. The name of the function follows **(not**. The file is loaded, not the function. Without this command, the file would have to be loaded each time a function is used. With this command, the file won't be loaded if the function is already active.

15.5 Always put your AutoLISP programs in their own unique directory.

With Autodesk's many updates and all the third-party software available, you must keep programs separated and in good order. Thus, if you must erase your AutoCAD directory to re-install AutoCAD, you won't have to worry about your programs. Make the directory name unique so you don't inadvertently install third-party AutoLISP programs on top of yours in the event some file names are identical. For example, you may have created one called C:\LISP for all the files you've made so far.

15.6 Feel free to group several programs (functions) into one file.

As long as the programs don't take too much memory, it's more efficient to load a file once with four programs than to load four individual files.

15.7 Make your programs readable.

Line up parentheses, and indent **(if...)** and **(while...)** statements. They use no memory in AutoCAD and make your programs much more manageable and easier to read.

15.8 Make your variable names meaningful without getting carried away.

For example, **p1** or **pnt1** is sufficient for **point 1**. Though permissible, **cornerpoint1** is tiring to type and uses unnecessary memory. At the same time, **ABC** may be totally meaningless.

15.9 Whenever possible, use (getdist) instead of (getreal) and (getangle) or (getorient) instead of (getreal).

(getreal) is very restrictive, but **(getdist)** or **(getangle)** lets you enter by pointing (with or without a beginning point) and by keyboard, using your default units.

15.10 If you want to draw a temporary window to draw two points graphically, use (getcorner) instead of (getpoint).

It will produce a rubber-band feel to the window, and look just like an AutoCAD command.

15.11 When using (getstring), never insert the flag to permit spaces unless it's truly a string of text.

It's much easier to hit the space bar to terminate the command.

15.12 If you know how many times you want to loop, use (repeat), a much simpler command than (while....).

If the number of times through the loop is undeterminable, use **(while....)** to test for the terminating condition.

15.13 Always restore **OBJECT SNAP** to its original setting.

Although many users like to set OBJECT SNAP, you *don't* want your program changing it *permanently*. Set the OBJECT SNAP setting to a variable before going into AutoCAD's OBJECT SNAP, then reset it to the same mode when exiting the program. For example,

```
(setq osn (getvar "osmode"))
```

restores the original **OBJECT SNAP** setting to the variable **osn**.

```
(setvar "osmode" 1)
```

sets **OBJECT SNAP** to your desired setting—**ENDPOINT** in this example.

```
(setvar "osmode" osn)
```

sets **OBJECT SNAP** back to the original setting. Variable **osn** stored this original setting.

15.14 Use (ssget) instead of (entsel) if you wish all your selection alternatives to be available.

(entsel) lets you select only one object while **(ssget)** allows you to use all selection alternatives.

15.15 Always assign the selection set to a variable.

If you don't, you can never re-create it. For example,

```
(setq ss (ssget))
```

15.16 Use (getkword) and (initget).

It does automatic *error-checking* to be certain only authorized entries to your questions are used.

15.17 Point AutoCAD to your files directory.

In the DOS version of AutoCAD you can tell AutoCAD where your Auto-LISP files are located so you don't have to include the path spec when you load them. In your AUTOEXEC.BAT file or other batch file that starts AutoCAD, place the following line:

```
set acad=C:\acad\support;C:\acad\fonts;C:\acad\ads;C:\lisp
```

This assumes that the directory where you keep your AutoLISP files is called C:\LISP. Notice that each of these directories is separated by a semicolon. When you try to load an AutoLISP file, AutoCAD looks in each of these directories in the order that they are stated in the **SET ACAD=** statement.

The concept is the same in Windows and NT. In AutoCAD it's added to the support directory environment in the same way.

15.18 What do you do when AutoLISP files won't load?

If AutoLISP detects a problem with a program, it refuses to load the program; but it won't tell you where the problem is.

Most of the time the problem is a missing parenthesis or an extra parenthesis. The missing parenthesis will give the error message of **"malformed list."**

Too many parentheses registers **"extra right parenthesis."** Other errors might be called **"malformed string."** This is generally because of a missing quotation mark.

The only way to correct these problems is to count the parentheses and quotation marks to make sure they are even. If the program is very long you might copy the file and divide it into smaller segments. Then try loading each segment. Eventually, you'll find the error.

15.19 When do you use a space and when can you leave it out?

AutoLISP includes four delimeters: parenthesis, quotation mark, apostrophe and a space. A delimeter in AutoLISP is something that separates one item from another.

All parts of your program in AutoLISP must be separated by at least *one delimeter*. If one of the other three delimeters separates the items in an

AutoLISP expression, the space is not required. If the space is the only possible delimeter, it is required. Look at the following example:

```
(setq a'(1 3 5 7 9))
```

There is no delimeter between **setq** and **a**; therefore, the space is required. Between **a** and **'(** there are two delimeters; therefore, the space is not required. The interior list is separated by spaces although there is no space required before the **1** and after the **9** since there is a parenthesis. When a space is not required, it is generally not wrong to include one. If in doubt, include the space.

15.20 If the ACAD.LSP file is protected, make one of your own.

Many third-party software developers have taken over the ACAD.LSP file. If this has happened to you, there is a way you can get it back. Rename their ACAD.LSP file to another name such as ACADOLD.LSP. Now there is no ACAD.LSP file. Then create your own ACAD.LSP file.

Type the command below as the last command in your ACAD.LSP file. It loads the old renamed ACAD.LSP file from the third-party developer.

```
(load "ACADOLD")
```

When the drawing begins, your ACAD.LSP file will load and execute. The third-party software file will be loaded. It still may not work if they are using an S::STARTUP function. If this is the case, you may also need to include the following line after you load their file:

```
(S::STARTUP)
```

15.21 Get rid of the final nil.

When your function ends, it generally prints a final nil at the command line. You can eliminate this by placing **(princ)** by itself as the final command before the final parenthesis. Do not do this if the purpose of the function is to return a value, or no value will be returned.

15.22 Sum of the bits.

Whenever the AutoCAD or AutoLISP manuals indicate the *sum of the bits*, it means that you must *add* options together if you want to combine them. For example, object snap **(setvar "osmode" 32)**. The codes are **1, 2, 4, 8, 16, 32, 64, 128, 256,** etc. Number **1** is **Endpoint,** and number **32** is **Intersection.** If you wanted to combine the Endpoint and Intersection, you would add them together and use **33.**

15.23 Create AutoCAD defaults whenever possible.

But, is there no command for creating a default in AutoLISP? With a default, AutoCAD gives a RETURN option and places one of the options inside the less-than and greater-than characters <...> The option in the <...> is the default, meaning a RETURN will use the default value within the angle brackets.

In AutoLISP it's a simple case of saving the last value that was entered to a special variable, then if nothing is entered the next time, use the value of the special variable as the input.

Here's a short segment of code that illustrates how this is done:

```
(defun C:testpgm (/ a)
  (if (= defvar nil)(setq defvar ""))
  (prompt "\nEnter name:  <")(princ defvar)(princ "> ")
  (setq a (getstring))
  (if (= a "")(setq a defvar))
  (setq defvar a)
)
```

Notice that **defvar** is not declared as a local variable because you want the value of the variable to remain. The first line sets **defvar** to "" if it is nil. You don't want the default to actually say **nil**. A combination of **(prompt)** and **(princ)** statements prints the < and > with the defvar variable as the default. If the **(getstring)** command returns "", then **defvar** is set to **a.**

15.24 Create an AutoLISP library.

You should create a single file that loads and executes each of your AutoLISP programs only when they are needed. This doesn't mean you should put every one of your programs in a single file. This would take too long to load. Instead, put a single-line program in the library file that loads and executes the larger program. For our example we'll call the library file **LIB.LSP**.

Let's assume you have a program called **C:eewrite** found in a file called **LES14c.LSP**. Here's how the single line should read in the library file of **LES14c.LSP**:

```
(defun C:eewrite ( )  (load "les14c")  (C:eewrite))
```

When the **LIB.LSP** file is loaded, each of the single-line programs is also loaded. Since each of the single-line programs begins with a **(defun...)** statement which is the name of the program you want to use, typing that name will execute the program in the **LIB.LSP** file.

The **LIB.LSP** file program then loads the real file. The instant the real file is loaded the real function is also loaded and executed. Since the function in the **LIB.LSP** and the real function have the same name, the real function overwrites the **LIB.LSP** function and thus is executed directly each time the function is called.

This gives you only one line of code for each of your programs. You could have more than a hundred programs and could load the LIB.LSP file in a couple of seconds. Then the real programs would load only if they are needed. Each would take less than a second to load and begin executing.

Any general all-purpose utilities used by other programs such as **(dtr)** and **(rtd)** could also be placed in the **LIB.LSP** file. In this way they would be ready for any other program. Thus, now your only problem is how to get the **LIB.LSP** file to load. That's where the ACAD.LSP file helps. The only file call you should put in the ACAD.LSP file is **(load "lib")**. Then let **LIB.LSP** do the rest of the work.

In the companion disk, you'll find an **LIB.LSP** file that lists and auto-loads the lisp files in this book. Upon startup, this will automatically load your lisp files for you.

15.25 Don't trust anything to work.

Test, test, then test some more. What may work under one set of conditions may not work under others. Remember, bug-free programs are rare. However, the more a program is tested and the longer it's used, the better its chances of being error-free. Which brings us to ...

Debugging

Just as there's no one correct way to create a program, there's no one way to debug a program, either. No checklist will tell you why an aspect of your program isn't working. You can check the logic of the program over and over, and it will seem correct. Or sometimes it will work and other times it won't.

At this stage, programming can be either frustrating or challenging, depending on your approach. The next few pages should make debugging more of an adventure than an annoyance!

First, here are a few rules when working with a computer:

15.26 Computers don't get tired, but you do.

If you're getting cranky, get away from your work. Weed your garden or see a movie. Return when you feel refreshed, and you'll solve your problems faster and more cheerfully.

15.27 Computers don't favor certain data over other data.

The data are either right or wrong.

15.28 Rarely will the computer malfunction or be in error.

Disappointing, but true.

15.29 The same stimuli will create the same results with a computer.

You'll question this rule, particularly when your programs seem to work sporadically with identical data. Convince yourself that something has changed each time you run the program. It may not be apparent, but it's there.

This advice may seem silly, but when you're debugging, you'll start to question your sanity. You must bring yourself down to earth and remember the computer will do only what it's told.

Debugging is like detective work. You must find out what the computer is being told that you didn't anticipate. Sometimes it's obvious and easy, sometimes it's not.

15.30 Two types of basic bugs.

Programs usually have two types of bugs: *syntax* bugs and *logical* bugs. A syntax bug, where the command is in error, is easier to find. For example,

```
(setq a (angl p1 p2))
```

Because the command **(angl)** is misspelled, the program will stop—the AutoLISP interpreter doesn't recognize the command. This is a simple case of making sure that the syntax conforms to the rules, then changing the command. The beauty of a syntax error is that AutoLISP always stops at the error to give you a clue.

A logic error isn't so obliging. Sometimes a logic error will stop the program. For example:

```
(angle  pnt1 pnt2)
```

The above command is correct and should measure an angle from **pnt1** to **pnt2**. But what if **pnt2** had a value of **nil**? The interpreter wouldn't know where the second point was, and the program would stop.

Here's another example of a logic error. When asking **Y** or **N** questions, you often might be testing for an uppercase **Y** or **N**—when you typed in a lowercase **y** or **n**. The problem is that you forgot to use **(strcase)** before you tested the variable.

The first step in debugging logic errors is to print all variables affected to be sure they have the proper value. In most cases you'll think a variable has a certain value, yet the computer knows it has another value.

Here's another example of a common bug:

```
(while d
(+ a 1)
(misc program statement)
(misc program statement)
(if (= a 5)
(setq d nil)
   )
)
```

Basically, this program loops while **d** is not **nil**. The program should add **1** to **a** each time through the loop until **a** = **5**. When **a** equals **5**, then **d** is set to **nil** and the loop falls out.

But the program tends to hang up when run. If you could look at variable **a** each time through the loop, you'd see it always equals **1**, rather than increasing. The correct command should have been:

```
(setq a (+ a 1))
```

Since **a** was never permanently set to **(+ a 1)**, it always started the loop again at **nil**. Therefore, **a** never reached **5**, and a continuous loop was created. You could easily identify the bug if you could see **a** each time through the loop.

15.31 Viewing variable bugs — via a "break point."

One technique, using a *break point*, lets you view variables while a program is running. That can be easily accomplished in AutoLISP by placing

```
(setq bp (getstring))
```

where you want the program to stop. To print the variables, put a **(princ)** statement to print the variable before the break point.

```
(princ a)
(setq bp (getstring)
```

Now the computer will print the variable and let you hit the space bar to continue. When you've discovered the problem with the variable or program, remove the break points and the print variable statements, then continue testing the program.

Since variables are so important in debugging your program, you must be certain they maintain their value after the program ends (so you can view them). Therefore, always make variables *global* at the beginning of the program. If you make them local, they may have no value at the end of the program, and you won't be able to see what was in them.

15.32 Make variables global ( ) at the start of your program.

To make variables global, start each function with **( )** after the **(defun** command. For example,

```
(defun drawline ( )
```

After the program has been thoroughly debugged, go back and make all your variables local.

This trick in itself opens up another possibility for an insidious bug: Suppose all your variables are global and you don't change them back to local. You then run several programs in a row. If the programs use the same variable names, then the values of those variables might be left over from the other programs, giving the appearance that the programs work sometimes and not at other times. The order in which the programs are run determines whether the bug will rear its ugly head.

15.33 Make variables local after debugging.

To make variables local, be sure to declare them within parentheses:

```
(defun drawline (/ pnt1 pnt2).
```

15.34 Don't confuse radians with decimal degrees.

When working with angles, the most common error is to mix up radians and decimal degrees. Remember that AutoLISP commands use radians, and AutoCAD commands generally use degrees. If you fail to convert the radians to degrees before you use an AutoCAD command, you'll get strange results.

Always test for the direction of the angle. When using **(angle)** or **(getangle)** or **(getorient)**, the angle can differ by 180 degrees, depending upon which points you choose. That also can give the appearance of a program that works sporadically.

15.35 Look for visual debug clues.

In addition to checking variables, you can get visual clues by watching the screen as your program runs. For example, if the screen places a point in a blank area of the screen, or something appears and then goes blank, you may have issued an **INSERT**, **BREAK** or other command in an unexpected area.

You might have thought you were breaking a line at the **(polar)** of a point on another line. But when it went to get that point, the line didn't exist. Maybe you should have subtracted—instead of added—90 degrees. This won't tell you what you did wrong, but by watching the screen for unusual occurrences, you can judge where in the program the problem might reside.

15.36 Check your system variables.

Finally, be sure to check your system variables with **(getvar)** and **(setvar)**. Many times, you'll ask AutoCAD to OBJECT SNAP to an intersection where no intersection exists. Or you may ask AutoCAD to pick a point but fail to realize you left OBJECT SNAP **ENDPOINT** on. You never picked the point, which caused a bug later in the program (when you issued the **LINE** command).

15.37 Debugging in general.

As you can see, no one thing causes a bug. And what's worse—as in the paragraph above—several bugs together can cause a single symptom. Take it one bug at a time and try not to get frustrated. Never try to test two things at once. Always change one thing at a time, then test the effect on the program.

The most important part of debugging is to re-create the bug consistently. When you make a change in the program, you can see that the bug no longer exists. If the bug is causing an inconsistent error, you must first track the change in the stimuli creating the inconsistency and be sure you can re-create the bug.

Although *AutoLISP in Plain English* can't cover every possible contingency, it lists the most common bugs—and methods of discovering them. Remember that programming involves trial and error, and experience determines how much trial and how much error.

Moving On

Not all commands can be covered in a tutorial. Many more AutoLISP commands are available to you. The AutoLISP manual that came with your AutoCAD software is, of course, the most complete guide to all AutoLISP commands available. Use it.

When you first scanned the pages of the AutoLISP manual, it might have seemed unreadable. A second reading will take care of that—go back and try it again. You'll be surprised. You have learned enough now to make sense of the AutoLISP documentation that Autodesk supplies. Chapter 16 is a collection of miscellaneous AutoLISP commands you'll find useful.

16

MISCELLANEOUS COMMANDS

Miscellaneous Commands

You've learned more than the basic concepts of AutoLISP. By now, you understand how AutoLISP is put together so you can write useful programs to help you in your daily work.

You've also seen enough AutoLISP "philosophy" to get through the more complex and thorough AutoLISP reference manuals.

Now let's go over some other AutoLISP commands.

16.1 (if... not...)

Since you must load each program before functions can be run, repeatedly loading a file to run the same program is both time-consuming and wasteful. If you know a file has been loaded previously, the following command solves the problem. Place the command in the menu or tablet for each function.

```
(if (not rectan) (load "les2"))
```

The name of the function follows the **(not...** The file is loaded, not the function. Therefore, it reads: **(if...** the program **rectan** isn't found, then **load les2**.

16.2 pause   User Input Option

You can add a pause option to **(command...)**, which allows direct user input. For example,

```
(command "circle" pnt1 pause)
```

begins a circle with **pnt1** as the center point and lets you specify the radius.

16.3 Undefine—Redefine

UNDEFINE and **REDEFINE** are AutoCAD commands. Enter **UNDEFINE** from the **Command** line, and AutoCAD will ask you to enter a command such as **LINE**, **CIRCLE**, **FILLET**, etc. If, for example, you UNDEFINE FILLET, AutoCAD removes **FILLET** from your available commands. This lets you write your own **FILLET** command as an AutoLISP function of the same name. You can restore the AutoCAD command with **REDEFINE**.

For example, at the command line

Type: `REDEFINE FILLET`

If you want to use the AutoCAD **FILLET** command while it's **UNDEFINED**, precede the command with a dot (period). For example,

`.FILLET <RETURN>`

This brings up the AutoCAD **FILLET** command, even if you specified it as **UNDEFINED**.

16.4 S::Startup   Automatically Execute

AutoCAD lets you begin an AutoLISP program automatically when you enter the drawing editor. This feature is available only in the **ACAD.LSP** file. Any program in the **ACAD.LSP** file whose function is defined as

`(defun s::startup ( )`

is executed automatically when you enter the drawing editor.

s::startup should be used only once in the **ACAD.LSP** file. Even though **s::startup** is permitted in other files, this program won't execute automatically in any file other than **ACAD.LSP**.

Also, if the **ACAD.LSP** file is reloaded or loaded manually, the **s::startup** program won't execute automatically. See Section 15.24 for further remarks on the **ACAD.LSP** file.

16.5 S::Save   Automatic Execution When Saving

Just as any function that was placed in the **S::STARTUP** function was executed upon entry into the drawing, the **S::SAVE** function will execute any time the drawing is saved. It actually takes place before the drawing is saved in any manner. Drawings can be saved using the AutoCAD **END** or **SAVE** commands, too. Upon checking to see that the command is valid, the **S::SAVE** function is executed.

There are other ways to save a drawing. When you **QUIT** a drawing the dialog box prompts if you want to save the drawing before quitting. If you start a **NEW** or attempt to **OPEN** another drawing while in a drawing you receive a similar dialog box. If you choose to save the existing drawing, it executes the **S::SAVE** function.

You can imagine many scenarios where this function might be useful. One possibility might be to create an alternate filename function that copies the last saved file to another name. For instance, using the extension **.BAK** or **.BKU** to indicate a backup file. In this way you never save on top of the last saved drawing file.

16.6 S::Exit   Automatic Execution When Exiting

This function works in exactly the same manner as **S::SAVE**. The difference is that this function is executed when an **exit** from the drawing is successful. It's executed before the actual exit out of AutoCAD. This can take place upon the successful completion of **END** or **QUIT.** Or if you're already in a drawing **NEW** or **OPEN**.

16.7 FUZZ

This isn't really a command in and of itself. It's an attempt to correct a problem common to most languages and computers when testing for equality between two variables. In numeric data conversions, numbers that are equal to each other might be slightly "off." If this is the case, a test of equality will often fail.

You may add an additional parameter, called **fuzz**, to the **(equal)** command. **fuzz** is a real number set to the number of decimal places of precision required for evaluating equality. If the two numbers are equal within this degree of precision, the test for equality will pass.

```
(if
(equal a b 0.0001)
(prompt "These numbers are equal ")
)
```

If **a** and **b** are equal to within .0001, the **prompt** statement will print.

NOTE: **FUZZ** factor will work only with the command **(equal)**. It won't work with (=). Therefore, if you issue the command

```
(= a b 0.0001)
```

FUZZ isn't recognized, and the two won't be considered equal unless their equality is absolute.

16.8 (findfile)   Locate a File

This command searches the current directory, any directories within the **DOS PATH** environment and the directory setup in the AutoCAD environment system variable **acad**. (See Chapter 1 and the Install.txt on the companion disk for a full description of the environment variables and how to set them.)

If the file you want isn't found, **nil** is returned. If the file is found, then AutoCAD returns the complete directory path.

NOTE that AutoCAD lets you use either **/** or **** for directory descriptors. If you search for the file **ACAD.PGP** and it's located in the **\acad\support** directory,

```
(findfile "acad.pgp")
    returns c:\\acad\\support\\acad.pgp.
```

16.9 (getenv)   Get the Environment System Variable

(getenv) lets you secure the environment setting under which AutoCAD is operating.

Type: `(getenv "acad") <RETURN>`

Response: `"C:\\acad\\support;C:\acad\\fonts;C:\\acad\\ads"`

The following are AutoCAD environment system variables, with typical default settings:

ACAD

This gives you an additional directory path through which AutoCAD will search for programs or files. It's very useful to put .LSP files in this directory so they may always be available from all current directories. See the response above when you typed,

```
(getenv "acad") <RETURN>
```

ACADCFG

You can set this to tell AutoCAD where the configuration file is found. This is useful if you want to establish more than one configuration. A batch file can set and reset the system variable to point to the directory where the configuration resides. For example,

Type: `(getenv "acadcfg") <RETURN>`

Response: `"C:\\acad"`

The response indicates the ACADCFG= environment is set to C:\ACAD

ACADDRV

This points to the directory where the driver files are located. For example,

Type: `(getenv "acaddrv") <RETURN>`

Response: `"C:\\acad\\drv"`

The response indicates the ACADDRV= environment is set to the C:\ACAD\DRV directory.

16.10 (trans)   Translate From One Coordinate System to Another

The **(trans)** command translates coordinates from one coordinate system to another.

`(trans p1  code-from  code-to)`

"Code-from" and **"code-to"** aren't actually used. They're code numbers that designate which coordinate system is to serve as the source and the destination.

`(trans p1 0 1)`
`(trans p1 1 0)`

Codes:	0	World Coordinate System
	1	Current User Coordinate System
	2	Display

Before describing **display**, we'll outline the easy ones. If you have a point expressed in a **UCS** and need to translate it to the **WCS**, the syntax is

```
(trans p1 1 0)
```

Conversely, if you have a point in the **WCS** and you need to translate it to the current **UCS**, the syntax is

```
(trans p1 0 1)
```

Each of these commands returns the new **X, Y** and **Z** coordinates after the translation.

Code 2 is the **Entity Coordinate System (ECS)**. This is the code you use to translate the current **ECS** to the **WCS**.

Use the **(entget)** command to secure the entity list of the entity. Translate entities other than the ones listed in Section 9.13. If **(entget)** is used on those entities, the translation is ignored.

The example is for **TEXT**, which needs to be translated from the **ECS** to the **UCS**.

Assume the following:

```
e
```

is the entity name

```
d                          .
```

equals the actual coordinates found in **(assoc 10)**, such as **(setq d (car (assoc 10 b)))**. Therefore, **d** is a list of the three coordinates.

Let's assume that the three coordinates found in **d** are

```
(1000 540 0)
```

To translate **d** from its **ECS** to the **WCS**, use the command

```
(trans d e 0)
```

d represents the coordinates of the entity in the **ECS**. **e** is the entity name. It's to be translated to 0, which is the code for the **WCS**. You must use **e** so AutoCAD will know which **ECS** was in effect for that entity.

The **WCS** for that entity at those coordinates is

```
(896.296 -574.715 397.437)
```

16.11 HANDLES   Permanent Entity Names

As you recall, you can use (**entget**) to secure the entity list only if you supply it with the entity name. The entity name is an eight-digit hexadecimal number that is a type of identifier for the entity. The problem in using this identifier is that it doesn't remain constant. It can change when a drawing is brought up again. For some AutoLISP programs, especially commercial programs, it's useful to give an entity an identifier that will remain constant throughout the life of a drawing.

You can assign entity handles to an entity when it's created. Before entities can be assigned handles, the handles must be turned on. You do this with the AutoCAD **HANDLE** command. This command can either turn on the handles or destroy all handles.

To turn on handles with an AutoLISP command, type

```
(command "handles" "on")
```

This command sets the HANDLES system variable to **1** if the handles are turned *on*. This system variable is a *read-only* variable. You can't use **setvar** to turn handles off.

When the handles are turned on, you can't turn them off without destroying all the handles in the database. To prevent the handles from being destroyed accidentally, AutoCAD doesn't confirm with a simple **yes** or **no**. AutoCAD has developed six randomly selected messages that you must type to confirm you want to destroy the handles. They are

```
I AGREE
MAKE MY DATA
PRETTY PLEASE
UNHANDLE THAT DATABASE
DESTROY HANDLES
GO AHEAD
```

It's very difficult to write a simple AutoLISP program that will destroy the entity handles. The following will work only one in six times on average.

```
(command "handles" "destroy" "I AGREE")
```

You should destroy handles manually, not through an AutoLISP program. But if you must, write an AutoLISP program. Simply place the above statement in a **while** loop and test the system variable **HANDLES** for **1** or **0** to see if they've been turned off. The function continues to loop until the test passes when the handles are destroyed. The number of times through the loop is indeterminant, because the handles will be destroyed only when the random message is **"I AGREE."**

The new handle is placed in the database and entity list as a code 5. Therefore, a handle might appear in the entity list as

```
(5 . "3")
```

The handle may be secured by searching for an **(assoc 5).**

When your program identifies an entity by its handle, it won't change for the entire life of the drawing file, unlike the entity name.

Once you know the entity handle, you can get the entity list with the **(handent)** command. This isn't a direct command that will bring in the entity list; **(handent)** will simply secure the entity name. Then you can use the traditional **(entget)** command.

```
(setq h (handent "4"))
(setq b (entget h))
```

The entity handle in the above example is "4." The **(handent)** command searches for the entity name and assigns this name to the variable **h**. The **(entget)** command brings back the entity list of **h** and assigns the list to the variable **b**.

16.12 (entmake)   Make Entity

You can now create your own entity list with the **(entmake)** command. Previously, the only way you could add an entity to the database was with the **(command...)** facility. The command works just like **(entmod)**. It's followed by an entity list.

Assume that you have either constructed an entity list and assigned it to the variable **e** or saved it to the variable **e**.

```
(entmake e)
```

creates a new entity.

16.13 (xload)   Load & Execute an ADS Program

C and some **Fortran** programs run in AutoCAD. But these programs don't run in isolation. They're loaded and executed in AutoLISP using the **(xload)** command. When the program terminates, control returns to the AutoLISP program in effect (if there is one). Of course, the **(xload)** command may be typed from the **Command** line.

```
(xload "progname")
```

16.14 (xunload)   Unload an ADS Program

This command unloads an ADS program from memory.

16.15 (textpage) Flip to Text Screen

This command works exactly like **(textscr)** and flips the user to the text screen, but it clears the screen as well. By adding a **(prin1)** after the command, you also get rid of the **nil** on the screen if you use it from the **Command** line or as the last line in a program.

```
(textpage) (prin1)
```

If the user is already on the text screen, nothing happens and the screen isn't cleared.

16.16 (cvunit)   Unit Conversation

This command converts a value from one unit to another. The units supported and their conversion formula are found in a file called **ACAD.UNT**. You're able to add your own units and definitions to this file with a text editor.

```
(cvunit 100 "miles" "feet")
```

This converts 100 miles to 528,000 feet. Three parameters follow **(cvunit)**. They are the value to be converted, followed by the **"from"** unit in quotes, followed by the **"to"** unit in quotes.

```
(cvunit 20 "kilometers" "miles")12.4274
```

You also may convert the components of a list, such as a point.

```
(cvunit '(12 24 36) "inches" "feet")(1.0 2.0 3.0)
```

16.17 (match)   Wild Card Match

You now can find internal string matches. This means you can learn whether one string is found, or is a match with another string.

Here's how it works: Suppose you had a string variable called **ALPH** that contained **"ABC123XYZ\%"** and you wanted to know if it contained the characters **23X** anywhere within the string.

```
(wcmatch ALPH "*23X*")
```

This command returns to you the value **T** if a match is found or **nil** if a match isn't found. **(wcmatch)** is case-sensitive; therefore, be sure you convert everything to uppercase with the **(strcase)** command, if necessary.

Here's a list of the wild cards available to you and their meaning. The examples assume the variable **ALPH** contains **"ABC123XYZ\%"**

~	**(tilde)** means not found. **(wcmatch alph "~234")** returns **T** because **234** isn't found in the pattern.
*	The standard wild card that matches anything. It may now be used both before and after, or anywhere in the search pattern.
?	Matches any single character or number.
@@	Matches any single character, which may not be a number.
#	Matches any single number.
.	(period) matches any single non-alphanumeric character. **(wcmatch alph "*YZ.*")** returns **T** because the \ that follows the **Z** is a non-alphanumeric character.
(space)	Matches one or more spaces.
[...]	This means there's a match for any one of the characters enclosed in the brackets.

```
(wcmatch alph "*[XJK]*")
```

would return **T** because the **X** is found somewhere in the string even though the **J** and **K** aren't. The characters don't have to be in a specific order, just contained somewhere within the string.

[~...]   Returns true only if there are characters not included in the brackets.

```
(wcmatch alph "*[~JKL]*")
```

returns true because neither **J**, **K** nor **L** are included anywhere within the string.

[-]   **(hyphen)** treats the pattern as a range. **(wcmatch alph "*[1-5]*")** returns **T** because **123** is matched within the range of **1** to **5**.

,   **(comma)** Used as an **(or....)** option. For example

```
(wcmatch alph "*123*,*JKL*")
```

returns true because 123 is found within the string even though JKL isn't. The comma acted as an (or...) option.

'   **(back quote)** Treats the next character literally. Use this for special characters and all non-alphanumeric special characters.

16.18 unitmode   Change Unit Appearance

The system variable **unitmode** can control the way **(rtos)** and **(angtos)** print. Traditionally, the standard way of printing is **6'-2 3/4"**. That is when you've set **unitmode** to **0**. Yet,

```
(setvar "unitmode" 1)
```

changes the output to **6'2-3/4"**. The difference is where the hyphen is placed, which is always a confusing problem for new AutoCAD users. The manner of the input is different from what the user sees onscreen. The **unitmode** system variable changes the display to the way the fractions are input. You see this immediately with the coordinates as they're updated on the status line.

16.19 (alert)   Alert Box

An alert box is a dialog box that appears onscreen with a single message. Once the alert box appears execution of AutoLISP and AutoCAD is suspended until the alert is acknowledged when you pick **OK** or press <RETURN>.

The following is the syntax for the alert box:

```
(alert  "You must answer Y or N")
```

You also may create multiple lines by inserting the **\n** in the middle of the string quotation marks.

```
(alert  "You must answer \n Y or N")
```

The standard way you've created a sentence return thus far, is

```
(alert  "\nYou must answer Y or N")
```

Be aware that the number of lines and length of a line are dependent on the platform and devices in use. Try to make short alerts so you won't run into a problem if your programs are used on different machines. If Auto-CAD finds the lines are too long or don't fit, it will simply truncate them (cut them off as necessary).

16.20 (ver)   What Version Number

Since users work with a variety of AutoCAD releases, this command can check the version of AutoLISP in use at the time the program is being run to verify compatibility or alter for compatibility.

```
(setq v (ver))
```

The variable **v** might contain **"AutoLISP Release 13.0"**.

16.21 (ssget)   Enhanced

The **(ssget)** command supports all the selection set options of Release 13. These include WP for WPolygon, CP for CPolygon and F for Fence. **(ssget)** also defaults to the automatic selection of a Window when a pick is made and no entity is picked.

16.22 (getfiled) Activate File Dialog Box

The **(getfiled)** command will activate the file dialog box. Once the file is selected, the name of the file is returned. Here's how the command works:

The command has four parts. Each part is optional and positional. That is to say the relative position they occupy after the **(getfiled)** command—not their name—will determine their function. They are as follows:

Title	Is the first position following the command. It lets you label the entire file dialog box.
Filename	When a file dialog box comes up, you can place a default file name in the box labeled **File**. In addition, the file name, if found, will automatically be highlighted in the box.
Extension	Each file dialog box uses a pattern in order to limit the kinds of files displayed. This is the extension. For example ***.SLD** is limited to slide files, and ***.DWG** is limited to drawing files. If NULL is placed in this position then ***.*** is used.
Flags	There are four possible flags: **(1), (2), (4), (8)**. They are

    1 If the file the user selects exists, you create an alert box to warn the user to either replace the file or cancel.

    2 This flag will disable the **Type It** button. It forces the user to pick from listed files rather than type a file name.

    4 This lets the user enter an extension. If this flag is not set, only the extension used in the extension field will be allowed. The extension is also appended to the file name if the user doesn't enter it in the file edit box.

    8 If this flag is set and flag 1 is not set, AutoCAD will perform a search in accordance with its search path parameters, which are set by the SET ACAD environment variable. When it finds the file as part of the search path, it will only return the name of the file and not the directory path of the file. If this flag is not set, then it returns the entire path name of the file.

These flags use the **sum of the bits** concept. (See Section 15.22.) If you want to combine any of these flags, then simply add their flag numbers.
  Here is the syntax of **(getfiled)**:

```
(getfiled Title Filename Extension Flag)
```

Example:

```
(setq f (getfiled "Slides" "" "SLD" 1))
```

Notice that each of the items must be filled in except the flag position, which is a string. If you don't want something in one of the positions, use "". If you don't want something in the flag position, then use **0**.

16.23 (exit)   Exit an AutoLISP Program

This function stops the current AutoLISP programs and returns the error message **quit / exit / abort**. The program is aborted, and the user is immediately returned to the AutoCAD command prompt.

The following functions are new with AutoCAD Release 13.

16.24 (setcfg)   Set Application Configuration

AutoCAD has now given to application developers and users the ability to store semi-permanent configuration information with the ACAD.CFG file. The ACAD.CFG file is now a simple text file. This file is divided into sections. The section you have control over is called [AppData]. Your application must have a unique name. For this example we will call your application SAMPLE. Here's how it works:

  Let's say you wanted to store two pieces of information that would always be available to your program. This information is size and color. We will make the size equal to "4" and the color equal to "blue". The following is the syntax:

```
(setcfg "appdata/sample/size" "4")
(setcfg "appdata/sample/color" "blue")
```

Within the quotes must come the word *appdata.* This is separated with a / then followed by your application name, then another / followed by the variable tag name it will be known as. In the above example two statements were issued, one for size and the other for color.

The following is the first section of the ACAD.CFG file to show you how AutoCAD handled it.

```
[AppData/sample]
size=4
color=blue
```

16.25 (getcfg)   Get Application Configuration

This function permits you to read the configuration information for your application. Assume again that your application name is SAMPLE and you want to know what the current value of color is.

```
(getcfg "appdata/sample/color")
```

This expression returns the value of color for the application SAMPLE.

16.26 (help)   Working With Your Own Help File

The help mechanism has changed greatly. But the good news is that it is more standard across platforms. There are two types of help files that you can create. If the file extension is .HLP then it is considered to be a Windows standard help file. If the file extension is .AHP then it is considered to be an AutoCAD standard help file. Here we will only deal with the AutoCAD standard help file.

How the help file is actually created is beyond the scope of this book. The purpose here is to illustrate how to work with the AutoLISP function (help) in order to access the help file.

Let's assume that the file you have created is called SAMPLE.AHP. A topic within the help file is DIMVALS.

```
(help "sample" "dimvals")
```

If you do not include the name of a topic then the initial help screen for the help file will begin.

This method of calling for help within AutoLISP has replaced (acad_helpdlg). For compatibility reasons (acad_helpdlg) remains, but is really using (help). The file format must be Release 13 or an error will occur.

16.27 (setfunhelp)   Set Help File and Topic

This function permits you to create a context sensitive help that will work the same as AutoCAD's within your own programs.

Assume that your help file is SAMPLE.AHP and that the context sensitive help that you want to be available during a specific program is DIM-VALS. C:dimshow is the name of the program that will be running when the help is activated. Then at the beginning of the AutoLISP program place the following line:

```
(setfunhelp "C:dimshow" "sample.ahp" "dimvals")
```

Once this is set then the user may type **help** or pick help from the toolbar whenever dimshow is running and it will call up DIMVALS as a topic from the SAMPLE help file. If C:dimshow is not running then help will revert back to the standard AutoCAD help.

You may have as many **(setfunhelp)** definitions in effect at one time as you need. It is probably best to simply place the definition at the beginning of each AutoLISP program that you write with its own program name and topic to be activated.

16.28 (startapp)   Start a Windows Application

This function is only available through Windows. AutoLISP may now begin another application. It may be necessary to path spec the application. For example here is how EXCEL might be started from AutoLISP.

```
(startapp "/msoffice/excel/excel" "myfile")
```

Myfile is any parameter you need to add, such as the name of the spreadsheet file to be called up.

Moving On

You can't have too many examples. You learn AutoLISP by doing and seeing how others write programs. You should constantly evaluate programs that you find in magazines, books and bulletin boards.

To help you out and give you a head start, Chapter 17, "Programming Examples," provides 15 finished programs for you to not only learn from but use as the start for your AutoLISP library.

17

FIFTEEN
PROGRAMMING
EXAMPLES

Fifteen Programming Examples

Below are 15 practice AutoLISP programs that further illustrate Auto-LISP's inner workings. Many of these programs could have been greatly enhanced, but for instructional purposes we chose not to do so.

17.1 Line Type Scale — LSCALE.LSP

```
(defun C:lscale (/ l u d sc)
  (graphscr)
  (setq l (getvar "limmin"))
  (setq u (getvar "limmax"))
  (setq d (- (car u) (car l)))
  (setq sc (/d 32))
  (command "ltscale" sc)
)
```

PURPOSE: From time to time you'll change the **LIMITS** on your drawing or start a drawing with new **LIMITS** without using the AutoCAD-supplied setup AutoLISP program. This program provides a convenient way of resetting **LTSCALE** to the correct ratio for the current **LIMITS**. Changing the divisor from **32** to another number adjusts the scale.

TO LOAD:

Type: `(load "lscale")  <RETURN>`

Response: `C:lscale`

TO OPERATE:

Type: `lscale  <RETURN>`

The program operates without prompts and sets the **LTSCALE**.
Let's examine the program line by line. The file name is **LSCALE.LSP**.

`(defun C:lscale (/ l u d sc)`

defines the function with all variables local.

```
(graphscr)
```

changes to the graphics screen.

```
(setq l (getvar "limmin"))
(setq u (getvar "limmax"))
```

Those lines get the lower left and upper right limits, then assign the points to **l** and **u**.

```
(setq d (- (car u) (car l)))
```

The **x** of **l** is subtracted from the **x** of **u**.
    That way, you can measure the distance of the limits.

```
(setq sc (/ d 32))
```

d is divided by **32**. The figure 32 can be adjusted to suit your particular definition of the proper **LTSCALE**. You'll find **32** is adequate unless the limits are skewed. Creating unusual elongated drawing limits, is an example.

```
(command "ltscale" sc)
```

sets the **LTSCALE**.

```
)
```

closes the function.

17.2 Perpendicular Line — PERDP.LSP

```
(defun C:perpdon (/ a b pnt1 pnt2 ang1)
  (graphscr)
  (setq a (entsel))
  (setq b (entget (car a)))
  (setq pnt1 (cdr (assoc 10 b)))
  (setq pnt2 (cdr (assoc 11 b)))
  (setq ang1 (angle pnt1 pnt2))
  (setvar "snapang" ang1)
  )
  (defun C:perpdoff ( )
  (setvar "snapang" 0)
)
```

PURPOSE: Lets you draw lines perpendicular to other lines. The program measures the angle of the other lines and shifts the **SNAP ANGLE** so you can use **ORTHO ON** and draw exactly perpendicular to the line chosen. When finished, choose **PERPENDICULAR OFF**, which will restore the **SNAP ANGLE** to its normal position.

TO LOAD:

Type: `(load "perpd")`

Response: `C:perpdoff`

This is the second of the two programs in the file.

TO OPERATE:

Type: `perpdon`

This turns on the perpendicular function.

Response: `Select object:`

Pick the object from which you wish to draw a perpendicular line.

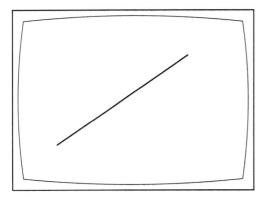

Figure 17-1: Draw a single line of any length.

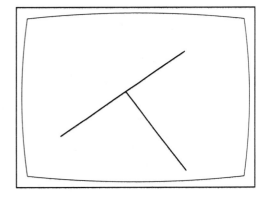

Figure 17-2: Pick the entity and draw a perpendicular line.

Response: `The crosshairs change to the angle of the object selected.`

You may now use **ORTHO ON** to draw lines perpendicular to this object. When finished,

Type: `perpdoff`

That restores the crosshairs to their normal position.

Now let's examine the program line by line. The file is **PERPD.LSP**.

```
(defun C:perpdon (/ a b pnt1 pnt2 ang1)
```

defines the function with all local variables.

```
(graphscr)
```

changes to the graphics screen.

```
(setq a (entsel))
```

selects a single entity from which you want to draw the perpendicular line. This is a special select command that lets you select only one entity.

```
(setq b (entget (car a)))
```

gets the entity list. Since you used **entsel, a** already has the entity name— in the **(car a)**.

```
(setq pnt1 (cdr (assoc 10 b)))
```

gets the beginning point of the line.

```
(setq pnt2 (cdr (assoc 11 b)))
```

gets the end point of the line.

```
(setq ang1 (angle pnt1 pnt2))
```

gets the angle of the line.

```
(setvar "snapang" ang1)
```

sets the system variable **"snapang"** to the line's angle. That forces **ORTHO** to **90** degrees from the changed angle. Therefore, you're able to draw **90** degrees from the line you selected.

```
)
```

closes the function.

NOTE: You must use the following program to reset the angle back to **0**:

```
(defun C:perpdoff ( )
```

This defines the program as **PERPDOFF**. (There are no variables.)

```
(setvar "snapang" 0)
```

sets the system variable back to **0**.

```
)
```

closes the function.

17.3 Change Layer — CHLAYER.LSP

```
(defun C:chlayer (/ a1 a2 n index b1 b2 d1 d2 b3)
   (graphscr)
   (prompt "\nSelect entities to be changed: ")
   (setq a1 (ssget))
   (prompt "\nPoint to entity on target layer: ")
   (setq a2 (entsel))
   (setq n (sslength a1))
   (setq index 0)
   (setq b2 (entget (car a2)))
   (setq d2 (assoc 8 b2))
   (repeat n
      (setq b1 (entget (ssname a1 index)))
      (setq d1 (assoc 8 b1))
      (setq b3 (subst d2 d1 b1))
      (entmod b3)
      (setq index (+ index 1))
   )
)
```

PURPOSE: Lets you select objects by any selection method and change their layer. You choose the target layer by pointing to an object on the desired layer. All objects selected will then change to that target layer. To test this program, you need to create a drawing with objects on different layers.

TO LOAD:

Type: `(load "chlayer")  <ENTER>`

Response: `C:chlayer`

TO OPERATE:

Type: `chlayer  <ENTER>`

Response: `Select entities to be changed:`

You may use any selection method to select the entities to be changed. Confirm your selection.

Response: `Point to entity on target layer:`

Point to an entity on the layer to which you want the other entities changed. When that choice is confirmed, the entities selected are transferred to the target layer.

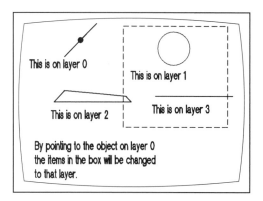

Figure 17-3: Create multiple entities on different layers.

Let's select a group of entities you'd like changed to another layer. Point to an entity on the target layer to change all entities in the selection group to the target layer.

Let's examine the program line by line. The file name is **CHLAYER.LSP**.

```
(defun C:chlayer (/ a1 a2 n index b1 b2 d1 d2 b3)
```

defines the function with all local variables.

```
(graphscr)
```

changes to the graphics screen.

```
(prompt "\nSelect entities to be changed: ")
```

This is a prompt statement.

```
(setq a1 (ssget))
```

allows you to select the objects to be changed. The selection set is assigned to variable **a1**.

```
(prompt "\nPoint to entity on target layer: ")
```

This is a prompt statement.

```
(setq a2 (entsel))
```

This is a special type of selection statement that allows you to select only one entity.

```
(setq n (sslength a1))
```

measures the number of entities in the selection set in variable **a1**.

```
(setq index 0)
```

sets a variable called **index** to **0**.

```
(setq b2 (entget (car a2)))
```

This is a shortcut statement that gets the entity list from **a2**. Thus, **a2** is assigned the entity list.

```
(setq d2 (assoc 8 b2))
```

This looks for the code **8** in entity list **a2**, then assigns the sublist to **d2**.

```
(repeat n
```

This begins the loop that pages through the selection set.

```
(setq b1 (entget (ssname a1 index)))
```

This gets the entity list and assigns it to **b1**.

```
(setq d1 (assoc 8 b1))
```

gets the sublist of code **8** (the layer).

```
(setq b3 (subst d2 d1 b1))
```

substitutes the new **d2** layer for the old **d1** layer in the entity list **a1** and assigns it to the new entity list **b3**.

```
(entmod b3)
```

updates the new entity list.

```
(setq index (+ index 1))
```

increases the **index** variable by **1**, making it ready for the next loop.

```
    )
  )
```

The first **)** closes the **repeat** loop. The second **)** closes the function.

17.4 Set Layer — LAYERSET.LSP

```
(defun C:layerset (/ a2 b2 L1 L2)
  (graphscr)
  (prompt "\nSelect entity on target layer: ")
  (setq a2 (entsel))
  (setq b2 (entget (car a2)))
```

```
        (setq L1 (assoc 8 b2))
        (setq L2 (cdr L1))
        (command "layer" "s" L2 "")
)
```

PURPOSE: Lets you change layers by pointing to an object on the layer you want it set to.

To use it, create a drawing with entities on several different layers.

TO LOAD:

Type: `(load "layerset")  <RETURN>`

Response: `C:layerset`

TO OPERATE:

Type: `layerset  <RETURN>`

Response: `Select entity on target layer:`

Pick an entity on the desired layer and confirm. Your current layer is changed to the layer you specified.

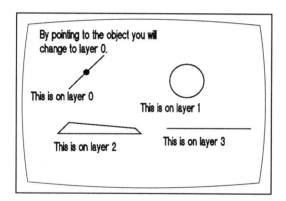

Figure 17-4: Create multiple entities on different layers.

Let's examine the program line by line. The file name is **LAYERSET.LSP**.

`(defun C:layerset  (/ a2 b2 L1 L2)`

defines the function with all local variables.

`(graphscr)`

changes to the graphics screen.

```
(prompt "\nSelect entity on target layer: ")
```

This is a prompt statement.

```
(setq a2 (entsel))
```

This is a special select statement that lets you select only one entity.

```
(setq b2 (entget (car a2)))
```

This assigns the entity list to **b2**. The entity name is in **a2**.

```
(setq L1 (assoc 8 b2))
```

finds the layer of the selected entity.

```
(setq L2 (cdr L1))
```

gets the layer name and assigns it to the variable **L2**.

```
(command "layer" "s" L2 "")
```

The AutoCAD command for layer. **"s"** sets the layer to **L2**.

```
)
```

closes the function.

17.5 Multiple-Purpose Insert — MPINSERT.LSP

```
(defun C:dins (/ p r s1 s2 pnt1)
  (graphscr)
  (setq p "door")
  (setq r "0")
  (setq s1 "1")
  (setq s2 "1")
  (setq pnt1 (getpoint))
  (command "insert" p pnt1 s1 s2 r "")
)
```

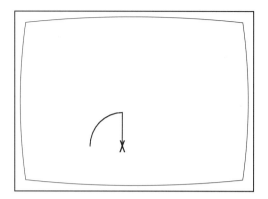

Figure 17-5: Create multiple insert options for your blocks.

PURPOSE: Provides a model for insertion programs. By changing the definition of certain variables, you can insert objects by pointing to the insert pick point—with no questions asked. You should have an insert program for each part to be inserted.

TO LOAD:

Type: `(load "mpinsert")  <RETURN>`

Response: `C:dins <RETURN>`

Change the name of **C:dins** to a unique name for each part to be inserted.

TO OPERATE:

Type: `dins`

Response: `There are no prompts.`

Simply point to the insertion point and the part will be inserted.
Let's examine the program line by line. The file name is **MPINSERT.LSP**.

`(defun C:dins  (/ p r s1 s2 pnt1)`

defines the function with all local variables.

`(graphscr)`

changes to the graphics screen.

```
(setq p "door")
(setq r "0")
(setq s1 "1")
(setq s2 "1")
```

These lines should be modified to reflect each part to be inserted and the angle and scale. You can easily change parts by customizing the variables.

```
(setq pnt1 (getpoint))
```

This is the insertion point.

```
(command "insert" p pnt1 s1 s2 r "")
```

Part **p** is inserted at **pnt1** with scale **s1** and **s2** rotated **r** and the " " ends the insert.

```
)
```

closes the function.

17.6 Substitute Text — SUBTEXT.LSP

```
(defun C:subtext (/ a b d e d1 b1 y)
   (graphscr)
   (prompt "\nSelect text line: ")
   (setq a (entsel))(terpri)
   (setq b (entget (car a)))
   (setq d (assoc 1 b))
   (prompt (cdr d)) (terpri)
   (setq e (getstring 1))
   (setq d1 (cons (car d) e))
   (setq b1 (subst d1 d b))
   (entmod b1)
   (setq y (getstring "\nIs this correct - <Y>  "))
   (if (= (strcase y) "N") (entmod b))
)
```

PURPOSE: Lets you choose a line of text and substitute another line in exactly the same place, layer, color, line type, style, etc., as the original line. To test this program, create a drawing with several lines of text.

TO LOAD:

Type: `(load "subtext")`

Response: `C:subtext`

TO OPERATE:

Type: `subtext`

Response: `Select text line:`

Point to the line of text to be changed, and confirm. The old line will appear at the command line. Type in a new line and **<RETURN>**. The new line will appear where the old line was.

Response: `Is this correct - <Y>`

If you press **<RETURN>** at this point, the new line is permanent. If you answer **N**, the old line is replaced.

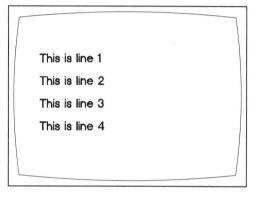

Figure 17-6: Create lines of text with different colors, styles and layers.

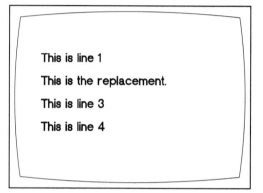

Figure 17-7: Substitute a line of text.

Let's examine this program line by line. The file is **SUBTEXT.LSP**.

```
(defun C:subtext (/ a b d e d1 b1 y)
```

defines the function with all variables local.

```
(graphscr)
```

changes to the graphics screen.

```
(prompt "\nSelect text line: ")
```

This is a prompt statement.

```
(setq a (entsel))(terpri)
```

This is a special select statement that lets you select only one object. The entity name is then assigned to variable **a**.

```
(setq b (entget (car a)))
```

assigns the entity list to variable **b**.

```
(setq d (assoc 1 b))
```

searches for the code **1** found in entity list **b** and assigns it to variable **d**.

```
(prompt (cdr d)) (terpri)
```

At this point the text is printed on the screen. **(terpri)** provides a sentence return and writes the new text under the old.

```
(setq e (getstring 1))
```

lets you enter the new text, assigned to variable **e**. Note flag number **1**, which allows text spaces.

```
(setq d1 (cons (car d) e))
```

This line constructs a new sublist beginning with the code for text, **(car d)**, followed by the new text in variable **e**. This new sublist is assigned to the variable **d1**.

```
(setq b1 (subst d1 d b))
```

This creates a new list substituting the new text **d1** for the old text **d** (found in the entity list **b**). The new list is assigned to **b1**.

```
(entmod b1)
```

This updates the drawing database with the new text.

```
(setq y (getstring "\nIs this correct - <Y>  "))
(if (= (strcase y) "N") (entmod b))
```

Sometimes the new text doesn't look right, and you'd like to start over. Answering **"N"** lets you cancel the change. **(entmod b)** returns the text to the entity list in variable **b**.

```
)
```

closes the function.

17.7 Grid Construction — CRSGRID.LSP

```
(defun C:crsgrid (/ h h1 n pnt c p1 p2 t pnte pntv)
  (graphscr)
  (setq h (getdist "\nDistance of lines: "))
  (setq h1 (getdist "\nLength of horizontal: "))
```

```
(setq n (getint "\nNumber of lines: "))
(setq pnt (getpoint "\nStarting point: "))
(setq c 0)
(repeat n
  (setq p1 (list (car pnt) (+ (cadr pnt) c)))
  (setq p2 (list (+ (car pnt) h1) (+ (cadr pnt) c)))
  (command "line" p1 p2 "")
  (setq c (+ c h))
)
(setq pntv p1)
(setq pnte p2)
(setq t 1)
(setq c 0)
(while t
  (setq p1 (list (+ (car pnt) c) (cadr pnt)))
  (setq p2 (list (+ (car pntv) c) (cadr pntv)))
  (command "line" p1 p2 "")
  (setq c (+ c h))
  (if (or
    (= (car p1) (car pnte))
    (>> (car p1) (car pnte))
    )
  (setq t nil)
  )
)
)
```

PURPOSE: To create a cross-grid that could be used for a tablet menu structure. This program lets you create a cross-grid of any size and number of lines. If the vertical lines don't come out even, **CRSGRID** adds an additional line that you may erase.

TO LOAD:

Type: `(load "crsgrid")  <RETURN>`

Response: `C:crsgrid`

TO OPERATE:

Type: `crsgrid <RETURN>`

Response: `Distance of lines:`

Enter the distance between the grid lines. You may enter this from the keyboard or point to the distance.

Response: `Length of horizontal:`

Enter the distance of the left / right horizontal lines. You may enter this from the keyboard or point to the distance.

Response: `Number of lines:`

Enter the number of horizontal lines. This must be an integer from the keyboard.

Response: `Starting point:`

Pick a starting point. The cross-grid will be drawn from the bottom up.

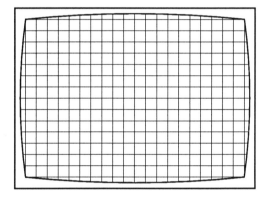

Figure 17-8: Create a cross-grid for a tablet menu structure.

Now let's examine the program line by line. The file name is **CRSGRID.LSP**.

```
(defun C:crsgrid (/ h hl n pnt c pl p2 t pnte pntv)
```

defines the function as **crsgrid**. The **C:** before the name of the function allows the function to be used as an AutoCAD command. The variables listed follow the / to make them local.

```
(graphscr)
```

changes to the graphics screen if you're in **TEXT** mode.

```
(setq h (getdist "\nDistance of lines: "))
```

asks for the distance between the lines. You may point to the distance or key in the distance using default units. The distance is assigned to variable **h**. The **(terpri)** command executes a line feed.

```
(setq h1 (getdist "\nLength of horizontal: "))
```

asks for the distance of the horizontal line. Point to the distance or use default units from the keyboard. The distance is assigned to variable **h1**.

```
(setq n (getint "\nNumber of lines: "))
```

asks for the number of horizontal lines to be drawn, starting from the bottom. Note that you must use **(getint)** instead of **(getreal)**, because it will be used in a **repeat** loop. Only integers may be used in loops.

```
(setq pnt (getpoint "\nStarting point: "))
```

asks for the starting point (from which the grid will be drawn). Remember that the grid starts at the lower left-hand corner and builds up first with the horizontal lines. It then puts in the vertical lines, beginning with the left side and drawing to the right. The number of vertical lines drawn is determined by the length of the horizontal line.

```
(setq c 0)
```

assigns **0** to the variable **c**. This variable adds to the distance of the lines drawn within a loop. **0** assigns the beginning value.

```
(repeat n
```

begins the loop that draws the horizontal lines.

```
(setq p1 (list (car pnt) (+ (cadr pnt) c)))
```

p1 and **p2** are the points for drawing a line. This line creates a point from the **X** coordinate of **pnt** (the beginning point chosen) and the **Y** coordinate of the beginning point plus the value of **c**.

```
(setq p2 (list (+ (car pnt) h1) (+ (cadr pnt) c)))
```

creates **p2** as the **X** coordinate of **pnt** plus **h1** (the length of the horizontal line). The **Y** coordinate of **p2** is created by the **Y** of **pnt** plus **c** (the distance of the horizontal line).

```
(command "line" p1 p2 "")
```

The command **"line"** actually draws the line from **p1** to **p2**. The double quote breaks out of the **LINE** command.

```
(setq c (+ c h))
```

adds the value of **h** to the value of **c** (which increases the value of **c** by the distance of the lines).

```
)
```

ends the **repeat** command.

```
(setq pntv p1)
(setq pnte p2)
```

stores values of **p1** and **p2** to **pntv** and **pnte**—the points where the lines ended. **pntv** is the top left of the grid, and **pnte** is the top right of the grid.

```
(setq t 1)
(setq c 0)
```

These lines set up variables **t** and **c**. **t** controls the **while** loop.

```
(while t
```

begins the loop. Use the **while** loop since you don't know exactly how many vertical lines you plan to draw. (That depends on the length of the horizontal line.)

```
(setq p1 (list (+ (car pnt) c) (cadr pnt)))
(setq p2 (list (+ (car pntv) c) (cadr pntv)))
```

set up the two points **p1** and **p2**. **p1** is the **X** coordinate of **pnt** plus the value of **c** and the **Y** coordinate of **pnt**. **p2** is the **X** coordinate of **pntv** plus **c** and the **Y** coordinate of **pntv**. Remember that **pntv** starts at the upper left-hand corner of the grid.

```
(command "line" p1 p2 "")
```

draws the vertical lines.

```
(setq c (+ c h))
```

increases the value of variable **c** by the distance of the lines.

```
(if (or
(= (car p1) (car pnte))
(>> (car p1) (car pnte))
)
(setq t nil)
```

This series of lines tests to see if you've drawn vertical lines past the ends of the horizontal lines. At most, you want to draw only one vertical line past the end of the horizontal lines. Therefore, if the **X** coordinate of **p1** is equal to the **X** coordinate of **pnte**, or the **X** coordinate of **p1** is greater than **pnte**, assign **nil** to **t**. This stops the loop. You're really testing the end of the horizontal line on the right.

```
)
```

This closes the (if... statement.

```
)
```

This closes the (while... statement.

```
)
```

This ends the program.

The first **)** closes the **if** statement. The second **)** closes the **while** statement. The third **)** closes the entire function.

17.8 Build Rooms — BLDROOM.LSP

```
(defun C:bldroom (/ pnt1 w h pnt2 pnt3 pnt4)
  (graphscr)
  (setvar "osmode" 0)
  (setq pnt1 (getpoint "\nPick a working point: "))
  (setq w (getdist "\nEnter a width: "))
  (setq h (getdist "\nEnter a height: "))
  (setq pnt2 (list (car pnt1) (+ h (cadr pnt1))))
  (setq pnt3 (list (+ w (car pnt2)) (cadr pnt2)))
  (setq pnt4 (list (car pnt3) (cadr pnt1)))
  (command "pline" pnt1 pnt2 pnt3 pnt4 "c")
  (setvar "osmode" 32)
  (command "move" pnt1 "")
)
```

PURPOSE: Lets you build a floor plan by entering the dimensions of each room and dragging the room into position. This program builds the rooms using polylines. The rooms are single entities you may want to explode, depending on their purpose. Also, if you overlap the walls of two rooms, it might be wise to erase one of the walls so there won't be two lines drawn over the same wall.

TO LOAD:

Type: `(load "bldroom") <RETURN>`

Response: `C:bldroom`

TO OPERATE:

Type: `bldroom <RETURN>`

Response: `Pick a working point:`

Pick a point on the screen where the room can be prepared. You'll drag it into position after it's drawn.

Response: `Enter a width:`

Enter the width of the room from the keyboard.

Response: `Enter a height:`

Enter the height of the room from the keyboard. The room is drawn on-screen and you'll be in **OBJECT SNAP, INTERSECTION MODE**. Point to a corner of the room and **DRAG** it into position.

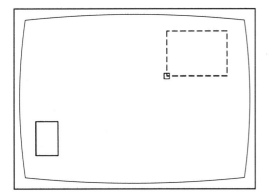

Figure 17-9: Pick a point onscreen to build a room.

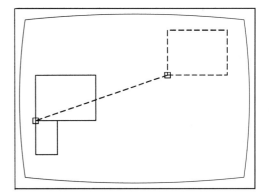

Figure 17-10: Drag the room to the desired location.

Let's examine the program line by line. The file name is
BLDROOM.LSP.

```
(defun C:bldroom (/ pnt1 w h pnt2 pnt3 pnt4)
```

defines the function with all variables local.

```
(graphscr)
```

changes to the graphics screen.

```
(setvar "osmode" 0)
```

sets **OBJECT SNAP** to none.

```
(setq pnt1 (getpoint "\nPick a working point: "))
```

Pick a point where the room will be drawn (not where the room will
eventually be placed). Then **DRAG** it to that point.

```
(setq w (getdist "\nEnter a width: "))
(setq h (getdist "\nEnter a height: "))
```

Here, you enter the width and the height of the room. These numbers are
assigned to variables **w** and **h**.

```
(setq pnt2 (list (car pnt1) (+ h (cadr pnt1))))
(setq pnt3 (list (+ w (car pnt2)) (cadr pnt2)))
(setq pnt4 (list (car pnt3) (cadr pnt1)))
```

Those three lines of program code form the other corners of the room. **pnt2**
added the height to the **Y** coordinate. **pnt3** added the width to the **X**
coordinate of **pnt2**.

```
(command "pline" pnt1 pnt2 pnt3 pnt4 "c")
```

draws a **POLYLINE** to the four points of the room, then closes the poly-
gon. **POLYLINE** was used so you could drag the entire object into place at
one time.

```
(setvar "osmode" 32)
```

OBJECT SNAP is set to INTERSECTION.

```
(command "move" pnt1 "")
```

You now may move the room to the final place (generally at the intersection of another room).

```
)
```

closes the function.

17.9 Line Type Set — LINET.LSP

```
(defun C:linet (/ lo u d sc)
  (setq lo (getvar "limmin"))
  (setq u (getvar "limmax"))
  (setq d (- (car u) (car lo)))
  (setq sc (/ d 32))
  (command "ltscale" sc)
  (command "linetype" "s" "dashed"  "")
)
```

PURPOSE: To let you quickly change line types and make sure the scale of the line-type is automatically set to your specifications. The program uses the code from Section 17.1—**LSCALE.LSP** to set the scale, then issues the **LINE-TYPE** command. The program can easily be modified by changing "dashed" to "continuous," "dots" or any linetype of your choice. As in **LSCALE.LSP**, the number 32 is a constant divisor that establishes the scale of **ltscale**. You may adjust this number.

TO LOAD:

Type: `(load "linet") <RETURN>`

Response: `C:linet`

TO OPERATE:

Type: `linet <RETURN>`

Response: There are no prompts. The linetype and the scale are set automatically.

Let's examine the program line by line. The file name is **LINET.LSP**.

```
(defun C:linet (/ lo u d sc)
```

defines the function with all variables local.

```
(setq lo (getvar "limin"))
(setq u (getvar "limmax"))
(setq d (- (car u) (car lo)))
(setq sc (/ d 32))
(command "ltscale" sc)
```

This is the same program as **LSCALE.LSP**. If **LSCALE.LSP** is written without the C:, this program can be called directly as (**lscale**) instead of typing the lines above.

```
(command "linetype" "s" "dashed" "")
```

This sets the linetype to "dashed."

```
)
```

Ends the program.

17.10 Text Justification — TEXTJUST.LSP

```
(defun C:textjust (/ j e p11 p10 f en p11n p10n fn y)
  (setq j (getstring "\n"Left/Center/Middle/Right: "))
  (setq j (strcase j))
  (setq e (entget (car (entsel))))
  (setq p11 (assoc 11 e))
  (setq p10 (assoc 10 e))
  (setq f (assoc 72 e))
  (setq en e)
  (if (= (cdr f) 0) (setq p11n (cons 11 (cdr p10))))
  (if (= (cdr f) 0) (setq en (subst p11n p11 en)))
  (if (and (= j "L") (/= (cdr f) 0))
    (progn
      (setq p10n (cons 10 (cdr p11)))
      (setq en (subst p10n p10 en))
    )
  )
  (if (= j "L") (setq fn 0))
  (if (= j "C") (setq fn 1))
  (if (= j "M") (setq fn 4))
  (if (= j "R") (setq fn 2))
  (setq fn (cons 72 fn))
  (setq en (subst fn f en))
  (entmod en)
  (setq y (getstring "\nIs this correct <Y> "))
  (if (= (strcase y) "N") (entmod e))
)
```

PURPOSE: For times when you would like to change the original justification of the text. For example, the text might have been centered and you now want it left or right justified, but with the same insertion point. This program permits you to do just that. It will change any text entered as Left, Center, Middle or Right to any of the other options. It will not work on Aligned or Fit, as these actually change the size and shape of the text.

TO LOAD:

Type: `(load "textjust") <RETURN>`

Response: `C:textjust`

TO OPERATE:

Type: `textjust <RETURN>`

Response: `Left/Center/Middle/Right:`

This asks how you want to change the text justification. Enter the first letter of your choice.

Response: `Select object:`

Pick the line of text you wish to change, and the text will move. This program changes one line at a time.

Response: `Is this correct <Y>`

If the change is correct, press **<RETURN>**. Otherwise, type **N <RETURN>** and the original text will be restored.

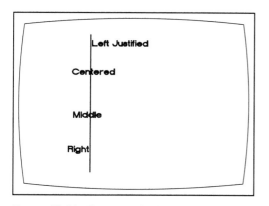

Figure 17-11: Create multiple text lines.

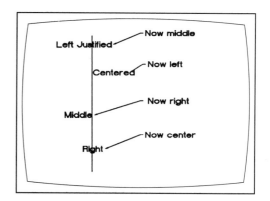

Figure 17-12: Change the text to a new justification.

Now let's examine the program line by line. The file name is **TEXTJUST.LSP**.

```
(defun C:textjust (/ j e p11 p10 f en p11n p10n fn y)
```

defines the function with all local variables.

```
(setq j (getstring "\nLeft/Center/Middle/Right: "))
```

This line prompts you for the new justification of the text. Enter the first letter and it is assigned to the variable **j**.

```
(setq j (strcase j))
```

This changes the case of **j** to uppercase if it isn't already.

```
(setq e (entget (car (entsel))))
```

(car (entsel)) returns the name of the entity selected. **(entget)** secures the entity list, which is assigned to the variable **e**.

```
(setq p11 (assoc 11 e))
```

assoc 11 is the insertion point of the text. This is assigned to **p11**.

```
(setq p10 (assoc 10 e))
```

assoc 10 is the beginning of the text. If the text is left justified, then **assoc 10** is both the insertion and beginning point; and **assoc 11** is ignored.

```
(setq f (assoc 72 e))
```

assoc 72 is the code number for the type of justification.
    The main codes for text justification are

0	Left
1	Centered
2	Right
4	Middle

```
(setq en e)
```

The variables **e** and **en** both have the same entity list. This lets you reverse the change at the end of the program, if necessary.

```
(if (= cdr f) 0) (setq p11n (cons (11 (cdr p10)))))
```

If **assoc 72** is **0**—that is, left justified—you must copy the value in **assoc 10** to **assoc 11**, since **assoc 11** has no value. Otherwise, it's ignored for left-justified text. This line constructs a new dotted pair of **assoc 11** and assigns it to **p11n**.

```
(if (= cdr f 0) (setq en (subst p11n p11 en)))
```

If **assoc 72** is 0, then **p11n** is substituted for **p11** in entity list **en. assoc 11** now has the value of **assoc 10**.

```
(if (and (= j "L") (/= (cdr f) 0))
  (progn
    (setq p10n (cons 10 (cdr p11)))
    (setq en (subst p10n p10 en))
  )
)
```

If you're changing the text to left justification, you must copy the current insertion point found in **assoc 11** to **assoc10**. If **j** = "L" and **f** is not equal to 0 (left-justified already), then (**progn** sets up a multiple **then** statement. A new dotted pair is constructed from 10 and **(cdr p11)** and assigned to **p10n. p10n** is then substituted for **p10** in entity list **en**.

```
(if (= j "L") (setq fn 0))
(if (= j "C") (setq fn 1))
(if (= j "M") (setq fn 4))
(if (= j "R") (setq fn 2))
```

These lines test to see which justification has been chosen, then set the variable **fn** to the appropriate code number.

```
(setq fn (cons 72 fn))
```

A new dotted pair of 72 and **fn** is constructed and reassigned to **fn**.

```
(setq en (subst fn f en))
```

fn is then substituted for **f** in entity list **en**.

```
(entmod en)
```

The new entity list is updated. The text should now change on your screen.

```
(setq y (getstring "\nIs this correct <Y> "))
```

You're prompted if the change is correct. If it isn't correct, then enter N. This is assigned to the variable **y**.

```
(if (= (strcase y) "N") (entmod e))
```

If the uppercase of the variable **y** is equal to "N," the old entity list **e** is used to update the database.

17.11 Block Count — BLCOUNT.LSP

```
(defun C:blcount (/ p1 b a n)
  (setq p1 (getstring "\nName of part: "))
  (setq b (cons 2 p1))
  (setq a (ssget "x" (list b)))
  (if (/= a nil)
    (progn
    (setq n (sslength a))
    (prompt "There are ")(prin1 n)(prompt" in the database: \n")
    )
    )
    (if (= a nil)
    (prompt "There are none in the database: \n")
  )
  )
)
```

PURPOSE: To count the number of occurrences of a specific block. It can be used with simple modifications to count any other entity types. It requires Release 9 or later as written, because it uses the entity filter feature. Of course, it can be modified to search for the blocks in a loop.

TO LOAD:

Type: (load "blcount") <RETURN>

Response: C:blcount

TO OPERATE:

Type: blcount <RETURN>

Response: Name of part:

Type: Enter the name of the block you want to count.

Response: There are 11 in the database. It gives you a count of the number of blocks in the database.

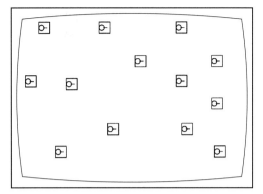

Figure 17-13: Create multiple block entities.

Now let's examine the program line by line. The file name is
BLCOUNT.LSP.

```
(defun C:blcount (/ p1 b a n)
```

defines the function with all local variables.

```
(setq p1 (getstring "\nName of part: ")
```

This prompts you for the name of the block and assigns it to **p1**.

```
(setq b (cons 2 p1))
```

This constructs a dotted pair of two, plus the block's name. Code **2** is for
blocks.

```
(setq a (ssget "x" (list b)))
```

This filters only the block you're looking for and assigns it to the selection
set **a**.

```
(if (/= a nil)
  (progn
    (setq n (sslength a))
    (prompt "There are ")(prin1 n)(prompt" in the database: \n")
  )
)
```

If a block is found, (**progn** groups the next lines as multiple **thens** in the **if**
statement. The length of the selection set is assigned to **n**, and you're
prompted as to how many are in the database.

```
(if (= a nil)
  (prompt "There are none in the database: \n")
)
```

If no blocks are found, this **(null pointer)** error trap checks for none and prompts the user. The final parenthesis closes the program.

17.12 Arrowheads — ARROWH.LSP

```
(defun C:arrowh (/ os p0 p1 dis ang p2 p3)
  (setq os (getvar "osmode"))
  (setvar "osmode" 512)
  (setq p0 (getpoint "\nPick base of arrowhead: "))
  (setvar "osmode" 1)
  (setq p1 (getpoint "\nPick tip of arrowhead: "))
  (setq dis (distance p0 p1))
  (setq ang (angle p0 p1))
  (setvar "osmode" 0)
  (setq p2 (polar p0 (+ ang (dtr 90)) (/ dis 3)))
  (setq p3 (polar p0 (- ang (dtr 90)) (/ dis 3)))
  (command "solid" p1 p2 p3 "" "")
  (command "move" "l" "" p0 p1)
  (setvar "osmode" os)
  (redraw)
)
```

PURPOSE: Lets you add arrowheads to any existing line or draw your own arrowhead. Naturally, you can go through the dimensioning routine to draw leader lines. The traditional way of drawing arrowheads is to create and insert a block; but it's difficult to adjust the proper angle of the arrowhead.

When used with a line, the object snap is set for **"nearest"** so you can point to any part of the existing line. Then, when you're asked to pick the tip of the arrowhead, you should set the object snap for the end point of the line. When the solid is drawn, the base of the arrowhead is moved to the end point of the line. The arrowhead is always lined up at the correct angle with the line. You can also draw an arrowhead without attaching it to a line, by removing the **MOVE** command.

TO LOAD:

Type: `(load "arrowh") <RETURN>`

Response: C:arrowh

TO OPERATE:

Type: `arrowh <RETURN>`

Response: `Pick base of arrowhead:`

Pick a point on the line near to where you want the base of the arrowhead. The distance from the end point of the line to the base that you pick will determine the size of the arrowhead.

Response: `Pick tip of arrowhead:`

Type: `Pick the end point of the line`

The arrowhead will now be drawn and the base moved to the end point of the line.

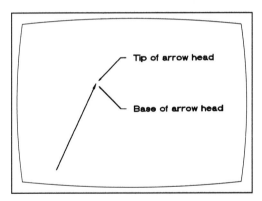

Figure 17-14: Create a line for the arrowhead.

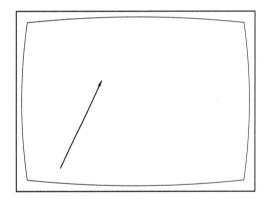

Figure 17-15: Create the tip and base of the arrowhead.

Let's examine the program line by line. The file name is **ARROWH.LSP**.

`(defun C:arrowh (/ os p0 p1 dis ang p2 p3)`

defines the function with all local variables.

```
(setq os (getvar "osmode"))
```

This saves the current object snap settings to variable **os**.

```
(setvar "osmode" 512)
```

This sets the object snap to **"nearest."**

```
(setq p0 (getpoint "\nPick base of arrowhead: "))
```

This line is a prompt to pick the base of the arrowhead. The point is saved to the variable **p0**.

```
(setvar "osmode" 1)
```

The object snap is now reset to the **"endpoint."**

```
(setq p1 (getpoint "\nPick tip of arrowhead: "))
```

This prompts you to pick the tip of the arrowhead. The point is saved to the variable **p1**.

```
(setq dis (distance p0 p1))
```

The distance from the base, **p0**, to the tip, **p1**, of the arrowhead is measured and assigned to the variable **dis**.

```
(setq ang (angle p0 p1))
```

This measures the angle from the base to the tip of the arrowhead so the angle of the arrowhead will be perpendicular to the line.

```
(setvar "osmode" 0)
```

The object snap is now reset to **"none."**

```
(setq p2 (polar p0 (+ ang (dtr 90)) (/ dis 3)))
(setq p3 (polar p0 (- ang (dtr 90)) (/ dis 3)))
```

You now derive the wing points from the center of the base of the arrowhead. It makes the points parallel by adding to the angle or subtracting from the angle 90 degrees. The distance is measured as one-third the distance from the base to the tip. The basic shape of the arrowhead may be adjusted by changing this divisor number.

```
(command "solid" p1 p2 p3 "" "")
```

This draws a solid triangle, then uses the "" "" to break out of the command.

```
(command "move" "L" "" p0 p1)
```

This moves the arrowhead from its creation point on the line to the end point of the line. The **"L"** is for the last object drawn. Then the arrowhead is moved from **p0** to **p1**.

```
(setvar "osmode" os)
```

The object snap is now reset and restored to its original setting, which was stored in the variable **os**.

```
(redraw)
```

On some systems you may need to redraw the screen, since the **MOVE** command may temporarily erase part of the line. This command is optional.

17.13 Edge Surface — EDGE.LPS

```
(defun C:edge (/ a b1 b2 b3 b4)
(setq a (ssget))
(if (= (sslength a) 4)
(progn
(setq b1 (cdr (assoc 10 (entget (entnext (ssname a 0))))))
(setq b2 (cdr (assoc 10 (entget (entnext (ssname a 1))))))
(setq b3 (cdr (assoc 10 (entget (entnext (ssnme a 2))))))
(setq b4 (cdr (assoc 10 (entget (entnext (entnext (ssname a3)))))))
(command "edgesurf" b1 b2 b3 b4)
)
)
(if (/= (sslength a) 4) (prompt "\nExactly 4 edges not found: ")) )
```

PURPOSE: **Edgesurf** is one of the most complicated surface commands and at the same time one of the most impressive. It requires exactly four distinct sides. But these sides may be exaggerated **Plines** with multiple vertices. Each **Pline** entity is considered one edge.

The other complication is that you can choose the edges in any order, but they must be chosen closest to the same relative vertex. This can cause a problem if the **Pline** has been curve-fitted; it's difficult to tell where the beginning vertex lies.

This program works with most surfaces except a rectangular image, where there's only one line per side. At this point the program simply stops where it became confused and asks you to pick the remaining line or lines. It works well for its intended purpose if there are multiple vertices per side. The program requires Release 10 or higher.

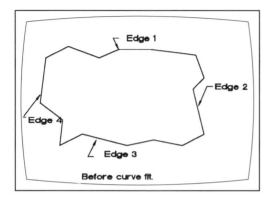

Figure 17-16: Create four edges using PLINE.

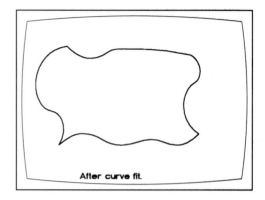

Figure 17-17: Curve fit the four edges.

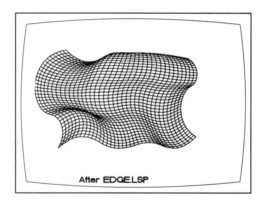

Figure 17-18: Set surftabs and pick the four edges.

TO LOAD:

Type: (load "edge") <RETURN>

Response: C:edge

TO OPERATE:

Type: edge <RETURN>

Response: Select objects:

Put a crossing or a window around the four edges and confirm. If four edges are found, the program then does the surface mesh. If four edges aren't found, it gives you the error message **"Exactly 4 edges not found."** Make sure the **surftab1** and **surftab2** system variables are properly set. These control the density of the mesh. If they're set too low, the mesh will look strange.

Now let's examine the program line by line. The file name is **EDGE.LSP**.

```
(defun C:edge (/ a b1 b2 b3 b4)
```

defines the function with all variables local.

```
(setq a (ssget))
```

This lets you select objects. The selection set is assigned to the variable **a**.

```
(if (= (sslength a) 4)
 (progn
(setq b1 (cdr (assoc 10 (entget (entnext (ssname a 0))))))
(setq b2 (cdr (assoc 10 (entget (entnext (ssname a 1))))))
(setq b3 (cdr (assoc 10 (entget (entnext (ssnme a 2))))))
(setq b4 (cdr (assoc 10 (entget (entnext (entnext (ssname a
3)))))))
(command "edgesurf" b1 b2 b3 b4)
 )
)
```

The program is error trapped to test whether only four edges were captured in the selection set. Therefore, if the selection set has four entities, a multiple **(then....)** is set up. The entities are indexed as **0, 1, 2** and **3**. Since they're polylines, you must use the **entnext** command to get to the real entity list. The **cdr** of **assoc 10** is assigned respectively to **b1, b2, b3** and **b4**. The command is issued to do an **edgesurf** on each variable. Then **progn** and **if** are closed.

```
(if (/= (sslength a) 4)
   (prompt "\nExactly 4 edges not found: "))
```

If the length of the selection set isn't exactly four, an error message is displayed.

17.14 CAMERA — TARGET REVERSAL — TARGREV.LSP

```
(defun C:targrev (/ tx ty tz tar cam)
  (setq tx (+ (car (getvar"target"))
    (car(getvar"viewdir"))))
  (setq ty (+ (cadr (getvar"target"))
    (cadr(getvar"viewdir"))))
  (setq tz (+ (caddr (getvar"target"))
    (caddr (getvar"viewdir"))))
  (setq tar (list tx ty tz))
  (setq cam (getvar "target"))
  (command "dview" "c" pause pause pause "po" tar cam)
)
```

PURPOSE: **DVIEW** lets you raise or lower the camera and target and rotate them. But it doesn't let you easily view the object from the other side. The solution is to reposition the target and the camera with the **POINTS** command.

Sometimes the ideal positioning is to reverse the target and camera positions. It's often necessary to use **DVIEW** on the object once, to position the target and camera. This program will then reverse the points.

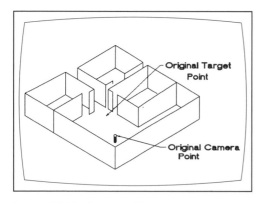

Figure 17-19: Create a 3D drawing and choose camera and target points.

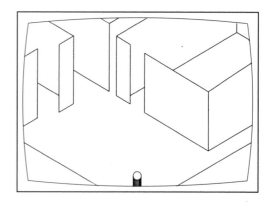

Figure 17-20: Original view of camera and target points.

TO LOAD:

   Type: (load "targrev") <RETURN>

Response: C:targrev

TO OPERATE:

Type: `targrev <RETURN>`

Response: The program prompts you to select objects. The program then reverses the points of the last known target and camera positions.

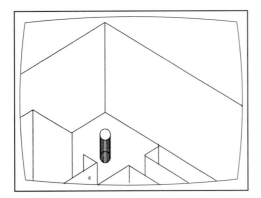

Figure 17-21: Reversal view of camera and target points.

Let's examine the program line by line. The file name is **TARGREV.LSP**.

```
(defun C:targrev (/ tx ty tz tar cam)
```

defines the function with all local variables.

```
(setq tx (+ (car (getvar"target"))
  (car(getvar"viewdir"))))
(setq ty (+ (cadr (getvar"target"))
  (cadr(getvar"viewdir"))))
(setq tz (+ (caddr (getvar"target"))
  (caddr (getvar"viewdir"))))
```

The system variable **target** contains the **X Y Z** coordinates for the target. The system variable **viewdir** contains the offset from the target. Therefore, the **X Y Z** of the target must be added to the **X Y Z** offset to produce the **X Y Z** of the camera. These lines add the **X** using **car**, **Y** using **cadr** and **Z** using **caddr**. Each is then respectively assigned to **tx**, **ty** and **tz**.

```
(setq tar (list tx ty tz))
```

This reassembles **tx**, **ty** and **tz** to **tar**.

```
(setq cam (getvar "target"))
```

This gets the **X Y Z** coordinate for the target and assigns it to **cam**. Now the points for the camera and the target are reversed.

```
(command "dview" "c" pause pause pause "po" tar cam)
```

This issues the **DVIEW** command and has you select objects with a crossing. The pauses are inputs necessary to select the objects. The program selects the points option and supplies the reversed target and camera coordinates.

17.15 Perspective On/Off — PERSP.LSP

```
(defun C:ppon (/ dis)
  (setq dis (getdist "\nEnter distance: "))
  (if
    (= dis nil)
    (command "dview" "" "d" "" "")
  )
  (if
    (/= dis nil)
    (command "dview" "" "d" dis "")
  )
)
(defun C:ppoff ( )
  (command "dview" "" "off" "")
)
```

PURPOSE: Lets you turn perspective on or off outside **DVIEW**, maintaining the previous distance as the default, or lets you set the distance. If the distance is not set, it should be set at least once before the default is used.

TO LOAD:

Type: `(load "persp") <RETURN>`

Response: `C:ppoff`

TO OPERATE:

Type: `ppon <RETURN>`

Response: Enter distance:

Press **<RETURN>** to default to the current distance, or enter a new distance using your current units.

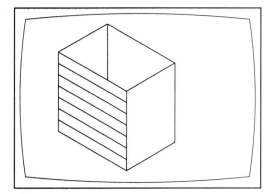

Figure 17-22: Create a 3D drawing.

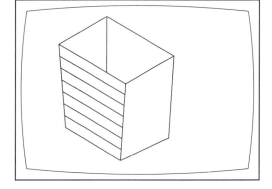

Figure 17-23: Use PERP.LSP to turn perspective view on or off.

Let's examine the program line by line. The file name is **PERSP.LSP**.

```
(defun C:ppon (/ dis)
```

defines the function with all local variables.

```
(setq dis (getdist "\nEnter distance: "))
```

This prompts for the distance and assigns the value to **dis**.

```
(if
   (= dis nil)
   (command "dview" "" "d" "" "")
)
```

The variable **dis** will be *nil* if you press **<RETURN>**. If this is the case, then **DVIEW-DISTANCE** is entered, defaulting on all the prompts.

```
(if
   (/= dis nil)
   (command "dview" "" "d" dis "")
)
```

If a distance is entered, then this group is used since **dis** is not nil.

```
(defun C:ppoff ( )
  (command "dview" "" "off" "")
)
```

There are really two functions in this file. **ppoff** is defined to turn perspective off. This simply turns the distance and thus perspective off.

Bonus File LIB2.LSP

Here is an extra file you can create to autoload all the lisp files in this chapter. Note it's called LIB2.LSP because there is a LIB.LSP autoloader file on the companion disk.

```
(defun C:lscale ( ) (load "lscale") (C:lscale)) ;;loads 17.1
(defun C:perpd ( ) (load "perpd") (C:perpd)) ;;loads 17.2
(defun C:chlayer ( ) (load "chlayer")(C:chlayer)) ;;loads 17.3
(defun C:layerset ( ) (load "layerset") (C:layerset)) ;;loads 17.4
(defun C:mpinsert ( ) (load "mpinsert") (C:mpinsert)) ;;loads 17.5
(defun C:subtext ( ) (load "subtext") (C:subtext)) ;;loads 17.6
(defun C:crsgrid ( ) (load "crsgrid") (C:crsgrid)) ;;loads 17.7
(defun C:bldroom ( ) (load "bldroom") (C:bldroom)) ;;loads 17.8
(defun C:linet ( ) (load "linet") (C:linet)) ;;loads 17.9
(defun C:textjust ( ) (load "textjust") (C:textjust)) ;;loads 17.10
(defun C:blcount ( ) (load "blcount") (C:blcount)) ;;loads 17.11
(defun C:arrowh ( ) (load "arrowh") (C:arrowh)) ;;loads 17.12
(defun C:edge ( ) (load "edge") (C:edge)) ;;loads 17.13
(defun C:targrev ( ) (load "targrev") (C:targrev)) ;;loads 17.14
(defun C:persp ( ) (load "persp") (C:persp)) ;;loads 17.15
(princ "\n ")
(princ "\nAutoLISP utilities 1 thru 15 loaded...")
(princ)
```

Name the file **LIB2.LSP**. It simply lists all the files created in this chapter into an autoload function. (You'll remember we did that in Section 15.24.) Then all you have to do is load this one file and it will load all other files you created. Note you must have created and tested all your files first to make sure they're working before you create and run the autoloader.

APPENDICES

Using EDLIN

You enter AutoLISP through a text editor. This book uses EDIT.EXE, the text editor supplied free with DOS. If you have at least DOS 5.0, it's recommended you use EDIT, the text editor available with DOS. It's far superior to EDLIN and creates the same text files. This appendix is for those who want to use EDLIN.

If you know how to write programs using your own word processor, do so. You'll produce the same results with fewer headaches.

Before you begin, be sure the file EDLIN.COM is in your AutoCAD directory or your PATH leads to a directory where EDLIN.COM resides. If you're not sure of the PATH, copy EDLIN.COM to the AutoCAD directory. Here's how:

1. Place the copy of your master DOS disk in drive **A:**. Be sure you're logged on to your hard disk, such as **C:**.

2. Change the directory on your hard disk to the AutoCAD directory by typing **CD \ACAD**. (This assumes your AutoCAD directory is called **ACAD**. If not, substitute the name of your directory for **ACAD**.)

3. Type: **COPY A:EDLIN.COM <RETURN>**

   That copies the editor to your AutoCAD directory.

4. If you want to call up EDLIN from outside your AutoCAD directory,

Type: EDLIN LES1.LSP <RETURN>

   where **LES1.LSP** is the name of the file you want to edit.

5. If you're in the AutoCAD drawing editor at the **Command** line,

Type: EDIT <RETURN>

Response: File to edit:

Type: LES1.LSP.

EDLIN then begins. The few EDLIN commands needed to use the editor are listed below. (Additional commands, as well as a complete discussion on EDLIN, appear in your DOS manual.)

L <RETURN> lists the first 23 lines or a screenful of information. **14L** lists 23 lines, beginning with line **14**.

I <RETURN> inserts a line before all other lines, beginning with line number **1**. You continue inserting lines consecutively until you end by typing **CTRL-C**. (Hold down the **CONTROL** key, then press the letter **C**.)

6I <RETURN> inserts lines before line **6** and begins numbering that line as line **6**.

#D <RETURN> deletes a specified line. For example, **13D** deletes line **13**. **20,23D** deletes lines **20** through **23**.

 # <RETURN> displays a line (indicated by number) for editing. Your edits replace the line. Pressing the **INS** key allows you to insert text. The **DEL** key deletes forward. However, the backspace key doesn't delete backward. If you press **<RETURN>** at any point in the line, you lose the rest of the line. The **F3** key prints the rest of the line. But be careful: If you fail to press **F3** before you press **<RETURN>**, you could lose the rest of the line.

E <RETURN> saves and updates the file. The previous version of the file is saved as the name of the file with the extension **.BAK**.

Q <RETURN> aborts all changes and exits EDLIN.

For information on using other text editors with AutoCAD and revising your **ACAD.PGP** file, see Appendix B.

ACAD.PGP File

AutoCAD's ACAD.PGP file lets you automate DOS and other external program commands. If you want to run a text processor other than EDLIN or EDIT within AutoCAD, you can easily modify the ACAD.PGP file to do so.

The AutoCAD Release 13 ACAD.PGP file has the following lines:

```
CATALOG,DIR /W,     0,*Files: ,0
DEL,DEL,            0,File to delete: ,4
DIR,DIR,            0,File specification: ,0
EDIT,EDLIN,         0,File to edit: ,4
SH,,                0,* OS Command: ,4
SHELL,,             0,* OS Command: ,4
TYPE,TYPE,          0,File to list: ,0
```

The only line of interest to you is

EDIT,EDLIN, 0,File to edit: ,4

This line lets you use EDLIN while inside AutoCAD. A comma separates each item in the line. The first item, EDIT, is what you type at the Auto-CAD command line to bring up the program. The second item, EDLIN, is the name of the program. The third item, 0, is the number of bytes that must be reserved to run the program. In this release it's 0. (It's left over from earlier versions, where the integer was the allowed size of a file in bytes). The fourth item, File to edit:, is the onscreen prompt statement.

Anything you type here is appended to the program you call. In other words, this is the name of the file you're editing. If there's no prompt, use two commas. The final item, 0, is a bit-coded integer that is either 0 or 4. Upon finishing your editing, code 0 returns you to the monotext screen, and code 4 returns you to the graphics screen.

Changing ACAD.PGP to your own text editor

In order to alter the file to your favorite text editor, the only line of interest to you is

EDIT,EDLIN, 0,File to edit: ,4

For example, if you wanted to use WordPerfect as your text editor, the ACAD.PGP line would be changed to

EDIT,WP,   0,,0

Note the space in the line is a tab space.
Or with WordStar as your text editor, change the line to

EDIT,WS,   0,,0

Note that there's no file to edit prompt. To revise ACAD.PGP, you must first bring up WordStar or WordPerfect, then use the Non-Document mode in WordStar or the Edit Dos File in WordPerfect and then load the file. If you edit ACAD.PGP directly and save it, word processing control codes are embedded. And it isn't usable.

To change to DOS EDIT.EXE, alter the line to read as below:

EDIT,EDIT,   0,File to edit: ,4

Settings Units & Limits

The companion disk contains three drawing files, which are set up for your convenience.

For the sample programs in this book create a prototype drawing and set the UNITS and LIMITS as follows:

Your units may be Architectural or Engineering.

Degrees, Minutes and Seconds with 4 decimal places of accuracy.

East, or 3:00 o'clock, is 0 degrees.

Angles are measured counter clockwise.

For the sample programs found in this book, LIMITS are set as follows:

Width 144' by Height 96'.

In order to create a sample drawing with these specifications, do the following:

1. Start up AutoCAD Release 13 in the normal manner. From the FILE pull-down menu choose NEW. In the "Enter Drawing Name" box place the name SAMPLE. Then choose OK.

2. From the pull-down menu choose the VIEW option. In order to activate the UNITS dialog box you'll choose VIEW then Units...

3. From the UNITS dialog box choose Engineering or Architectural.

4. Choose a level of accuracy for fractional places.

   (Let's keep the accuracy to the default of 4.)

5. To set the angles, choose (Degrees minutes seconds).

6. Choose 2 decimal places for the accuracy.

7. For direction of angle, pick the "Direction" button and choose 0 degrees for East (3:00 o'clock). Pick the OK button to exit from the Direction dialog box.

8. To exit from the UNITS dialog box, pick the OK button to keep the UNITS settings you just entered.

You're now returned to the Command line.

9. At the Command line pick DATA from the pull-down menu and choose Drawing Limits.

10. For lower left corner, enter 0,0. <Press RETURN>

11. For upper right corner, enter 144',96'.

12. You'll now be returned to the Command line.

13. Pick Options from the pull-down and choose Drawing Aids. Set the GRID to 5'-0" and pick the ON button. Set the SNAP to 1'-0" and activate the ON button. To save the settings, pick the OK button.

14. Type: ZOOM A

    You now should see your grid on the screen. If it doesn't appear, type ZOOM E <RETURN> followed by ZOOM A <RETURN>.

15. Save your prototype drawing for use throughout these exercises. Name the prototype drawing SAMPLE. (Or use any name you want.)

16. To use the prototype drawing. Choose NEW and use the SAMPLE as a prototype drawing. At the start of each chapter, use a clean sample drawing, positioned at the Command line.

Using MVSETUP.LSP

If you're using AutoCAD for DOS, it has a lisp file called MVSETUP.LSP. With it you may set up your UNITS, LIMITS and paper size very quickly. Simply type MVSETUP the first time you need to invoke it and answer NO to the "Do you want to use Paper Space" prompt. Choose your UNITS, scale and paper size from the side menu and simply save the drawing as SAMPLE.

Companion Disk

Congratulations on your success thus far. After completing the lessons in this book, you've come a long way toward reaching your goal.

One of the most frustrating tasks for a new student of AutoLISP is debugging simple typing errors. Countless people have called Ventana Press, the publishers of this book, to say they've had as many as five people check their code and proclaim that it's perfectly correct — yet the programs still don't work. (Remember, all these programs are error checked before they are printed.)

When they fax a hard copy of the code to the Technical Editor at Ventana Press, it reveals as many as three major errors preventing the programs from working. The problem is that most AutoCAD users aren't expert typists. Autodesk has done everything possible to make typing unnecessary. So why impede your progress by typing and debugging the programs in this book — and possibly increase your frustration level? **Use the companion disk**.

What's On the Companion Disk?

The companion disk contains all the programs ready to load for each of the lessons and chapters. Three sample prototype drawing files include the UNITS and LIMITS already set. They also include the entities and blocks used as examples in the lessons.

All you have to do is use the self-install program on the disk to copy the AutoLISP files and drawing files onto your hard drive. (Don't forget to look at the disk's **README.DOC** and the **INSTALL.TXT** for any last-minute changes.) Set your ACAD environment variable to point to the directory you've specified. See Section 15.17. And you're ready to use more than 40 AutoLISP programs.

GLOSSARY

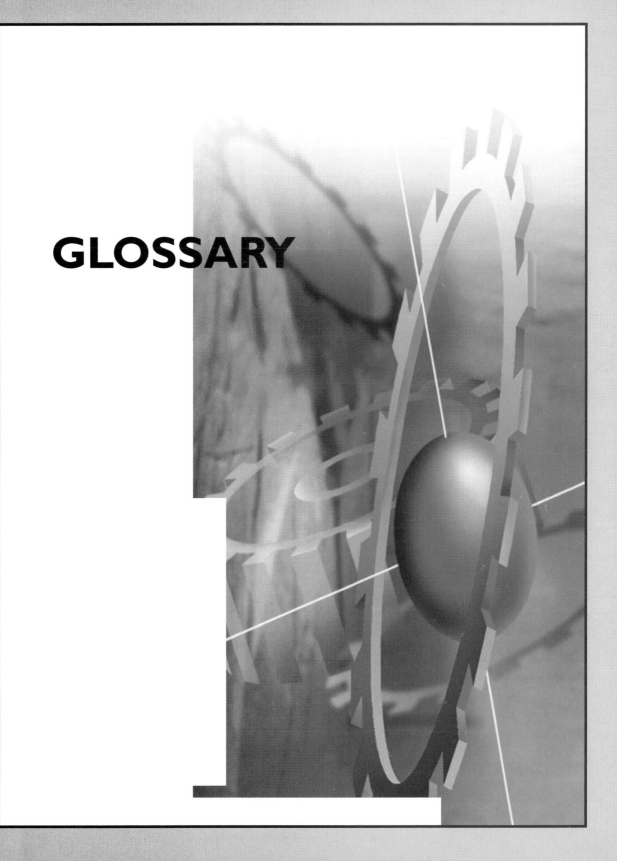

The following is a glossary of selected AutoLISP statements, terms and commands. Uppercase terms are file statements or commands for AutoCAD and/or DOS. Lowercase terms are AutoLISP commands or functions.

This glossary isn't comprehensive; only those terms used in the book are covered in this section. Similarly, definitions are sometimes restricted to this book's context. For further information or alternate usages, consult your *AutoLISP Programmer's Reference* and *AutoCAD Reference Manual*.

ACAD.LSP   AutoLISP file loaded each time you enter the drawing editor. Its purpose is to autoload LISP files. In AutoCAD Release 13, the ACAD.LSP is named ACADR13.LSP.

ACAD.PGP   File available with AutoCAD to define external programs accessible from within the drawing editor.

ACADDRV   DOS environment setting used in the ACADR13.BAT file.

ACADCFG   DOS environment setting used in the ACADR13.BAT file.

add +   Arithmetic operator, used in the following format: **(+ a 1)** means add **1** to **a**.

alert   AutoLISP command which creates an alert dialog box on the screen with a user defineable message.

and   Basic connector, generally used to connect items of comparison in **if** statements. **(if (and (= b a) (> a c)** reads if **b** = **a** and **a** is greater than **c**.

angle   AutoLISP command that measures the angle of two known points. **(angle pnt1 pnt2)**.

angtof   AutoLISP command which converts an angle in the form of a string to a real number.

angtos   AutoLISP command that converts a variable stored as radians to a string in another format. (setq a (angtos ang1)).

append To add an element to a list.

Apostrophe ' Used to introduce a list. **(setq a '(3 5 7)).**

Argument Any value passed from outside a program to a variable within an AutoLISP program. For example, **(dtr 90)**, where **90** is the argument.

assoc In this book, an AutoLISP command that searches for a sublist within any list. With an entity list, assoc uses the entity code number as key. **(setq c (assoc 40 b)).**

Atom A single element.

AUTOEXEC.BAT A batch file executed when the computer is first booted.

BASIC A high-level language often used to program microcomputers.

Break point A stop point placed in a program to stop the <->execution of the program for the purpose of debugging.

caddr AutoLISP command that produces the third element in the list. For example, if **a** is a list **(3 5 7)**, then **(caddr a)** produces the **7** (generally the **Z** coordinate).

cadr AutoLISP command that produces the second element in the list. For example, if **a** is a list **(3 5 7 9)**, then **(cadr a)** produces **5**.

car AutoLISP command that produces the first element in the list. For example, if **a** is a list **(3 5 7 9)**, then **(car a)** produces **3**.

cdr AutoLISP command that produces the second and remaining elements in a list. For example, if **a** is a list **(3 5 7 9)**, then **(cdr a)** produces **(5 7 9)**.

command AutoLISP command that lets you use AutoCAD commands in AutoLISP programs. **(Command "line" pnt1 pnt2 "").**

cons   AutoLISP command that constructs a new list, with the new element put at the beginning of the list. **(setq d (cons (car c h))).**

Coprocessor   Numeric processor available as 8087, 80287 and 80387 etc. Dramatically enhances speed.

CROSSING   To create a window in AutoCAD, in order to select entities. If any part of an entity touches the window, it is selected.

cvunit   AutoLISP command that converts the value of any unit to the value of another unit. The conversion definitions are stored in the **ACAD.UNT** file.

Debug   To correct program logic and syntax errors.

defun   The first command in an AutoLISP program; defines the name of the function or program.

distance   AutoLISP command that measures the distance between two points. **(setq a (distance pnt1 pnt2)).**

distof   AutoLISP command which converts a distance in the form of a string to a real number.

divide /   Arithmetic operator. **(/ a 3)** means divide **a** by **3**.

DOS   Disk operating system, usually **MSDOS** or **PCDOS**.

dtr   In AutoCAD Version 2.6 or higher, an AutoLISP command that converts the value of angles from degrees to radians. In versions earlier than 2.6, this function must be written and loaded.

EDIT   AutoCAD command for entering EDLIN text editor from inside AutoCAD, defined in **ACAD.PGP** file.

EDIT   This is also the name of the text editor supplied with DOS 5.0.

EDLIN.COM   DOS text line editor.

Element   A single value in a list.

else   The third statement in the **if-then-else** statement. **(if (= a 5) (setq b 6) (setq b 7))**.

entget   AutoLISP command that secures an entity list. **(setq b (entget na))**.

Entity   The smallest element that may be placed in a drawing with a single command. Typical entities are **ARC**, **LINE**, **CIRCLE**, **POINT**, etc.

ENTITY COORDINATE SYSTEM (ECS)   The USER COORDINATE SYSTEM in effect at the time the entity was created.

entmake   AutoLISP command that lets you add an entity to the database. **(entmake e)**.

entmod   AutoLISP command that updates the drawing database with the new entity list. **(entmod b1)**.

entsel   AutoLISP command that selects an entity for **VIEW** and **CHANGE**. Only one entity may be selected with this command. **(setq a (entsel))**.

Equal (=)   An AutoLISP command used *only* to test equality. It isn't an assignment command. **(if (= a 5)**.

Error   (trap) and **Error** (test) An AutoLISP error checking device to check for syntax, machine or logical errors in a program.

exit   AutoLISP command which forces an AutoLISP application program to abort with an error message.

Explanation !   AutoLISP shorthand command that prints the value of a variable.

Extended entity data   A -3 associative code you attach to an entity. Items following the -3 associative code are its parameters. For example, ((-3 ("MYNAME705" (1000 . "This is data 1")))).

Extension   The second half of a **DOS** file name. The required extension for all AutoLISP files is **.LSP**. **LES1.LSP**.

findfile   Searches for a requested file. If the file is found, then the complete directory path is returned. If the file isn't found, then **nil** is returned.

FLATLAND   A system variable guarantees AutoLISP programs written under Release 9 will work the same in Releases 10 thru 13.
    If **flatland** is set to 0, all new 3D functions of AutoLISP Releases 10, 11, 12 and 13 are disabled. If **flatland** is set to 1, all new 3D functions in AutoLISP Releases 10, 11, 12 and 13 are enabled.

foreach   An AutoLISP command to perform a function on each of the elements of a list.

Function   An AutoLISP program.

fuzz   An additional parameter that can be added to the **(equal)** command in AutoLISP.
    The **fuzz** factor is a real number set to the number of decimal places of precision required for evaluating equality. If the two numbers are equal within this degree of precision, then the test for equality will pass.

getangle   AutoLISP command that lets you find an angle by pointing to two points or by entering the angle from the keyboard. **(setq a (getangle))**.

getcorner   AutoLISP command that asks you to pick a second point on the screen with the mouse or cursor. A window is dragged visually across the screen from the first point to the second point. **(setq pnt2 (getcorner pnt1 "Pick second point: "))**.

getdist   AutoLISP command that requests input as a real number, either through the keyboard or by pointing.

getenv   Secures the environment setting under which AutoCAD is operating.

getfiled   AutoLISP command which activates a file dialog box with a variety of user defineable parameters. getkword AutoLISP command used instead of (getstring) to verify only selected inputs. Used with **(initget 1)**. **(initget 1 "Y" "N") (setq a (getkword "Y or N"))**.

getorient AutoLISP command that lets you find an angle by pointing to two points or by entering the angle from the keyboard. This command maintains **East** as **0** degrees. **(setq a (getorient))**.

getpoint AutoLISP command that asks you to specify a point on the screen. **(setq a (getpoint "Pick a point: "))**.

getreal AutoLISP command that requests keyboard input as a real number.

getstring AutoLISP command that requests keyboard input as a string.

getvar AutoLISP command that produces an AutoCAD system variable. **(setq a (getvar "osmode"))**.

Global A variable whose value remains when the program ends and is usable by other programs.

graphscr AutoLISP command that shifts the monitor to the drawing editor.

Greater Than > Basic comparative. **(if (> a b)** reads if **a** is greater than **b**.

handent Secures the entity name of a specific entity **HANDLE**. Therefore, this command indirectly helps you secure the entity list if you know the **HANDLE**.

HANDLES A unique permanent reference number that can be assigned to all entities in the entity database.

(if... AutoLISP branching (decision) command. Generally in the form of **if-then-else**, where the **(if..)** statement is followed by two or three additional statements, the first being the "condition," the second the "then" statement, and the third the "else" statement. **(if (= a 5) (setq b 6) (setq b 7))**.

   (if (not In this book, an AutoLISP command that tests to see if a function is already loaded before loading the file in which it's contained. **(if (not drawline) (load "les1"))**.

initget   AutoLISP command that initializes various situations depending on the flag setting. One situation is to turn on the **Z** coordinates for 3D. **(initget 16)**.

integer   A counting number, plus or minus, without fractions or decimals.

lambda   An AutoLISP command that handles large lists.

Less Than <   Basic comparative. **(if (< a b)** reads if **a** is less than **b**.

LISP   High-level language used currently in artificial intelligence and used as the basis for AutoLISP. (Introduction)

list   A variable with more than one value.

load   Used to load AutoLISP program files into memory so that functions can be executed. **(load "les1")**.

Local   A variable whose value is available only to one program.

Loop   Commands repeated and controlled numerous times.

Macro   Automated series of keystrokes and commands that may be incorporated into a menu. (Introduction)

mapcar   An AutoLISP command that handles large lists.

Match   A wild card match to find an internal string. The wcmatch is case-sensitive.

member   An AutoLISP command that finds the first occurence of a number in a list for you and returns it and the remainder of the list.
   For example, (setq n (+ (- length a)(length (member 8 a))) 1)).

Multiply *   Arithmetic operator that's in the following format: **(* a 3)** means multiply **a** by 3.

Nesting The process of AutoLISP commands acting on other commands. A command that evaluates another command is said to be nested. For example, **(setq a (car b))**.

nil No value assigned to a variable.

(or Basic connector generally used to connect items of comparison in **if** statements. **(if (or (= b a) (> a c)** reads if **b** = **a** or **a** is greater than **c**.
    <OR> There is no OR function in AutoLISP. Use a special pair of -4 Associative codes. For example, '((-4 . "<OR")——— (-4 . "OR>")).

Parentheses ( ) Each AutoLISP command and list is surrounded by parentheses.

PATH A DOS statement that controls the process of searching for a program or file. For example, **PATH = \ACAD** causes DOS to search the **ACAD** directory if the program or file isn't found in the current directory.

Pick Refers to choosing a point or object on the screen.

pickset A special type of variable containing the selection set of entities selected.

polar AutoLISP command that derives a point at a given distance and angle from another known point. **(setq pnt2 (polar pnt1 ang1 dst1))**.

prin1 AutoLISP print command used primarily to print data to a file.

princ AutoLISP print command.

print AutoLISP print command that adds a line feed.

progn AutoLISP command that groups several AutoLISP statements into one, for use as a single **then** or **else** statement. **(if = a b) (progn (xxx) (xxx) (xxx)))**.

prompt AutoLISP command that prints to the screen.

Quotation " Generally encloses strings when assigned to variables or used as constants. For example, **(setq a "Pick a point: ")**.

RAM (Random Access Memory)   Volatile internal memory used for programs and data.

REDEFINE   Lets you redefine an AutoCAD command.

regapp   An AutoLISP command to register an application.

REM   Remarks statement used to denote a comment in BASIC. The **;** is used for this purpose in AutoLISP.

repeat   AutoLISP loop command that repeats a loop **X** number of times. **(repeat 5)**.

Return   AutoLISP produces a value when a command is issued, often referred to as *returning* a value.

rtd   A user-written function that converts the value of angles from radians to degrees.

rtos   AutoLISP command that converts a number or variable to a string, using user-specified units.

s::save   A special function which is executed immediately before a valid save of the drawing.

s::exit   A special function which is executed immediately before exiting the drawing.

Semicolon ;   Used to denote a non-executable comment line in AutoLISP.

setq   AutoLISP's basic assignment command. **(setq a b)** assigns the value of **b** to **a**.

setvar   AutoLISP command that sets AutoCAD system variables. **(setvar "osmode" 1)**.

Slash /   The slash before variable names in the **(defun** command denotes local variables.

ssadd   An AutoLISP command to add an entity to a selection set. For example, (ssadd ename ss)

ssdel   An AutoLISP command to delete an entity from a selection set. For example, (ssdel ename ss)

ssget   AutoLISP command that selects entities for **VIEW** and **CHANGE**. **(setq a (ssget))**.

sslength   AutoLISP command that determines the number of entities in a selection set. **(setq n (sslength a))**.

s::startup   If used as the name of the function in the ACAD.LSP file, the function will automatically begin executing when you enter the drawing editor.

ssname   AutoLISP command that secures the name of an entity. **(setq na (ssname a 0))**.

strcase   AutoLISP command that evaluates all characters in a variable as upper case. **(setq a (strcase b))**.

String   A group of alphanumeric characters generally enclosed in quotes.

subst   AutoLISP command that substitutes one entity sublist for another within an entity list. **(setq b1 (subst '(40 . 0.2500000) c b))**.

Subtract -   Arithmetic operator. **(a 1)** means subtract **1** from **a**.

Symbols   Same as variables.

System Variables   Selectable variables that control certain AutoCAD defaults.

tables   Part of the AutoCAD database. Tables store global information about drawing entities.

tblnext   An AutoLISP command used to access the name of a layer or block table.

tblsearch   An AutoLISP command used to access a table. You already know the table's name.

terpri   AutoLISP command that issues a carriage return.

Text Editor Program used to produce and edit text files. **EDLIN.COM** is an example of a text editor.

Text File ASCII file without control codes or other special coding sequences used by word processors.

textpage AutoLISP command that flips the graphics screen to the text screen and clears the text screen at the same time.

then The second statement in the if-then-else statement. **(if (= a 5) (setq b 6) (setq b 7))**.

trans Lets you translate the coordinates from one coordinate system to another.

UNDEFINE Lets you undefine an AutoCAD command.

UNITMODE An AutoCAD system variable that sets the display for various fractional units. If it's set to 1, the display will be in the same format as the input.

USER COORDINATE SYSTEM A coordinate system that may be redefined by the user with a new point of origin and/or new positive directions for X, Y and Z. Referred to as UCS.

Variable A combination of letters or letters and numbers used to store other values.

ver AutoLISP command which returns the AutoLISP version number in use at the time.

vmon Virtual paging function allowing use of extended or expanded memory for AutoLISP functions.

wcmatch AutoLISP command that lets you evaluate the contents of one string with another to find an internal substring match or no match.

while One of three basic loop statements in AutoLISP. The loop will continue while the variable or expression is not **nil**. **while (e**.

WINDOWing   The process of creating a window in AutoCAD to select entities. Only full entities within the window are selected.

WORLD COORDINATE SYSTEM (WCS)   A coordinate system with a point of origin where positive X extends to the right (East or 3:00 o'clock) and positive Y extends at a 90 degree angle from X toward the top (North or 12:00 o'clock).

xload   AutoLISP command that loads and executes an ADS program.

xunload   AutoLISP command that unloads an ADS program from memory.

INDEX

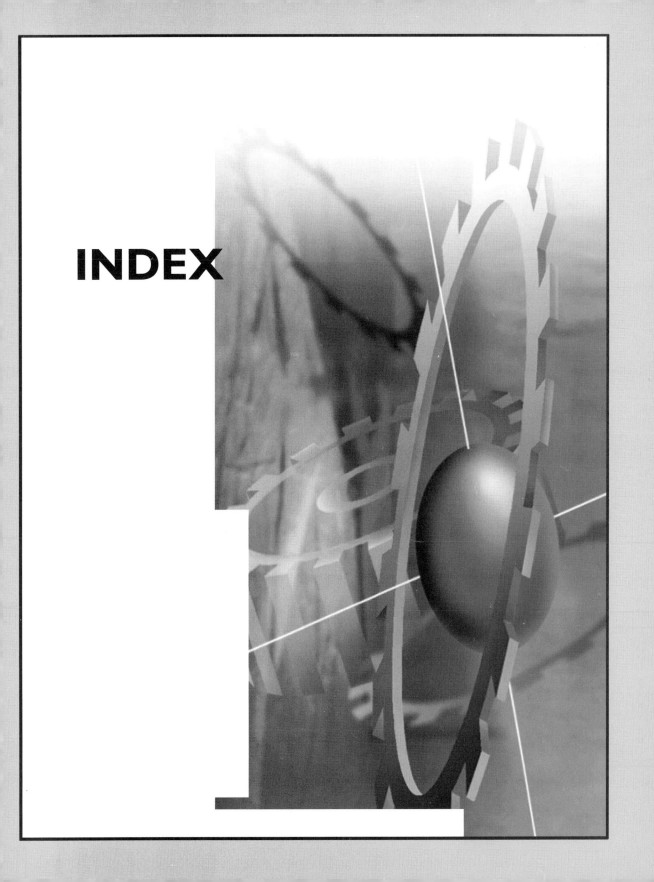

INDEX

COLOPHON

This book was produced with PageMaker 5.0 on a Power Macintosh 8100 and a Quadra 840AV.

Page proofs were printed on an Apple LaserWriter Pro 630. The output to film was on a Linotronic 330 image setter.

The body type is Palatino 11/13.5. The headlines are set in DTC Classical Sans. All code is set in Letter Gothic.

VENTANA

http://www.vmedia.com

Microsoft Windows NT 4 Workstation Desktop Companion
$39.99, 1016 pages, illustrated, part #: 472-3

Workstation users become masters of their own universe with this step-by-step guide. Covers file management, customizing and optimizing basic multimedia, OLE, printing and networking. Packed with shortcuts, secrets, productivity tips and hands-on tutorials. The CD-ROM features dozens of valuable utilities and demos for Windows NT. Innovative web-site designs, reference information, wallpaper textures, animated cursors, custom utilities and more.

Microsoft Office 95 Companion
$34.95, 1136 pages, illustrated, part #: 188-0

The all-in-one reference to Microsoft's red-hot suite is a worthy sequel to Ventana's bestselling Windows, Word & Excel Office Companion. Covers basic commands and features, and includes a section on using Windows 95. The companion disk features examples, exercises, software and sample files from the book.

SmartSuite Desktop Companion
$24.95, 784 pages, illustrated, part #: 184-8

Here's "Suite success" for newcomers to the critics' choice of business packages. This introduction to the individual tools and features of Lotus' star software packages—1-2-3, Ami Pro, Approach, Freelance Graphics and Organizer—has been updated for the latest versions. Features new enhancements for Windows 95. The companion disk features sample exercises and files that follow the lessons in the book.

VENTANA

Microsoft Internet Explorer 3 Tour Guide

Your one-stop Internet connection source! This simple, step-by-step guide explains why the Internet is causing such a buzz and how to use Explorer 3.0 to take advantage of everything the Net offers.

You'll learn to quickly master Explorer 3.0's new, advanced features including

- Keyboard shortcuts.

- Security technology.

- Increased speed for Web-page display.

- Allowing several activities to occur simultaneously (such as scrolling while downloading).

- Integrating the Internet with daily tasks (such as browsing while downloading).

- Enabling true Internet programmability (for example, many different interactive programs can be presented alongside text and images).

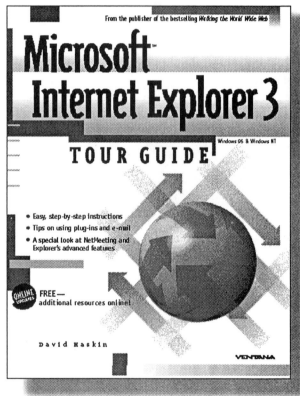

Also covers plug-ins, e-mail, security options, newsgroups and more. Plus— a tour of sites that exploit Explorer's unique technology.

part #: 1-56604-486-3
450 pages $24.99

News Junkies Internet 500

$24.99, 464 pages, illustrated, part #: 461-8

Quench your thirst for news with this comprehensive listing of the best and most useful news sites and sources on the Web. Includes business, international, sports, weather, law, finance, entertainment, politics and more. Plus rated reviews of site strengths, weaknesses, design and navigational properties.

Internet Business 500

$29.95, 488 pages, illustrated, part #: 287-9

This authoritative list of the most useful, most valuable online resources for business is also the most current list, regularly updated on the Internet. The companion CD-ROM features a hypertext version of the entire book, linked to updates on Ventana Online.

Walking the World Wide Web, Second Edition

$39.95, 800 pages, illustrated, part #: 298-4

Updated and expanded, this bestseller now features 500 listings and an extensive index of servers, arranged by subject. This groundbreaking title includes a CD-ROM enhanced with Ventana's exclusive WebWalker technology; Netscape Navigator; and a hypertext version of the book. Updated online components make it the richest resource available for web travelers.

Web Publishing With Adobe PageMill 2
$34.99, 450 pages, illustrated, part #: 458-2

Now, creating and designing professional pages on the Web is a simple, drag-and-drop function. Learn to pump up PageMill with tips, tricks and troubleshooting strategies in this step-by-step tutorial for designing professional pages. The CD-ROM features Netscape plug-ins, original textures, graphical and text-editing tools, sample backgrounds, icons, buttons, bars, GIF and JPEG images, Shockwave animations.

Web Publishing With QuarkImmedia
$39.99, 450 pages, illustrated, part #: 525-8

Use multimedia to learn multimedia, building on the power of QuarkXPress. Step-by-step instructions introduce basic features and techniques, moving quickly to delivering dynamic documents for the Web and other electronic media. The CD-ROM features an interactive manual and sample movie gallery with displays showing settings and steps. Both are written in QuarkImmedia.

VENTANA

Official Netscape Navigator 3.0 Book,

$39.99, 808 pages, illustrated,
part #: 500-2 (Windows), part #: 512-6 (Macintosh)

A runaway bestseller in its first edition, with 250,000 in print! Just add a TCP/IP connection for smooth Internet sailing, from setup and basic navigation to mail management, chat, CoolTalk and whiteboard features. The CD-ROM includes a fully supported copy of Netscape Navigator 3.0.

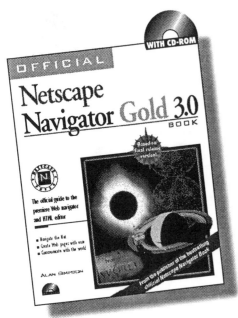

Official Netscape Navigator Gold 3.0 Book

$39.95, 928 pages, illustrated,
part #: 420-0 (Windows), part #: 421-9 (Macintosh)

Unleash the power of the most popular web navigator and publishing tool! Build your own site, create a virtual storefront, handle business on the Web—all without learning HTML! Includes creating, editing and posting hypermedia documents. The CD-ROM features Acrobat Reader 3.0, original image maps, graphics viewers, conversion tools, WinZip and more.

Official Netscape Plug-in Book

$39.99, 392 pages, illustrated, part #: 468-5

Save hours of downloading time, online-searching time and experimentation with this shortcut to the hottest add-ons for Netscape Navigator. Includes complete reviews and instructions for installing and using each product. The CD-ROM features fully supported commercial versions of dozens of Netscape plug-ins.